FLAKE

FLAKE

MATTHEW DOOLEY

JONATHAN CAPE
LONDON

A BIG THANK YOU TO MUM, DAD, PHILIPPA, KATE,
DAN FRANKLIN, CLARE BULLOCK, SAM COPELAND,
FRED HOLLIS AND KIRK CAMPBELL.

5 7 9 10 8 6 4

JONATHAN CAPE, AN IMPRINT OF VINTAGE
20 VAUXHALL BRIDGE ROAD,
LONDON, SW1V 2SA

JONATHAN CAPE IS PART OF THE PENGUIN RANDOM HOUSE GROUP OF COMPANIES
WHOSE ADDRESSES CAN BE FOUND AT GLOBAL.PENGUINRANDOMHOUSE.COM.

Penguin
Random House
UK

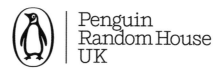

FIRST PUBLISHED BY JONATHAN CAPE IN 2020

PENGUIN.CO.UK/VINTAGE

A CIP CATALOGUE RECORD FOR THIS BOOK IS AVAILABLE FROM THE BRITISH LIBRARY

ISBN 9781787330580

PRINTED AND BOUND IN CHINA BY C&C OFFSET PRINTING CO., LTD

PENGUIN RANDOM HOUSE IS COMMITTED TO A SUSTAINABLE FUTURE FOR OUR
BUSINESS, OUR READERS AND OUR PLANET. THIS BOOK IS MADE FROM FOREST
STEWARDSHIP COUNCIL © CERTIFIED PAPER

FSC
www.fsc.org
MIX
Paper from
responsible sources
FSC® C018179

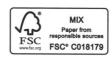

FOR CLAIRE

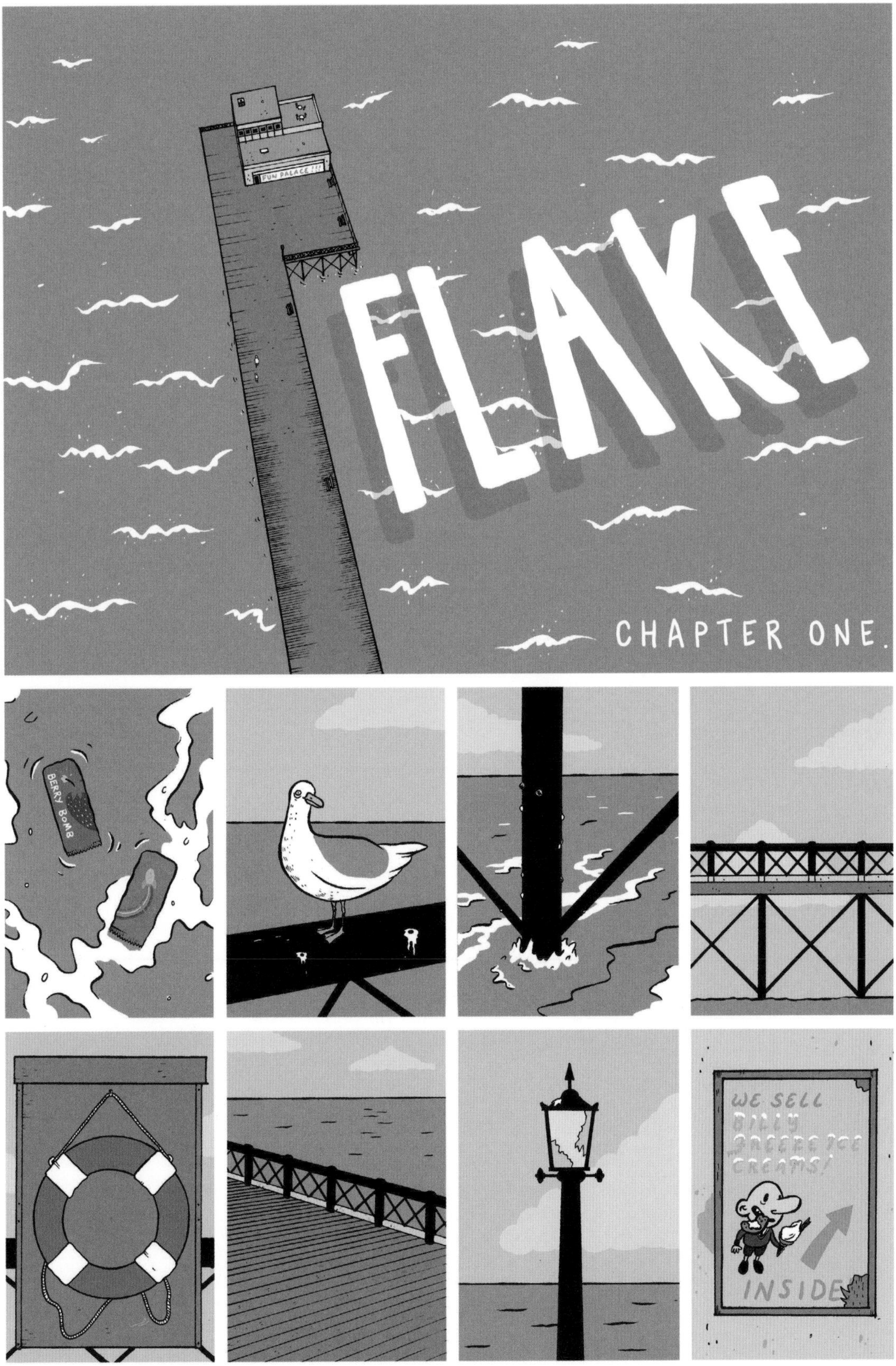
FUN PALACE!!!
FLAKE
CHAPTER ONE.
BERRY BOMB
WE SELL
BILLY
BREEZE ICE
CREAMS!
INSIDE

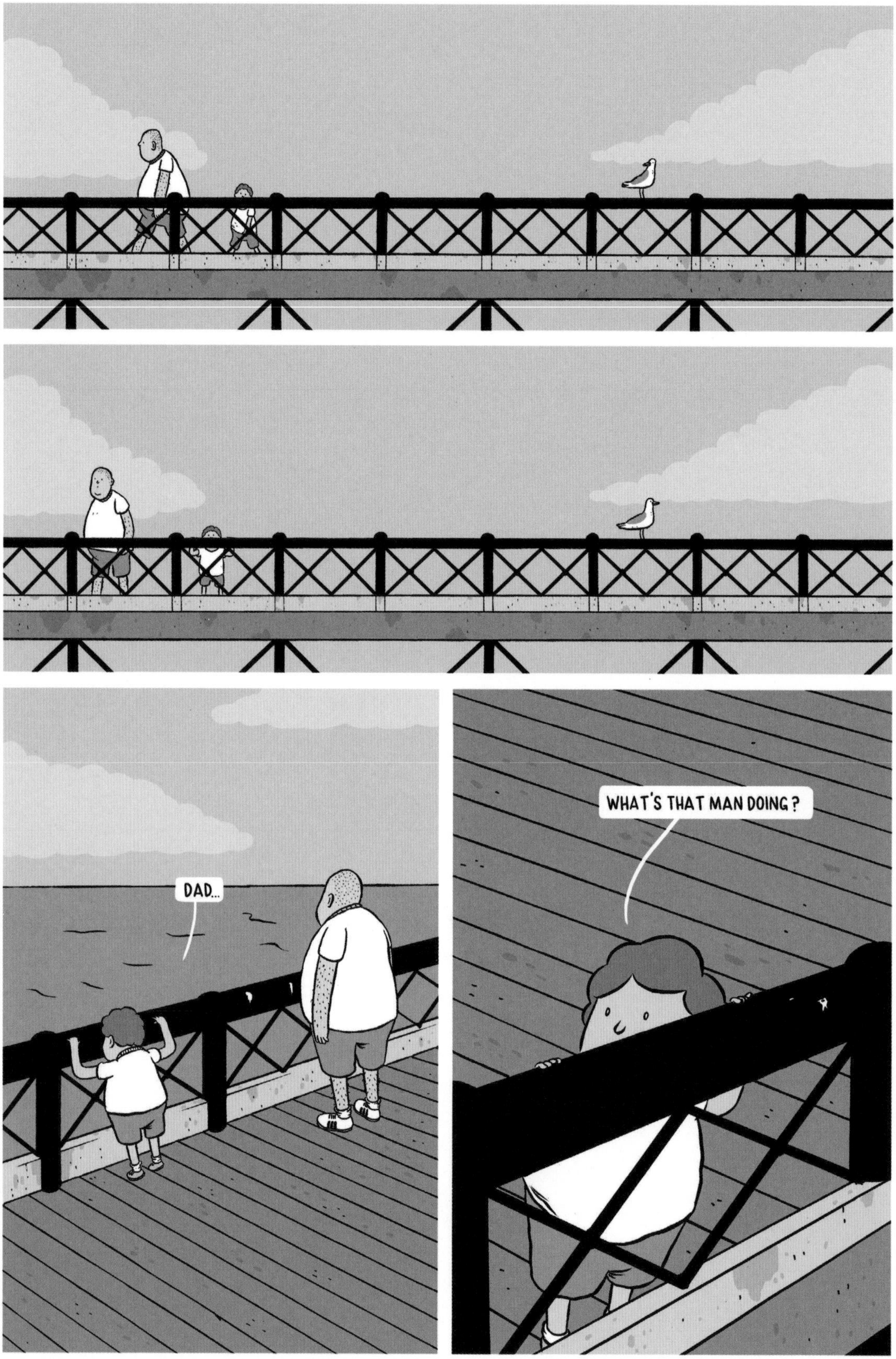
DAD...
WHAT'S THAT MAN DOING?

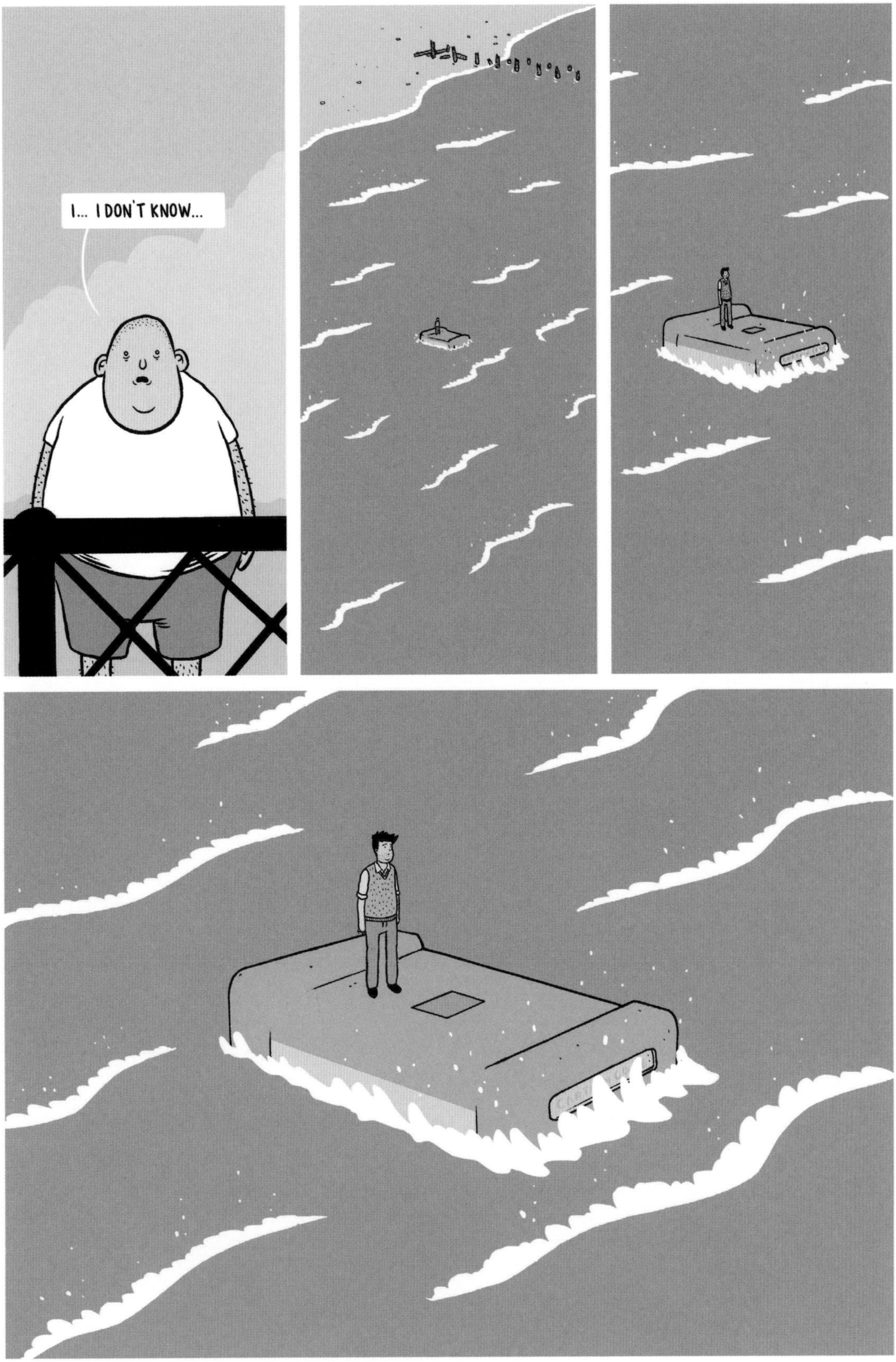
I... I DON'T KNOW...

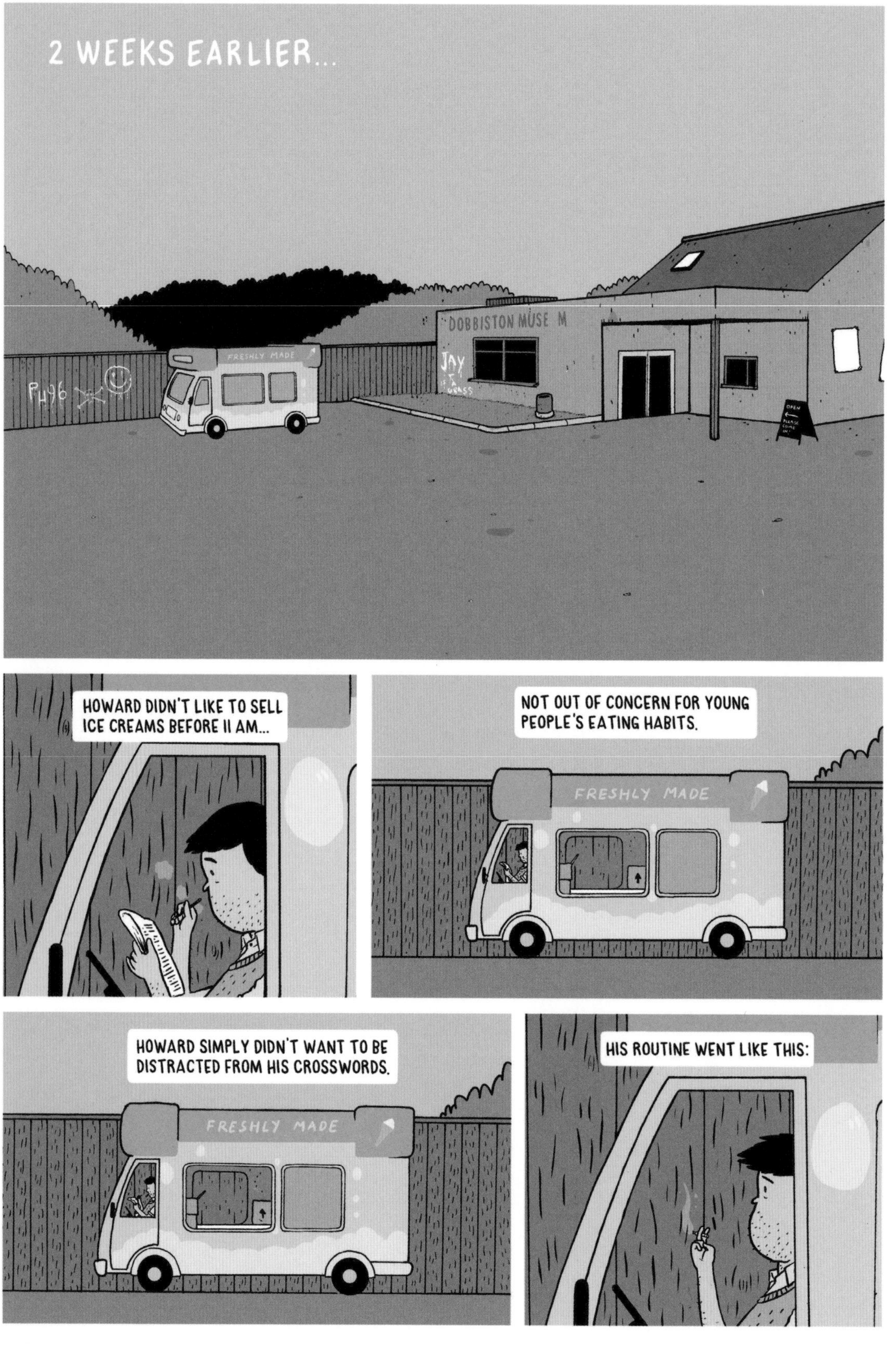
2 WEEKS EARLIER...
FRESHLY MADE
DOBBISTON MUSE M
PH96
JAY
HOWARD DIDN'T LIKE TO SELL ICE CREAMS BEFORE 11 AM...
NOT OUT OF CONCERN FOR YOUNG PEOPLE'S EATING HABITS.
FRESHLY MADE
HOWARD SIMPLY DIDN'T WANT TO BE DISTRACTED FROM HIS CROSSWORDS.
FRESHLY MADE
HIS ROUTINE WENT LIKE THIS:

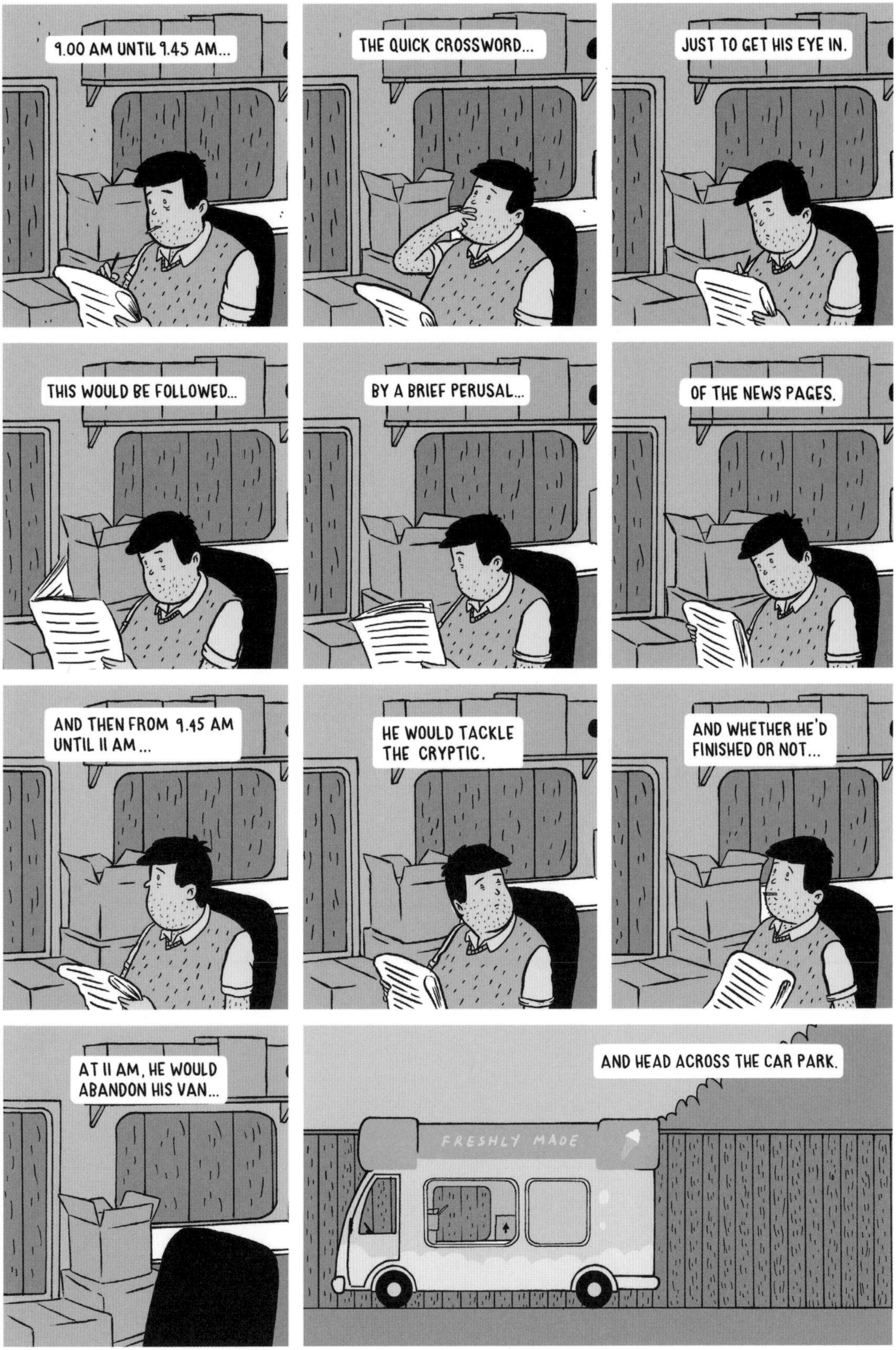
9.00 AM UNTIL 9.45 AM...
THE QUICK CROSSWORD...
JUST TO GET HIS EYE IN.
THIS WOULD BE FOLLOWED...
BY A BRIEF PERUSAL...
OF THE NEWS PAGES.
AND THEN FROM 9.45 AM UNTIL 11 AM...
HE WOULD TACKLE THE CRYPTIC.
AND WHETHER HE'D FINISHED OR NOT...
AT 11 AM, HE WOULD ABANDON HIS VAN...
AND HEAD ACROSS THE CAR PARK.
FRESHLY MADE

OPENING TIMES
ENTRANCE
OPEN
BECOME A
UPCOMING EXHIBITIONS
POTTERY SHARDS OF WEST LANCASHIRE
WICKER BASKETS - A HISTORY
IT'S £1 FOR CONCESSIONS...
MEMBER TODAY
ASK AT THE DESK FOR
LANCASHIRE
WICKER BASKETS - A HISTORY
THIS IS JASPER.
50P FOR A MAP.
TWO CONCESSIONS AND A MAP PLEASE.
RIGHT...
MUSEUM
ENTRANCE
GIFTSHOP
CARPARK
JASPER HAS WORKED IN THE MUSEUM FOR THE LAST TWENTY YEARS,
ENJOY!
ASIDE FROM A SIX MONTH STAY IN A FRENCH PRISON...
FOR TRYING TO CONVERT CONTINENTAL ROAD SIGNS FROM METRIC TO IMPERIAL.
TRAVECY 1.242
ST QUENTIN 13.0488
VENDEUIL 3.1069
UPCOMING EXHIBITIONS
POTTERY SHARDS OF WEST LANCASHIRE
WICKER BASKETS A HISTORY
ASK AT THE DESK FOR DETAILS
RIGHT JASPER, I NEED TWO!
TRICKY ONE TODAY, ME TOO!
6 DOWN?
TONDO.
12 ACROSS?
BUTTRESS.

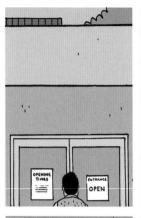

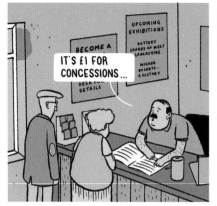

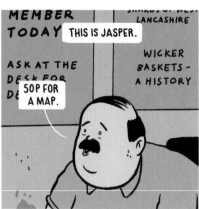

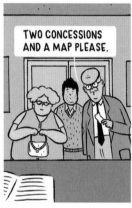

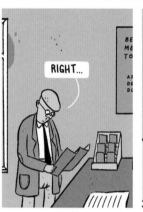

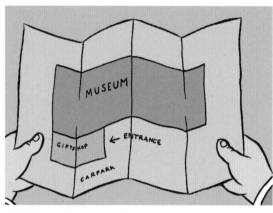

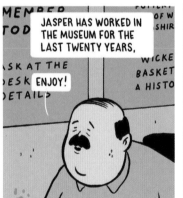

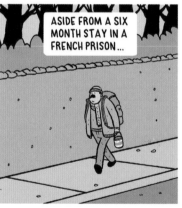

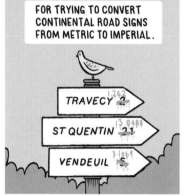

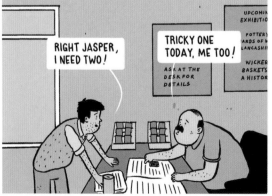

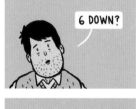

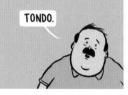

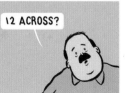

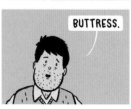

19 DOWN?
TODAY!
MMM... STILL WORKING ON THAT... CUPPA?
DETAILS
ALEX! WATCH THE TILL...
SO, HOW'S THE NEW GIRL?
ALEX?
FINE.
STUDENT. HISTORY.
MEDIEVAL.
I'M YET TO GIVE HER MY THEORY ABOUT GRAIN PRICES AND THE FALL OF THE PLANTAGENETS.
SHE'S IN FOR A TREAT...
HAROLD WILSON
LANCASHIRE'S GREATEST FUEL CAPS
ER... WHAT ARE THESE?
DON'T GET YOUR PRINTS ON THEM!
DMRS
GIVE US BACK OUR MOUNTAIN

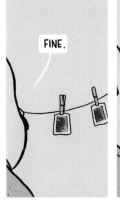

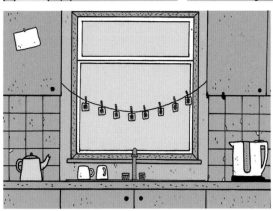

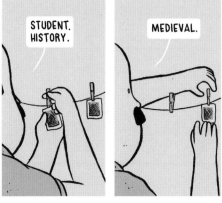

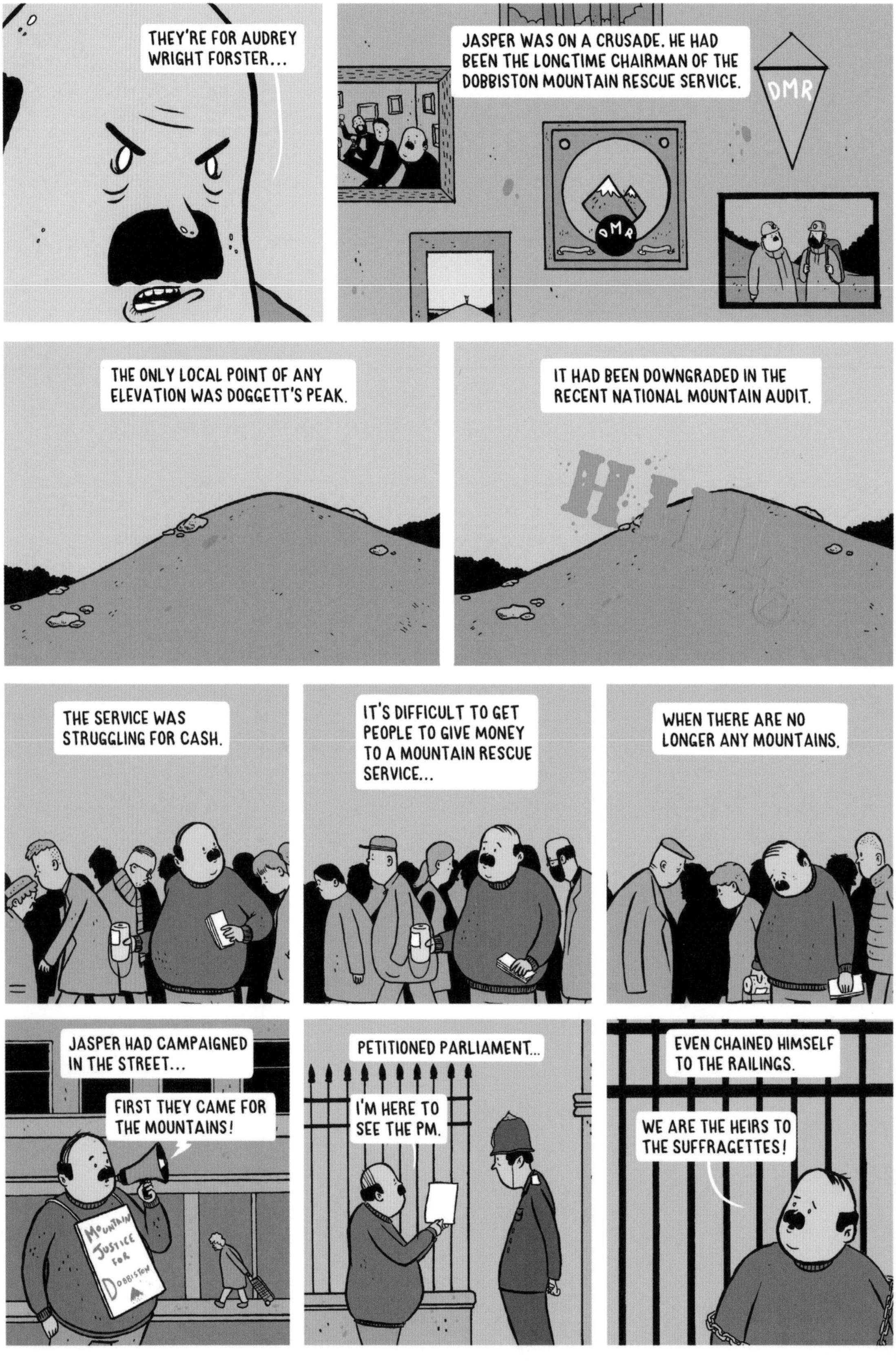
THEY'RE FOR AUDREY WRIGHT FORSTER...
JASPER WAS ON A CRUSADE. HE HAD BEEN THE LONGTIME CHAIRMAN OF THE DOBBISTON MOUNTAIN RESCUE SERVICE.
DMR
DMR
THE ONLY LOCAL POINT OF ANY ELEVATION WAS DOGGETT'S PEAK.
IT HAD BEEN DOWNGRADED IN THE RECENT NATIONAL MOUNTAIN AUDIT.
HILL
THE SERVICE WAS STRUGGLING FOR CASH.
IT'S DIFFICULT TO GET PEOPLE TO GIVE MONEY TO A MOUNTAIN RESCUE SERVICE...
WHEN THERE ARE NO LONGER ANY MOUNTAINS.
JASPER HAD CAMPAIGNED IN THE STREET...
FIRST THEY CAME FOR THE MOUNTAINS!
MOUNTAIN JUSTICE FOR DOBBISTON
PETITIONED PARLIAMENT...
I'M HERE TO SEE THE PM.
EVEN CHAINED HIMSELF TO THE RAILINGS.
WE ARE THE HEIRS TO THE SUFFRAGETTES!

THE TARGET OF THESE PROTESTS WAS AUDREY WRIGHT FORSTER, CHAIR OF THE UK MOUNTAIN COMMITTEE.

IT'S ALL POLITICS.

SHE'S IN THE POCKET OF THE HILL LOBBY, ALWAYS HAS BEEN.

YOU'VE USED PERSONALISED STATIONERY.

AREN'T THESE MEANT TO BE ANONYMOUS?

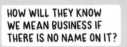

HOW WILL THEY KNOW WE MEAN BUSINESS IF THERE IS NO NAME ON IT?

I GUESS...

ANYWAY... I'M HEADING TO THE LODGE LATER... WANT ME TO TAKE A COLLECTION?

YES PLEASE.

SEE YOU LATER, ALEX!

LATER!

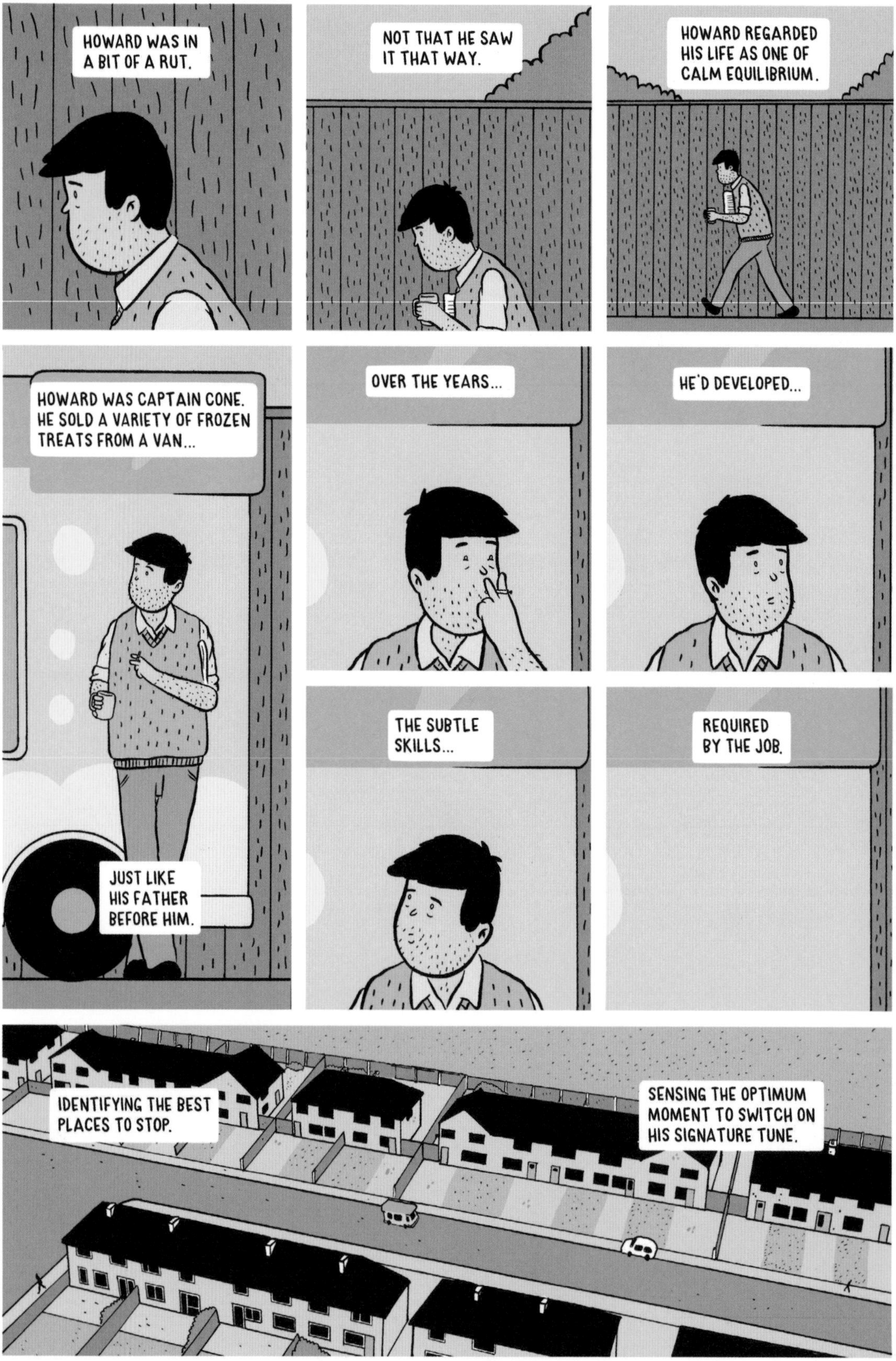
HOWARD WAS IN A BIT OF A RUT.
NOT THAT HE SAW IT THAT WAY.
HOWARD REGARDED HIS LIFE AS ONE OF CALM EQUILIBRIUM.
HOWARD WAS CAPTAIN CONE. HE SOLD A VARIETY OF FROZEN TREATS FROM A VAN...
JUST LIKE HIS FATHER BEFORE HIM.
OVER THE YEARS...
HE'D DEVELOPED...
THE SUBTLE SKILLS...
REQUIRED BY THE JOB.
IDENTIFYING THE BEST PLACES TO STOP.
SENSING THE OPTIMUM MOMENT TO SWITCH ON HIS SIGNATURE TUNE.

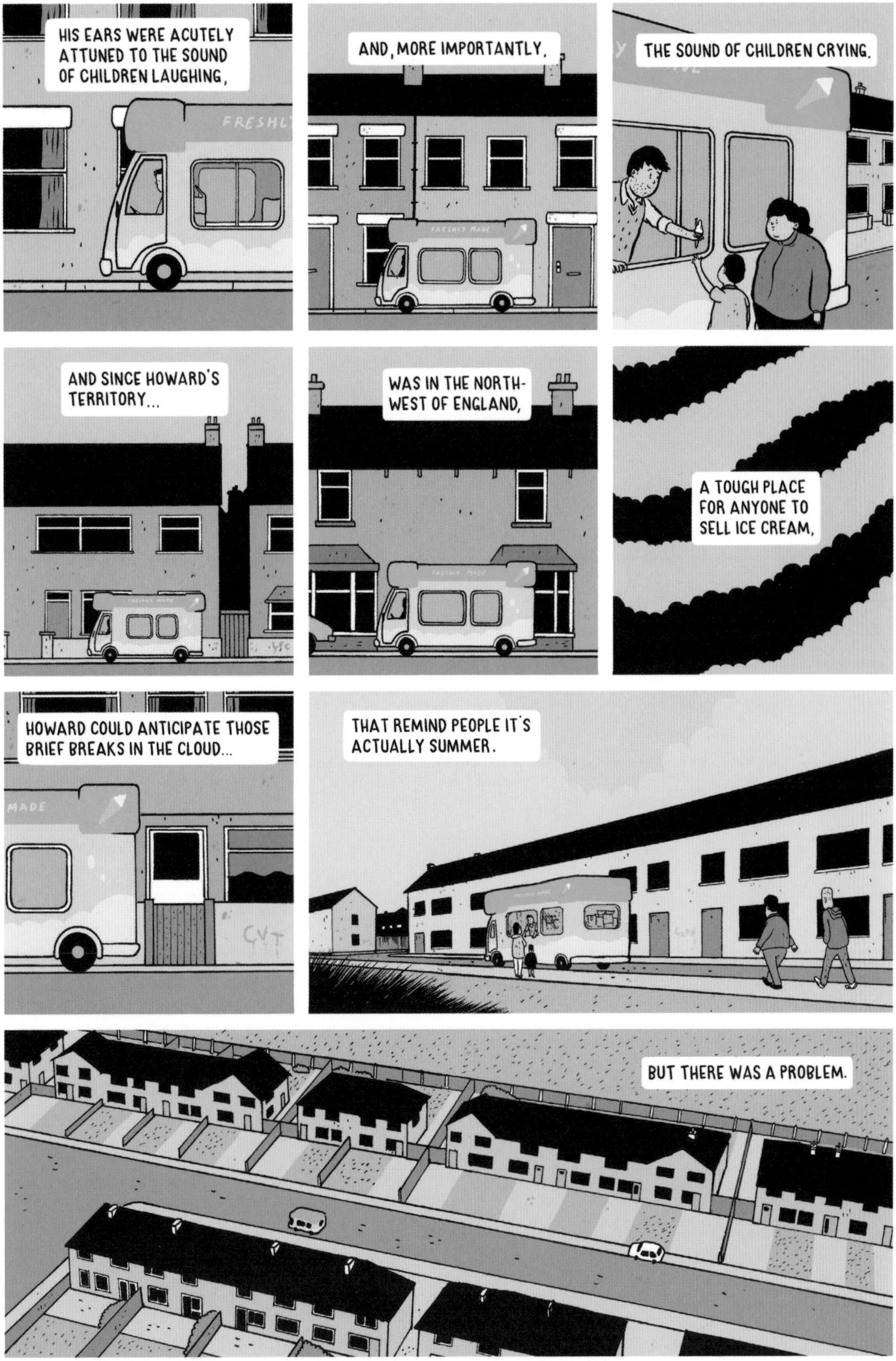
HIS EARS WERE ACUTELY ATTUNED TO THE SOUND OF CHILDREN LAUGHING,
AND, MORE IMPORTANTLY,
THE SOUND OF CHILDREN CRYING.
AND SINCE HOWARD'S TERRITORY...
WAS IN THE NORTH-WEST OF ENGLAND,
A TOUGH PLACE FOR ANYONE TO SELL ICE CREAM,
HOWARD COULD ANTICIPATE THOSE BRIEF BREAKS IN THE CLOUD...
THAT REMIND PEOPLE IT'S ACTUALLY SUMMER.
BUT THERE WAS A PROBLEM.

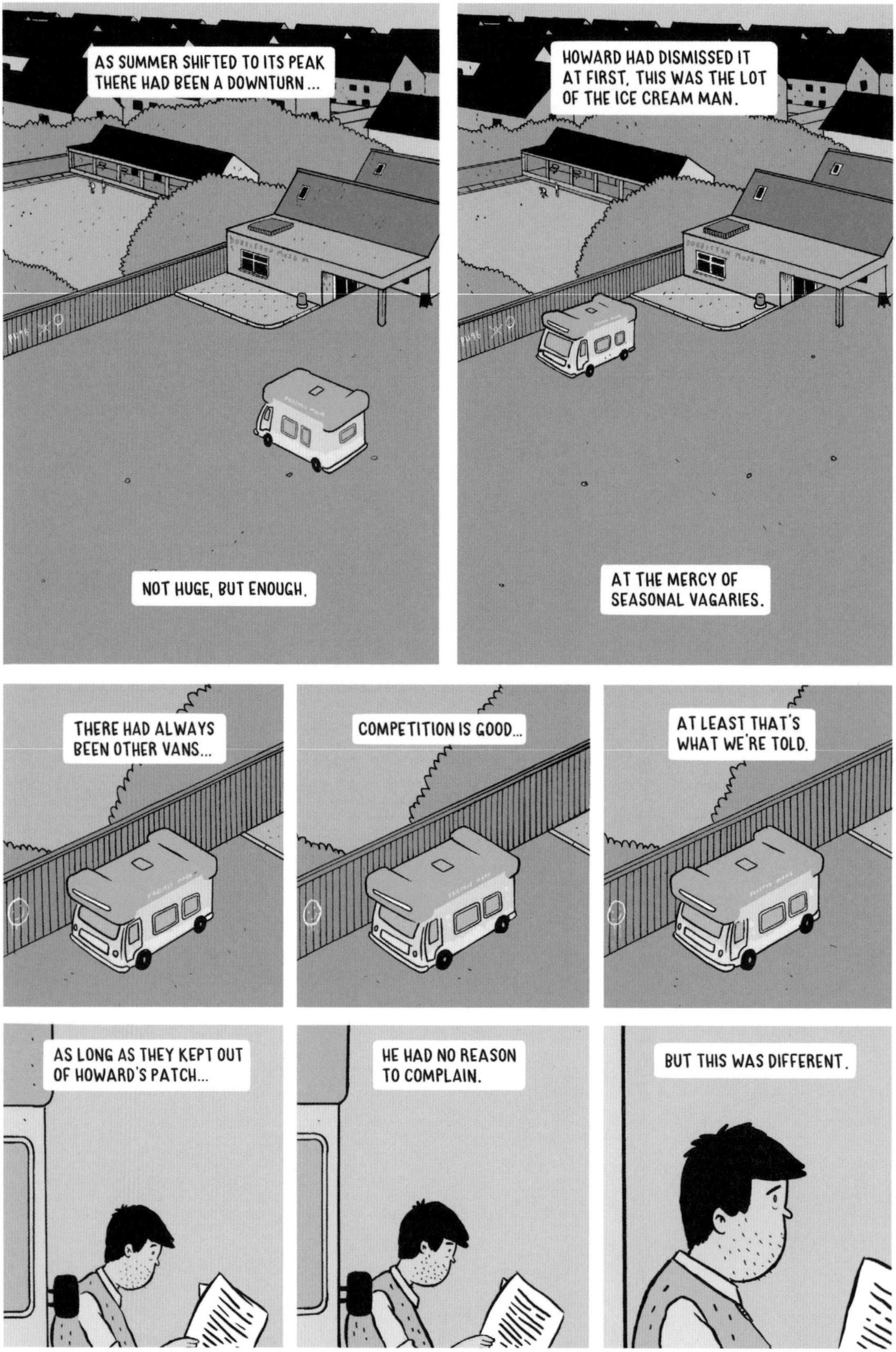
AS SUMMER SHIFTED TO ITS PEAK THERE HAD BEEN A DOWNTURN...
NOT HUGE, BUT ENOUGH.
HOWARD HAD DISMISSED IT AT FIRST, THIS WAS THE LOT OF THE ICE CREAM MAN.
AT THE MERCY OF SEASONAL VAGARIES.
THERE HAD ALWAYS BEEN OTHER VANS...
COMPETITION IS GOOD...
AT LEAST THAT'S WHAT WE'RE TOLD.
AS LONG AS THEY KEPT OUT OF HOWARD'S PATCH...
HE HAD NO REASON TO COMPLAIN.
BUT THIS WAS DIFFERENT.

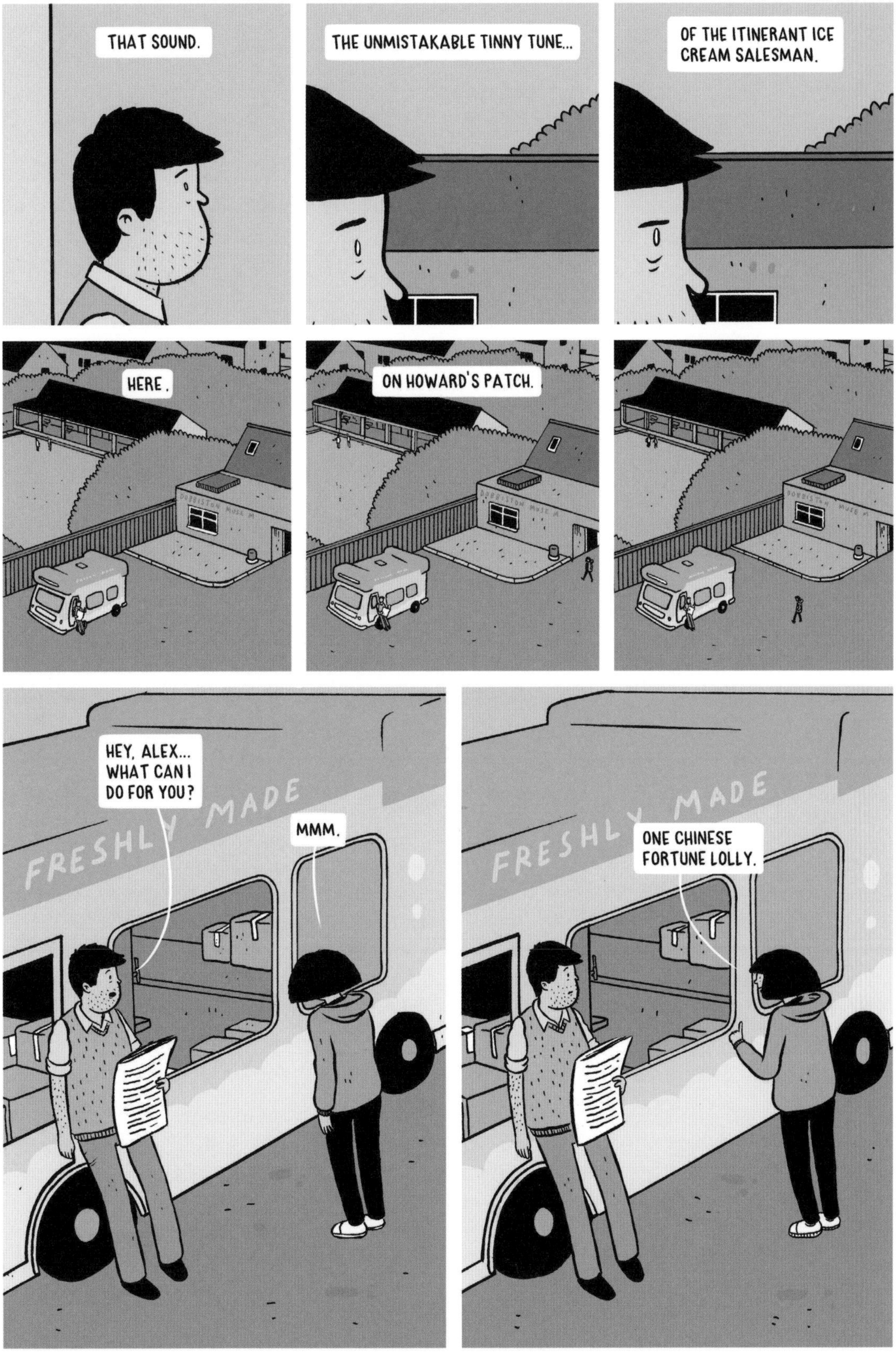
THAT SOUND.
THE UNMISTAKABLE TINNY TUNE...
OF THE ITINERANT ICE CREAM SALESMAN.
HERE.
ON HOWARD'S PATCH.
HEY, ALEX... WHAT CAN I DO FOR YOU?
FRESHLY MADE
MMM.
FRESHLY MADE
ONE CHINESE FORTUNE LOLLY.

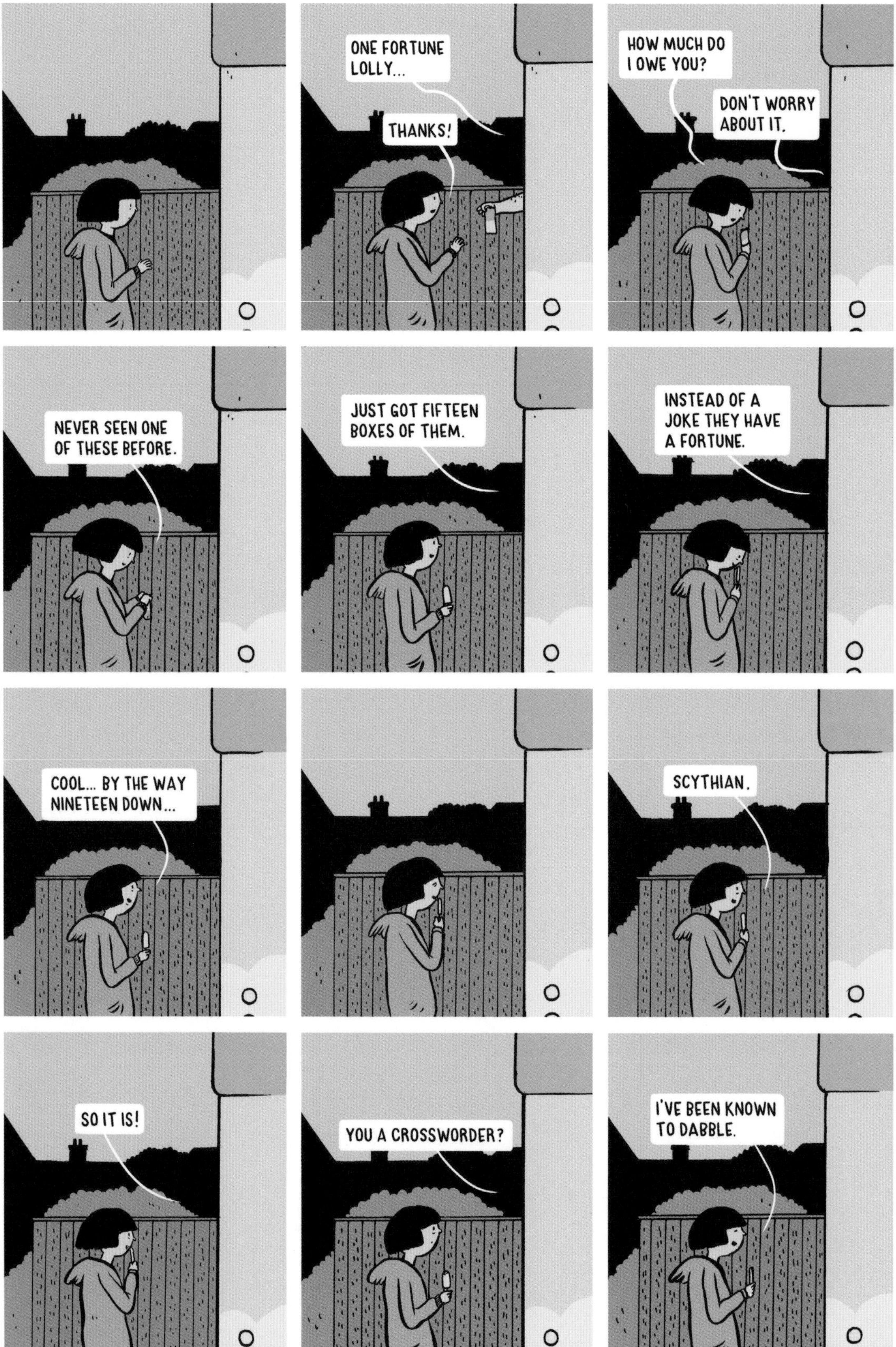
ONE FORTUNE LOLLY...
THANKS!
HOW MUCH DO I OWE YOU?
DON'T WORRY ABOUT IT.
NEVER SEEN ONE OF THESE BEFORE.
JUST GOT FIFTEEN BOXES OF THEM.
INSTEAD OF A JOKE THEY HAVE A FORTUNE.
COOL... BY THE WAY NINETEEN DOWN...
SCYTHIAN.
SO IT IS!
YOU A CROSSWORDER?
I'VE BEEN KNOWN TO DABBLE.

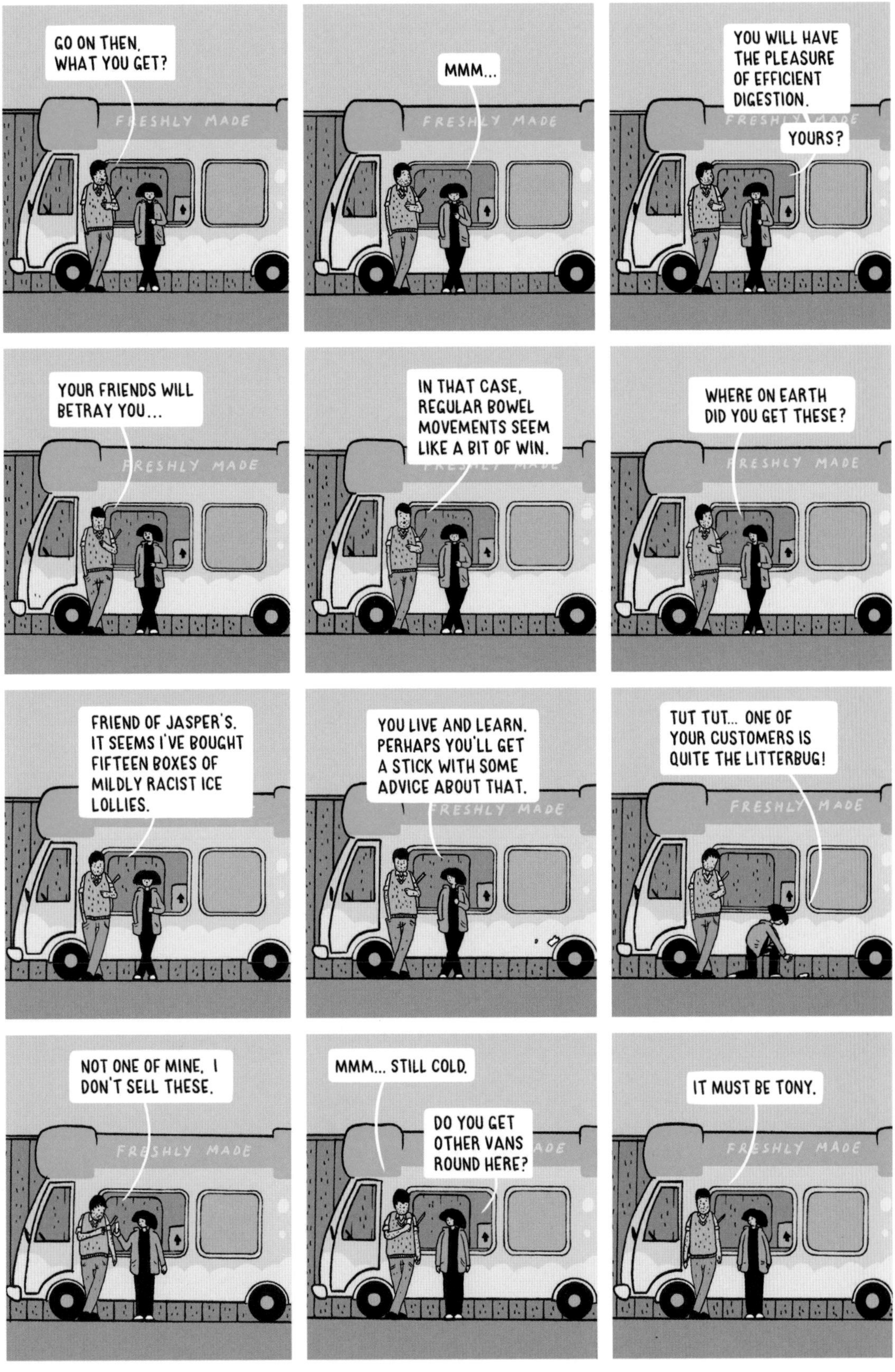
GO ON THEN, WHAT YOU GET?
MMM...
YOU WILL HAVE THE PLEASURE OF EFFICIENT DIGESTION.
YOURS?
YOUR FRIENDS WILL BETRAY YOU...
IN THAT CASE, REGULAR BOWEL MOVEMENTS SEEM LIKE A BIT OF WIN.
WHERE ON EARTH DID YOU GET THESE?
FRIEND OF JASPER'S. IT SEEMS I'VE BOUGHT FIFTEEN BOXES OF MILDLY RACIST ICE LOLLIES.
YOU LIVE AND LEARN. PERHAPS YOU'LL GET A STICK WITH SOME ADVICE ABOUT THAT.
TUT TUT... ONE OF YOUR CUSTOMERS IS QUITE THE LITTERBUG!
NOT ONE OF MINE, I DON'T SELL THESE.
MMM... STILL COLD.
DO YOU GET OTHER VANS ROUND HERE?
IT MUST BE TONY.

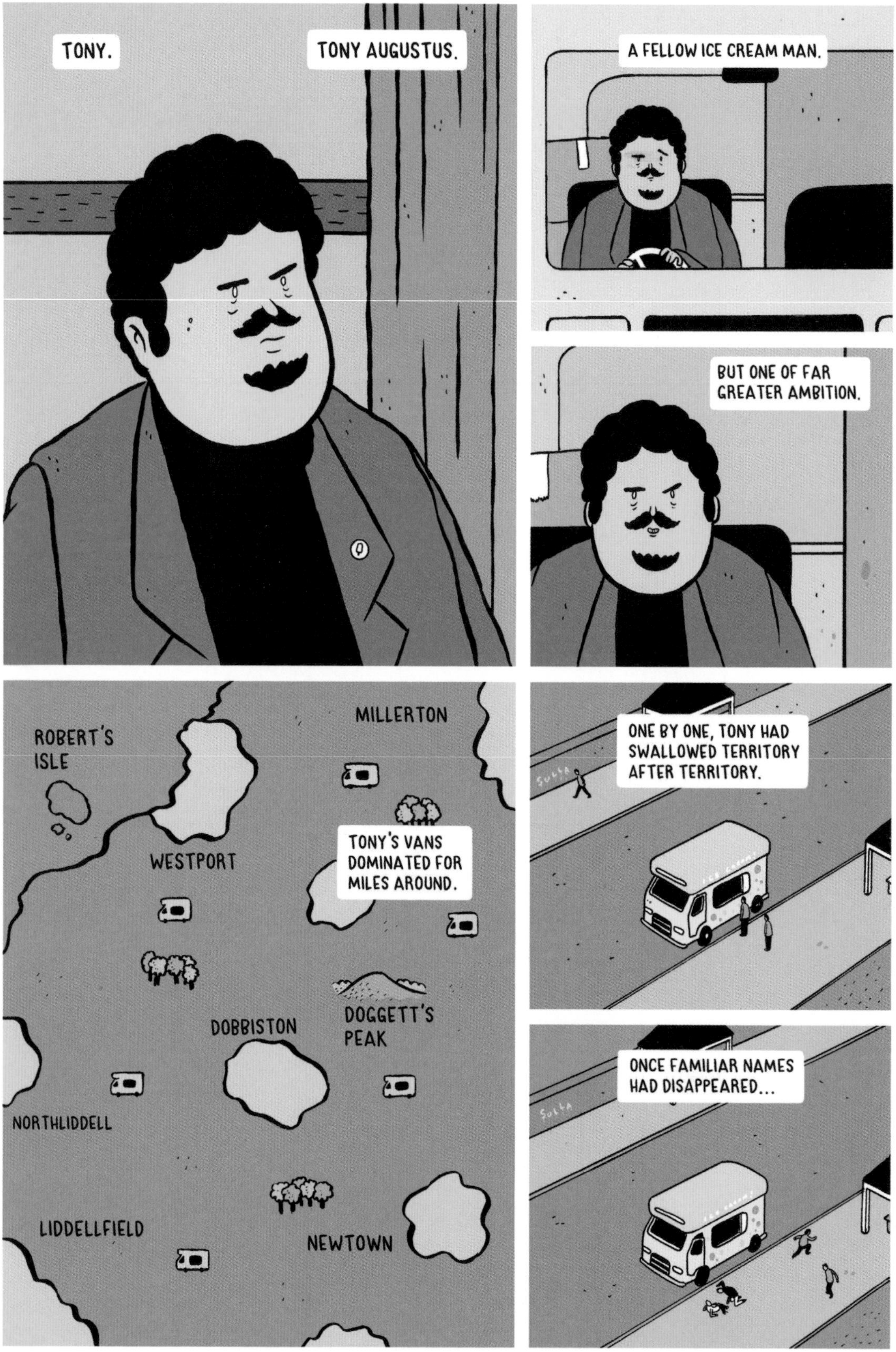
TONY.
TONY AUGUSTUS.
A FELLOW ICE CREAM MAN.
BUT ONE OF FAR GREATER AMBITION.
ROBERT'S ISLE
MILLERTON
WESTPORT
TONY'S VANS DOMINATED FOR MILES AROUND.
DOBBISTON
DOGGETT'S PEAK
NORTHLIDDELL
LIDDELLFIELD
NEWTOWN
ONE BY ONE, TONY HAD SWALLOWED TERRITORY AFTER TERRITORY.
ONCE FAMILIAR NAMES HAD DISAPPEARED...

BARRY'S ICES

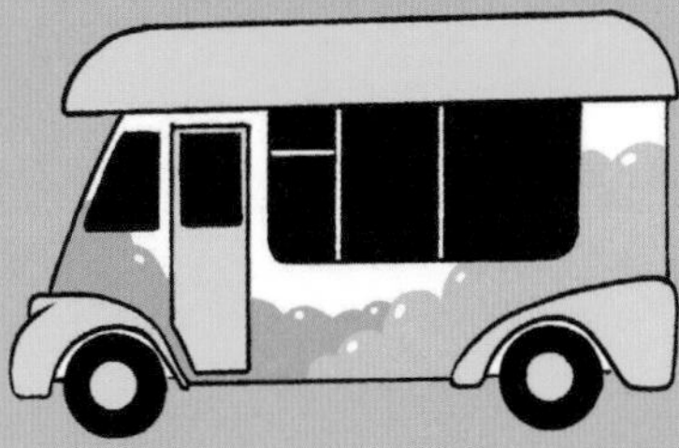

MR CREAMY

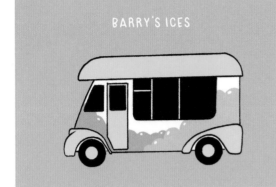

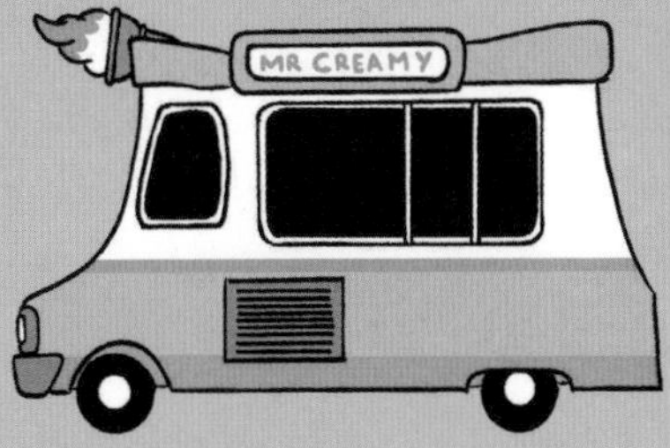
MR CREAMY

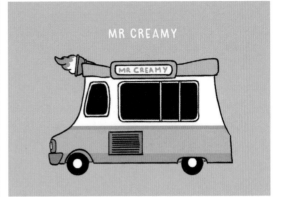

WALT WHIPMAN

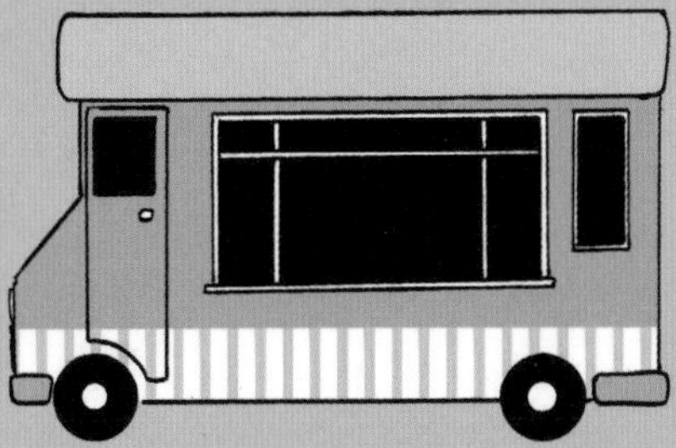

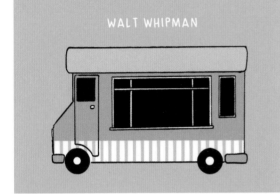

DR FRISBEE'S ICE-CREAMS
OF DISTINCTION

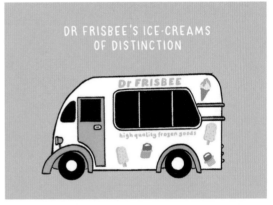

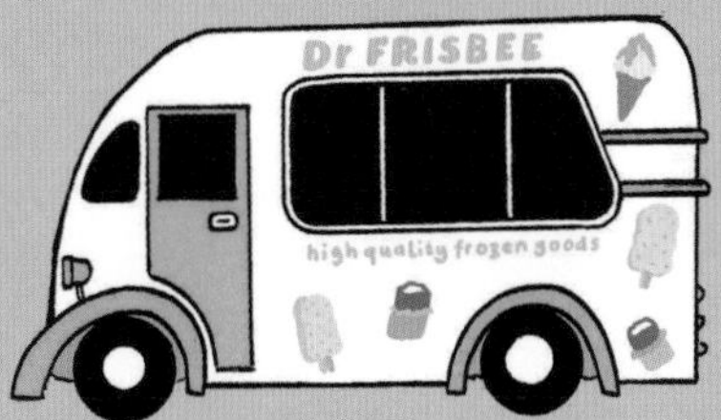
Dr FRISBEE
high quality frozen goods

PROFESSOR SCRUMPTIOUS

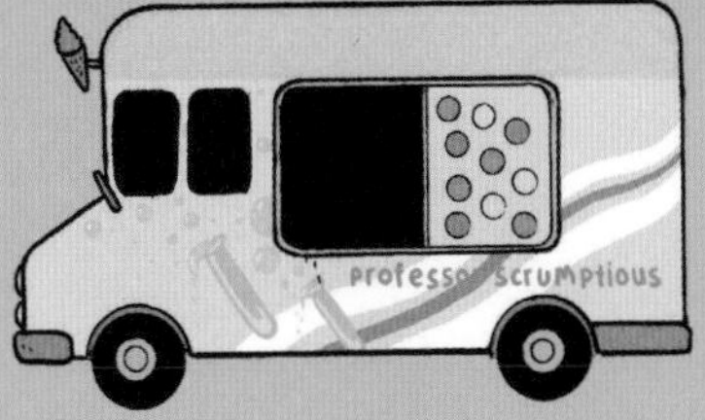
Professor Scrumptious

CAMELOT CREAMS

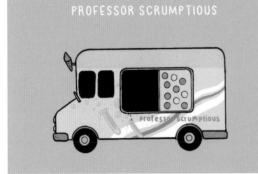

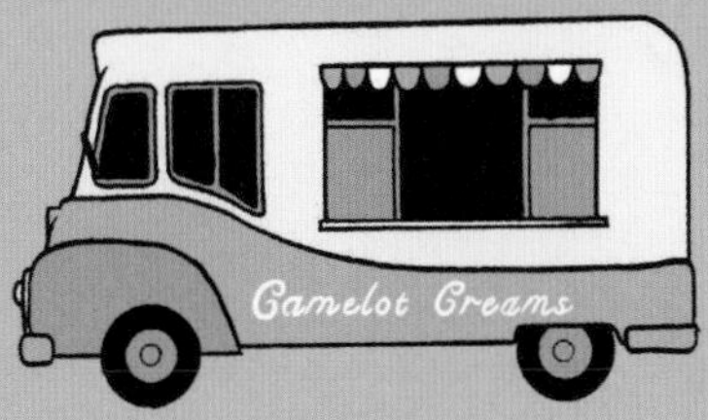
Camelot Creams

THE SHERBETMOBILE

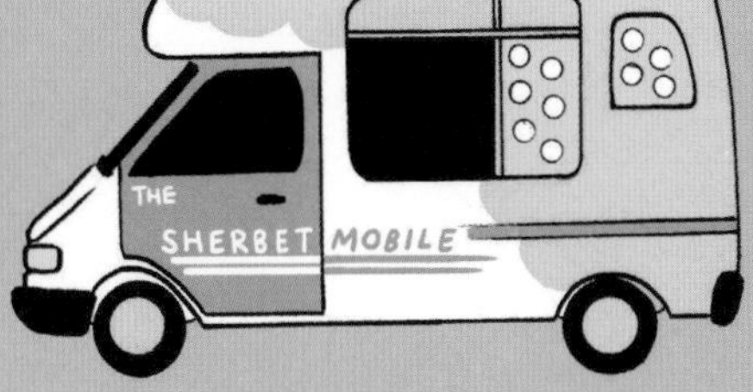
THE
SHERBET MOBILE

GOOD GOLLY MISS LOLLY

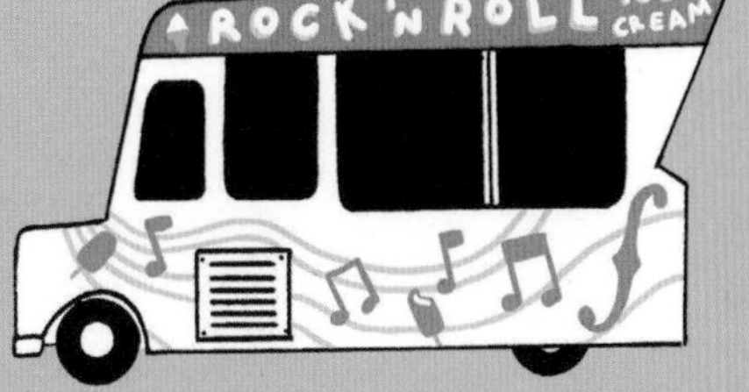
ROCK 'N ROLL ICE CREAM

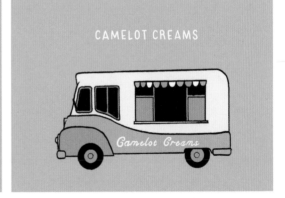

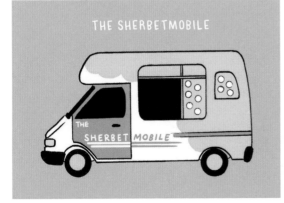

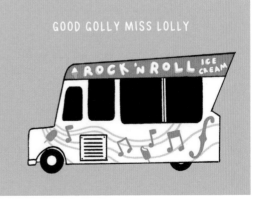

ALL GONE.

THEIR DOMAINS SUBSUMED BY TONY'S ICE CREAM EMPIRE.

ALL ASIDE FROM HOWARD.

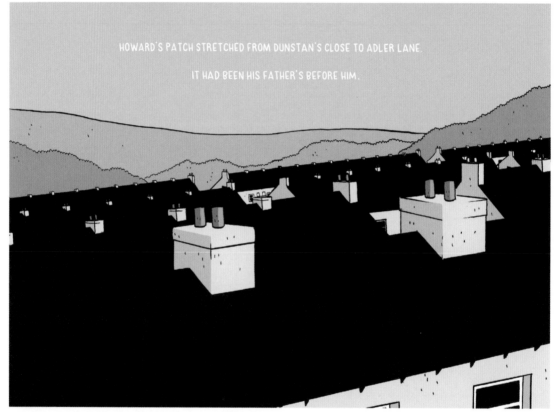

HOWARD'S PATCH STRETCHED FROM DUNSTAN'S CLOSE TO ADLER LANE.

IT HAD BEEN HIS FATHER'S BEFORE HIM.

AND PERHAPS THAT IS WHY TONY COVETED IT SO MUCH.

TONY WAS HOWARD'S HALF BROTHER.

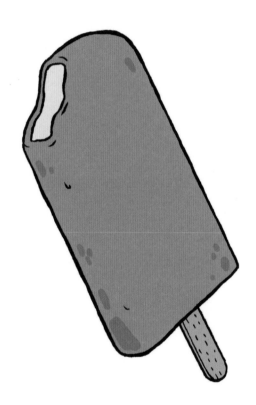

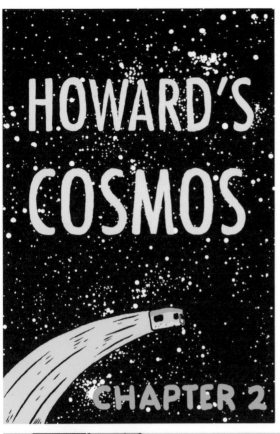

HOWARD'S COSMOS
CHAPTER 2
EVERY SIGNIFICANT MOMENT OF HOWARD'S LIFE HAD HAPPENED IN DOBBISTON.
ALL OF THE FORGETTABLE ONES HAD TOO.
DOBBISTON IS A SMALL MARKET TOWN IN THE NORTH-WEST OF ENGLAND...
EBABS
D-ZINER
BOOZE 'N FAGS
SALE
SUPERC
HOME TO AROUND THIRTY THOUSAND PEOPLE.

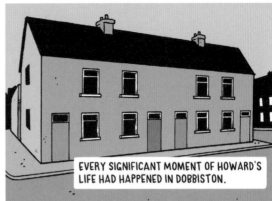

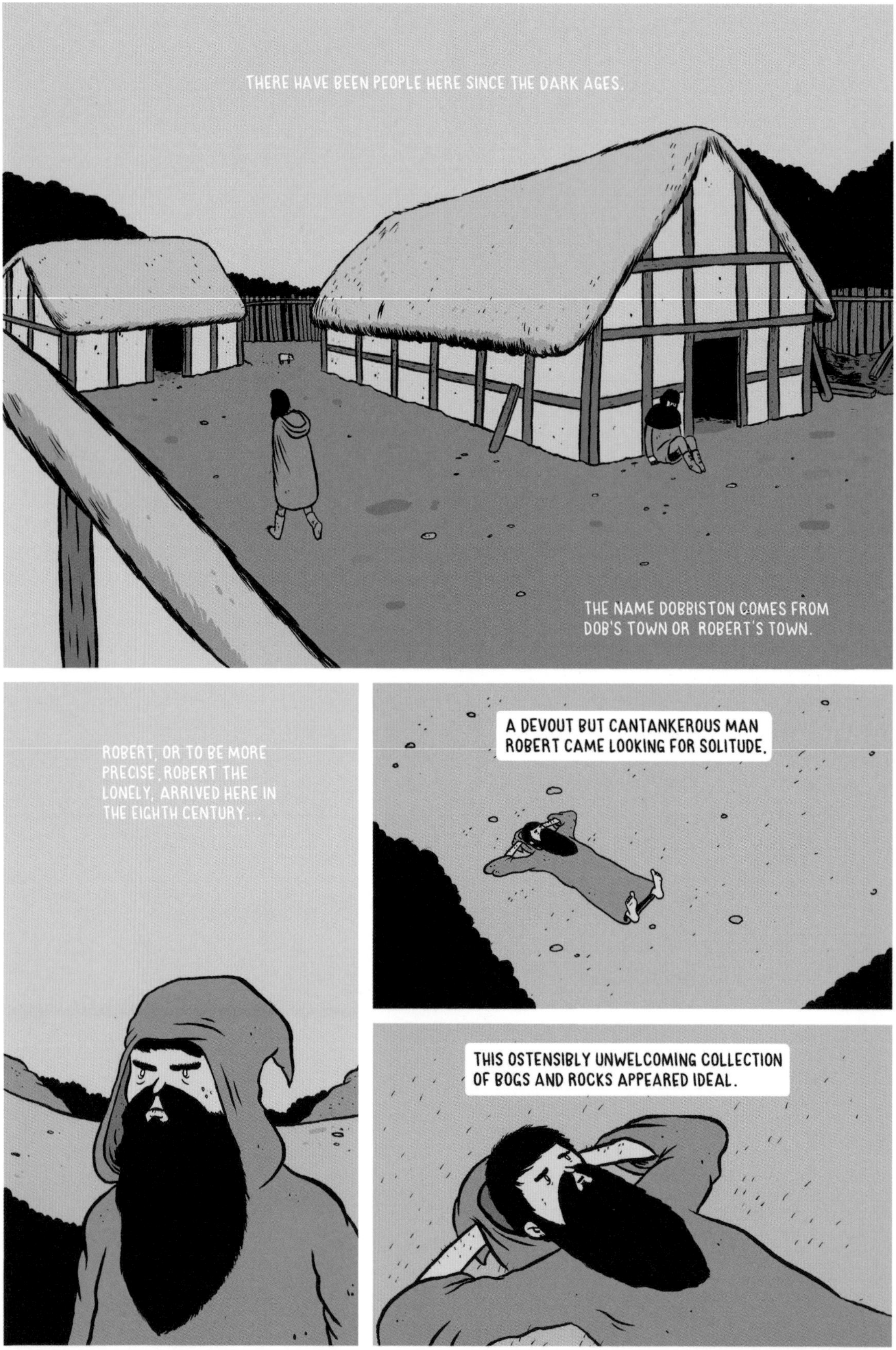
THERE HAVE BEEN PEOPLE HERE SINCE THE DARK AGES.
THE NAME DOBBISTON COMES FROM DOB'S TOWN OR ROBERT'S TOWN.
ROBERT, OR TO BE MORE PRECISE, ROBERT THE LONELY, ARRIVED HERE IN THE EIGHTH CENTURY...
A DEVOUT BUT CANTANKEROUS MAN ROBERT CAME LOOKING FOR SOLITUDE.
THIS OSTENSIBLY UNWELCOMING COLLECTION OF BOGS AND ROCKS APPEARED IDEAL.

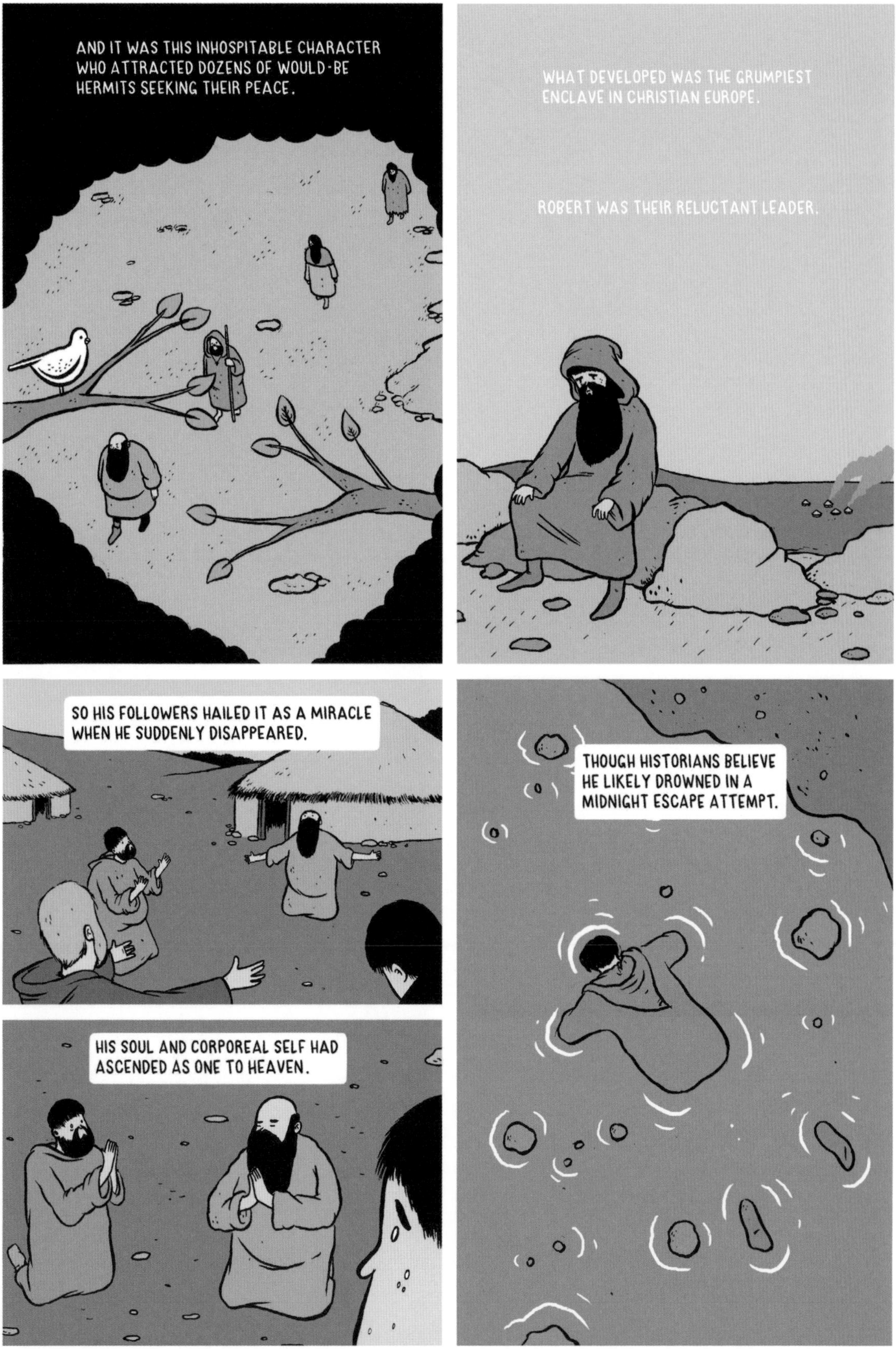
AND IT WAS THIS INHOSPITABLE CHARACTER WHO ATTRACTED DOZENS OF WOULD-BE HERMITS SEEKING THEIR PEACE.
WHAT DEVELOPED WAS THE GRUMPIEST ENCLAVE IN CHRISTIAN EUROPE.
ROBERT WAS THEIR RELUCTANT LEADER.
SO HIS FOLLOWERS HAILED IT AS A MIRACLE WHEN HE SUDDENLY DISAPPEARED.
HIS SOUL AND CORPOREAL SELF HAD ASCENDED AS ONE TO HEAVEN.
THOUGH HISTORIANS BELIEVE HE LIKELY DROWNED IN A MIDNIGHT ESCAPE ATTEMPT.

THE ALLEGED MIRACLE ATTRACTED MORE PEOPLE TO DOBBISTON.

BY THE TIME OF THE DOMESDAY BOOK, IT WAS HOME TO A COUPLE OF HUNDRED PEOPLE.

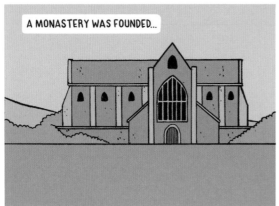

A MONASTERY WAS FOUNDED...

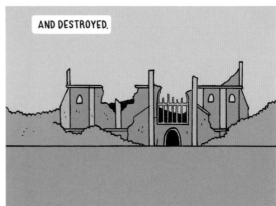

AND DESTROYED.

AND ASIDE FROM GLADSTONE REFERRING TO IT AS...

THE MOST POINTLESS PLACE I HAVE EVER KNOWN.

NOT A GREAT DEAL HAD HAPPENED HERE IN THE INTERVENING CENTURIES.

FOR MANY OF ITS RESIDENTS...

THAT WAS ITS CHIEF VIRTUE.

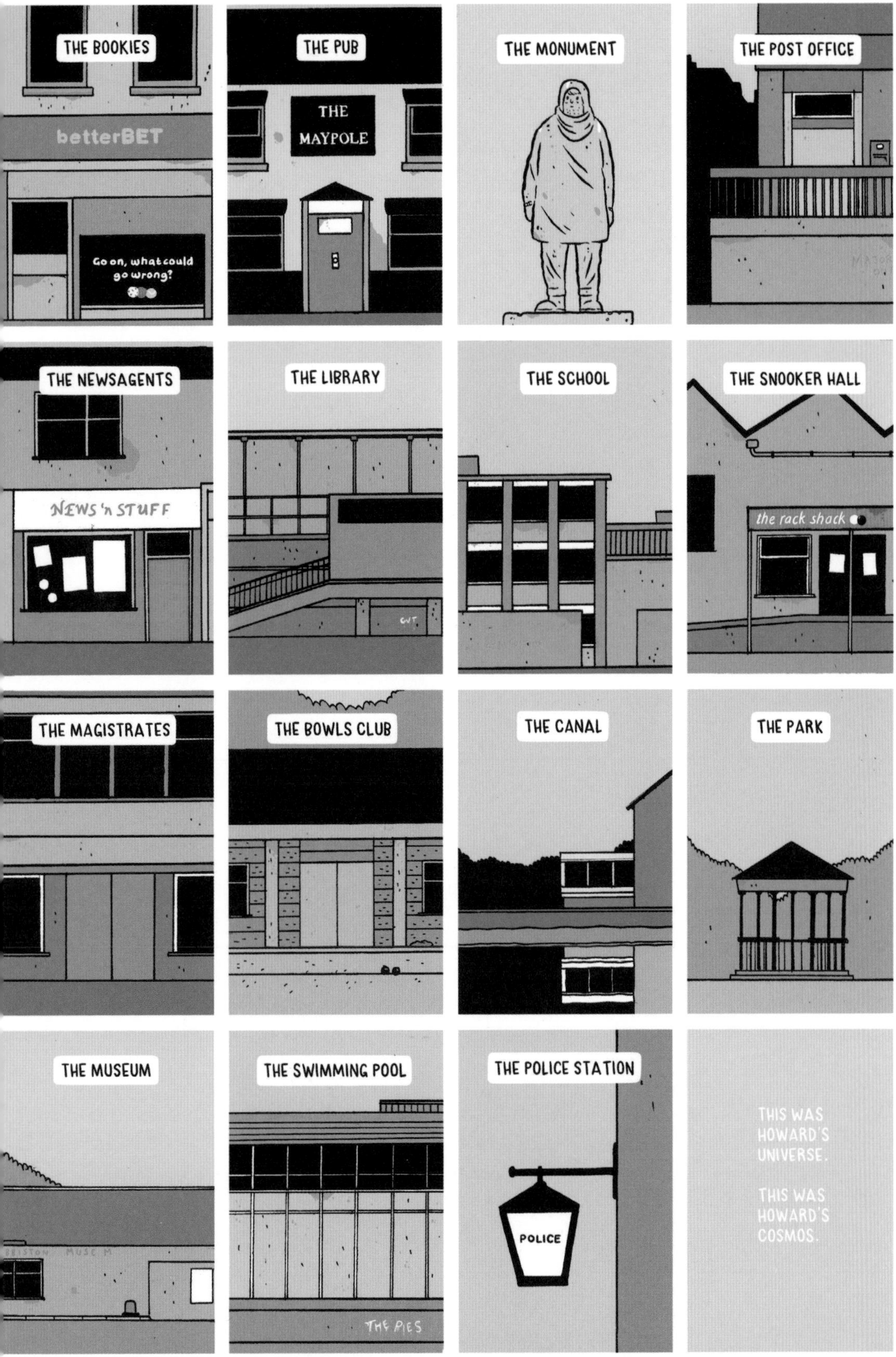
THE BOOKIES
betterBET
Go on, what could go wrong?
THE PUB
THE MAYPOLE
THE MONUMENT
THE POST OFFICE
THE NEWSAGENTS
NEWS 'n STUFF
THE LIBRARY
THE SCHOOL
THE SNOOKER HALL
the rack shack
THE MAGISTRATES
THE BOWLS CLUB
THE CANAL
THE PARK
THE MUSEUM
THE SWIMMING POOL
THE POLICE STATION
POLICE
THIS WAS HOWARD'S UNIVERSE.
THIS WAS HOWARD'S COSMOS.

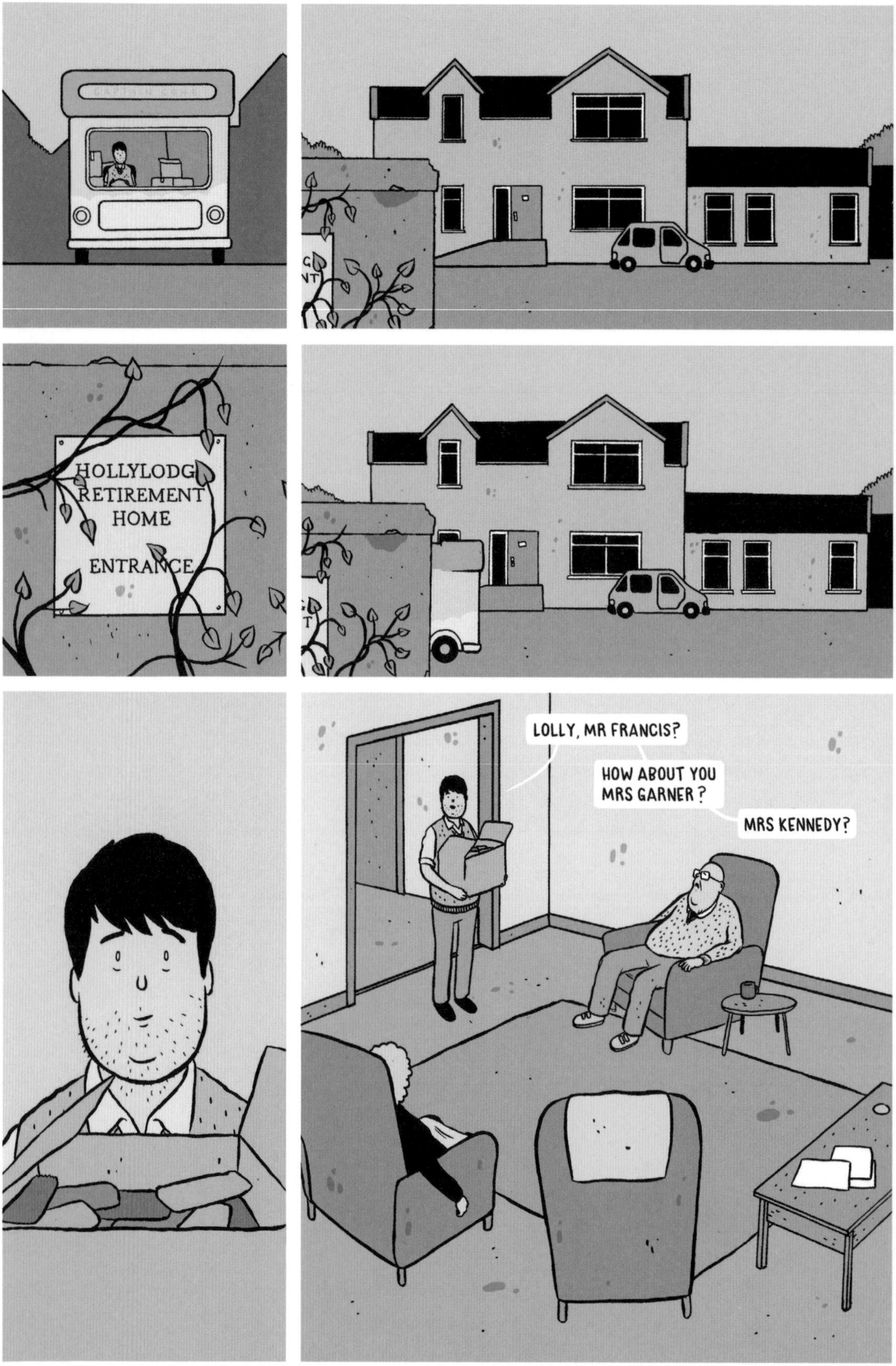
HOLLYLODGE
RETIREMENT
HOME
ENTRANCE
LOLLY, MR FRANCIS?
HOW ABOUT YOU MRS GARNER?
MRS KENNEDY?

OH... YES PLEASE, DEAR.

OH MY...

DO YOU HAVE ONE THAT'S A LITTLE WARMER?

ER... NO... SORRY.

I'M GOING TO LEAVE A COLLECTION TIN FOR THE MOUNTAIN RESCUE SERVICE.

THEY NEED THE MONEY SO ANY SPARE CHANGE WOULD BE GREAT...

YOU CAN COUNT ON US! MY RODNEY WAS ALWAYS A GREAT SUPPORTER OF THE SERVICE...

VERY SNEAKY THINGS, THESE MOUNTAINS...

YOU CAN BE SAT HERE, WATCHING YOUR PROGRAMMES...

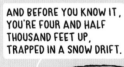

AND BEFORE YOU KNOW IT, YOU'RE FOUR AND HALF THOUSAND FEET UP, TRAPPED IN A SNOW DRIFT.

THAT'S WHY I ALWAYS KEEP ONE OF THESE IN MY HANDBAG...

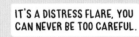

IT'S A DISTRESS FLARE, YOU CAN NEVER BE TOO CAREFUL.

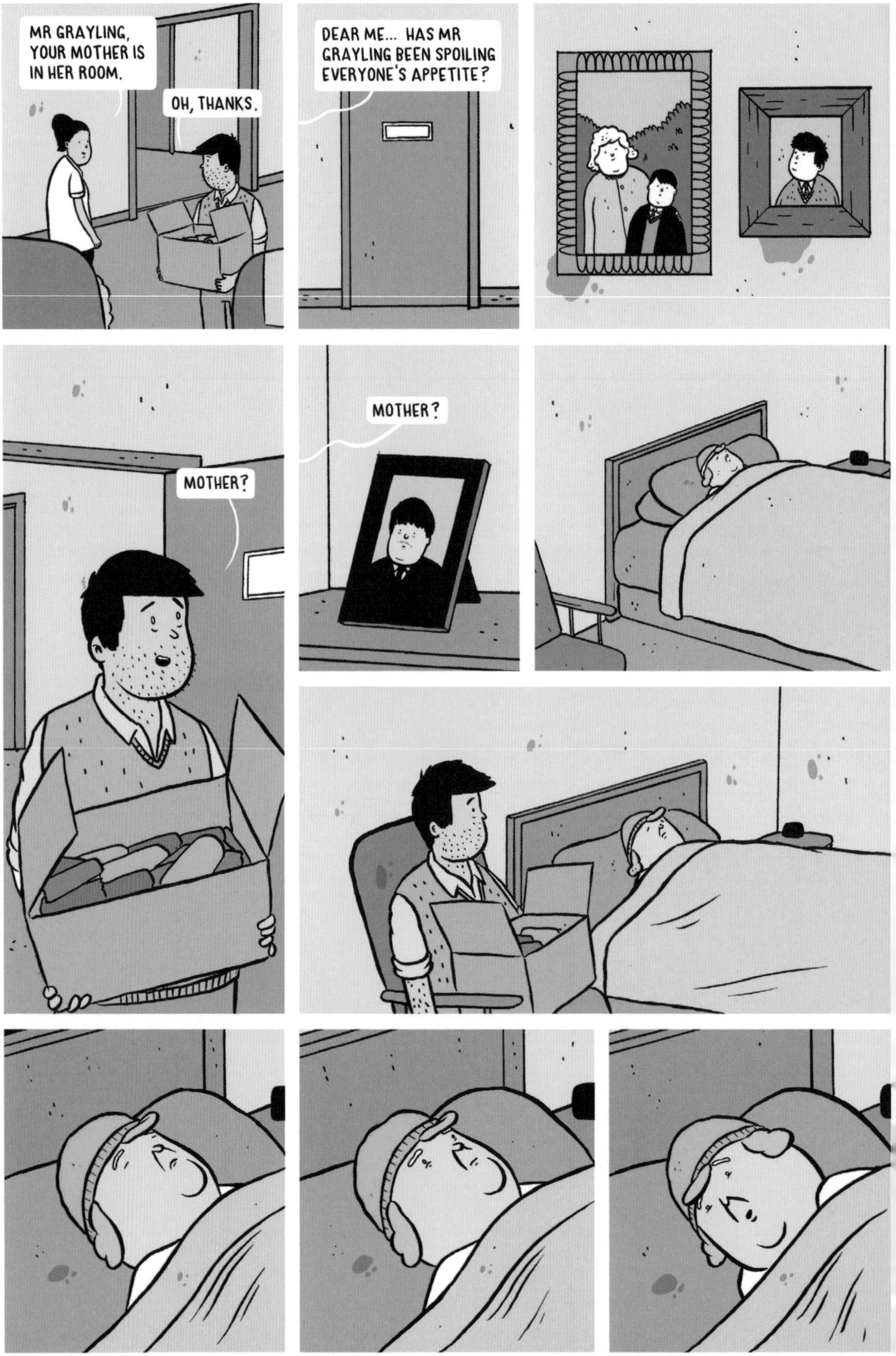
MR GRAYLING, YOUR MOTHER IS IN HER ROOM.
OH, THANKS.
DEAR ME... HAS MR GRAYLING BEEN SPOILING EVERYONE'S APPETITE?
MOTHER?
MOTHER?

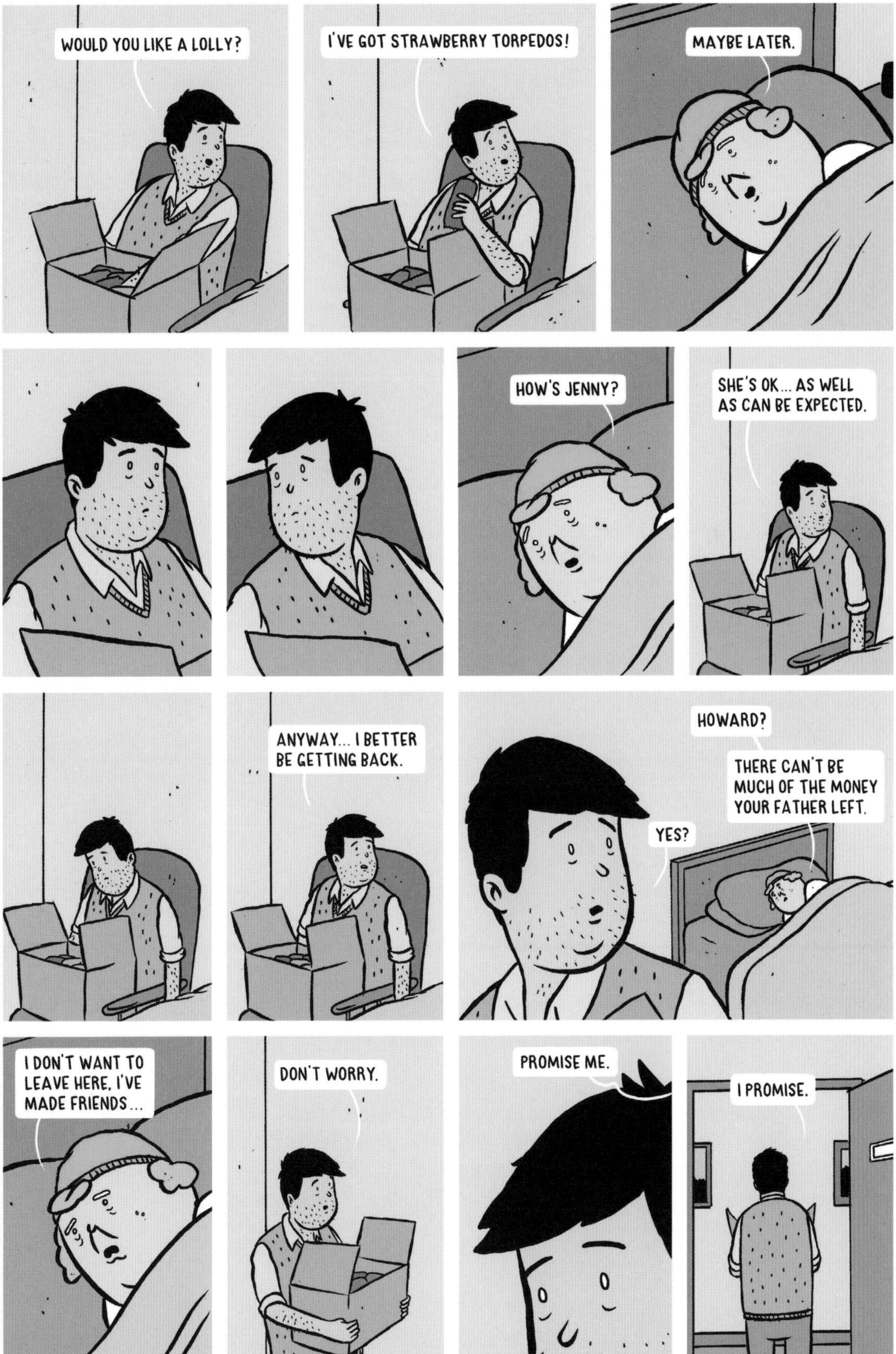
WOULD YOU LIKE A LOLLY?
I'VE GOT STRAWBERRY TORPEDOS!
MAYBE LATER.
HOW'S JENNY?
SHE'S OK... AS WELL AS CAN BE EXPECTED.
ANYWAY... I BETTER BE GETTING BACK.
HOWARD?
YES?
THERE CAN'T BE MUCH OF THE MONEY YOUR FATHER LEFT.
I DON'T WANT TO LEAVE HERE, I'VE MADE FRIENDS...
DON'T WORRY.
PROMISE ME.
I PROMISE.

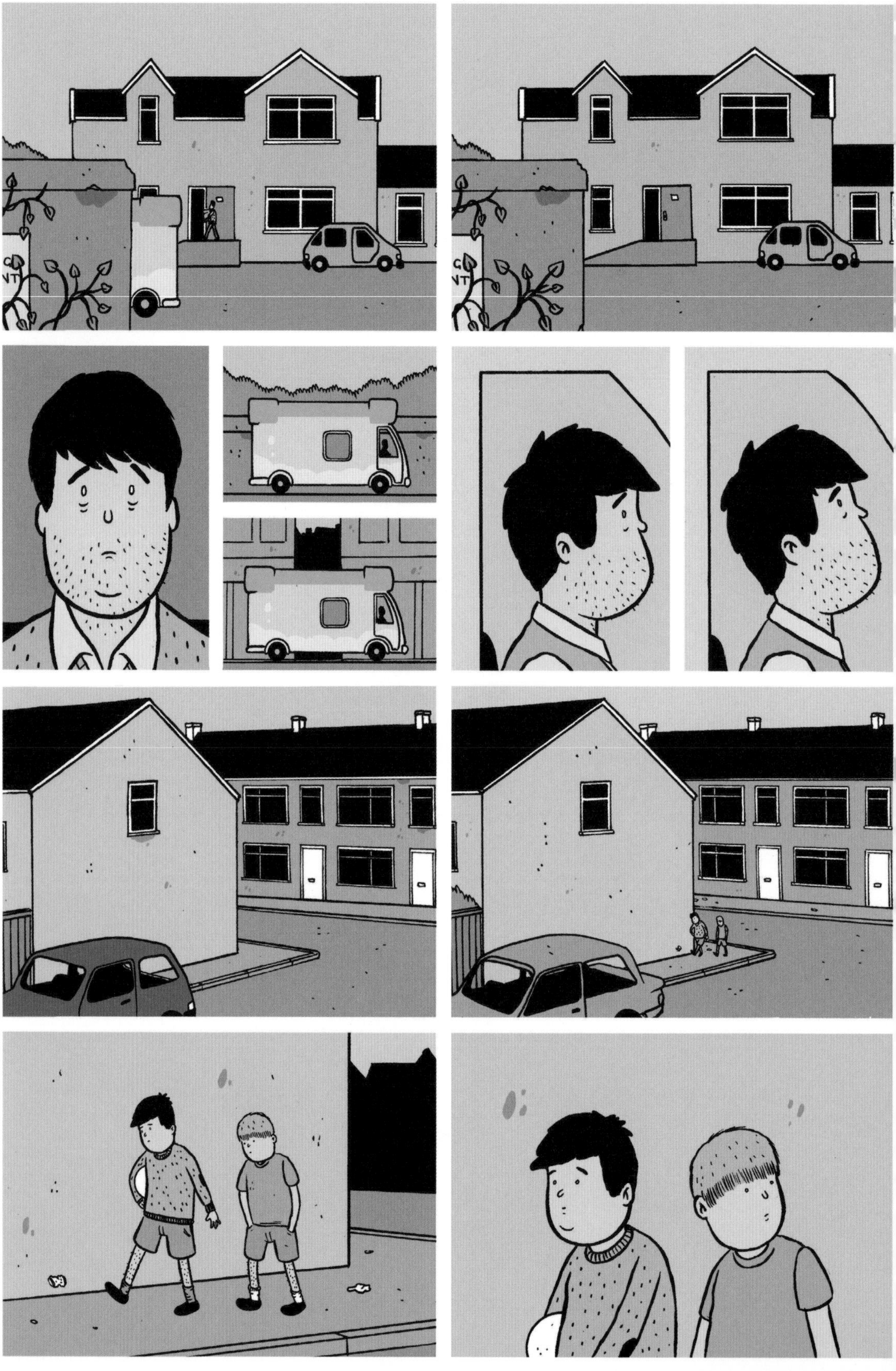

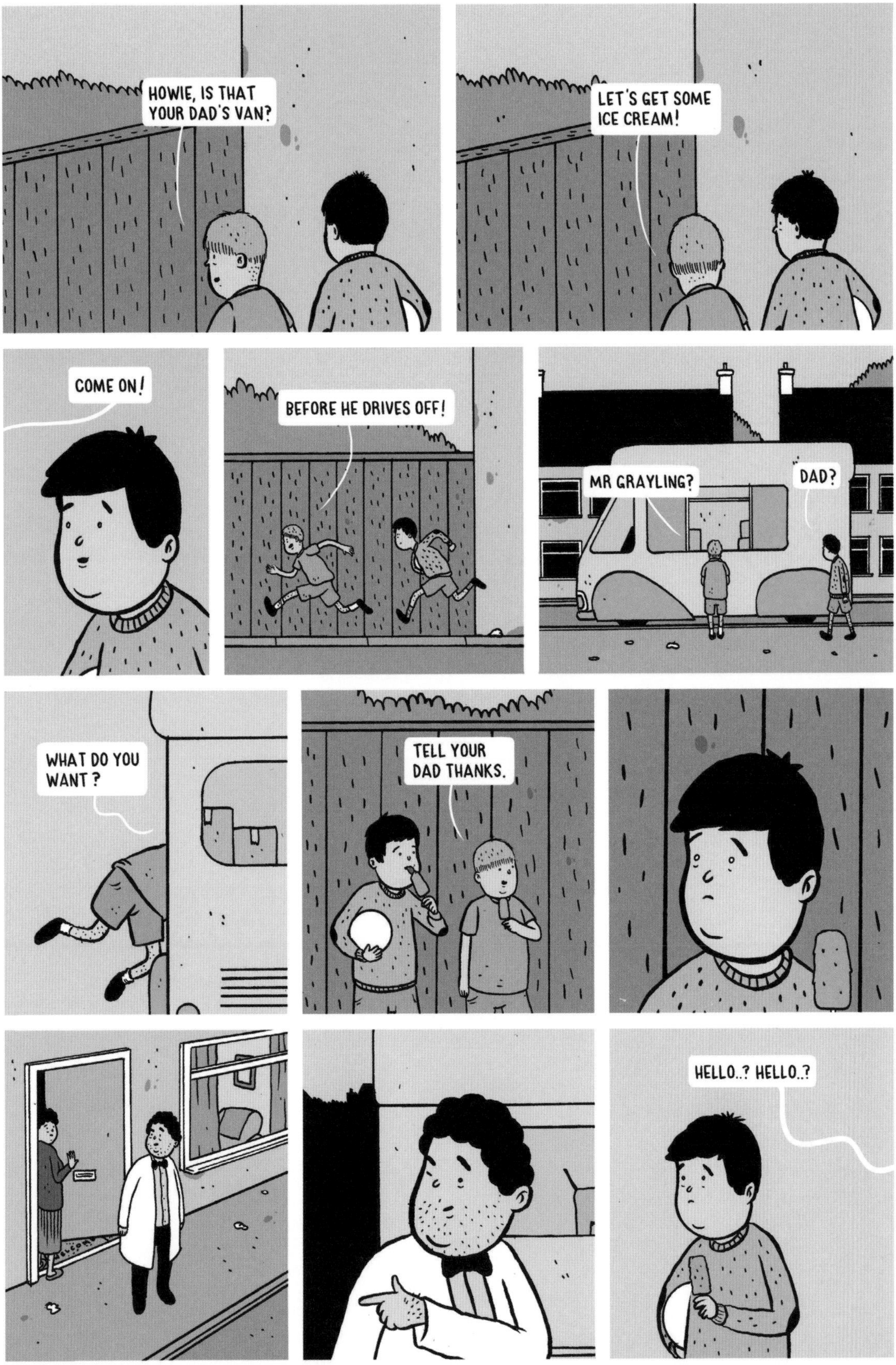
HOWIE, IS THAT YOUR DAD'S VAN?
LET'S GET SOME ICE CREAM!
COME ON!
BEFORE HE DRIVES OFF!
MR GRAYLING?
DAD?
WHAT DO YOU WANT?
TELL YOUR DAD THANKS.
HELLO..? HELLO..?

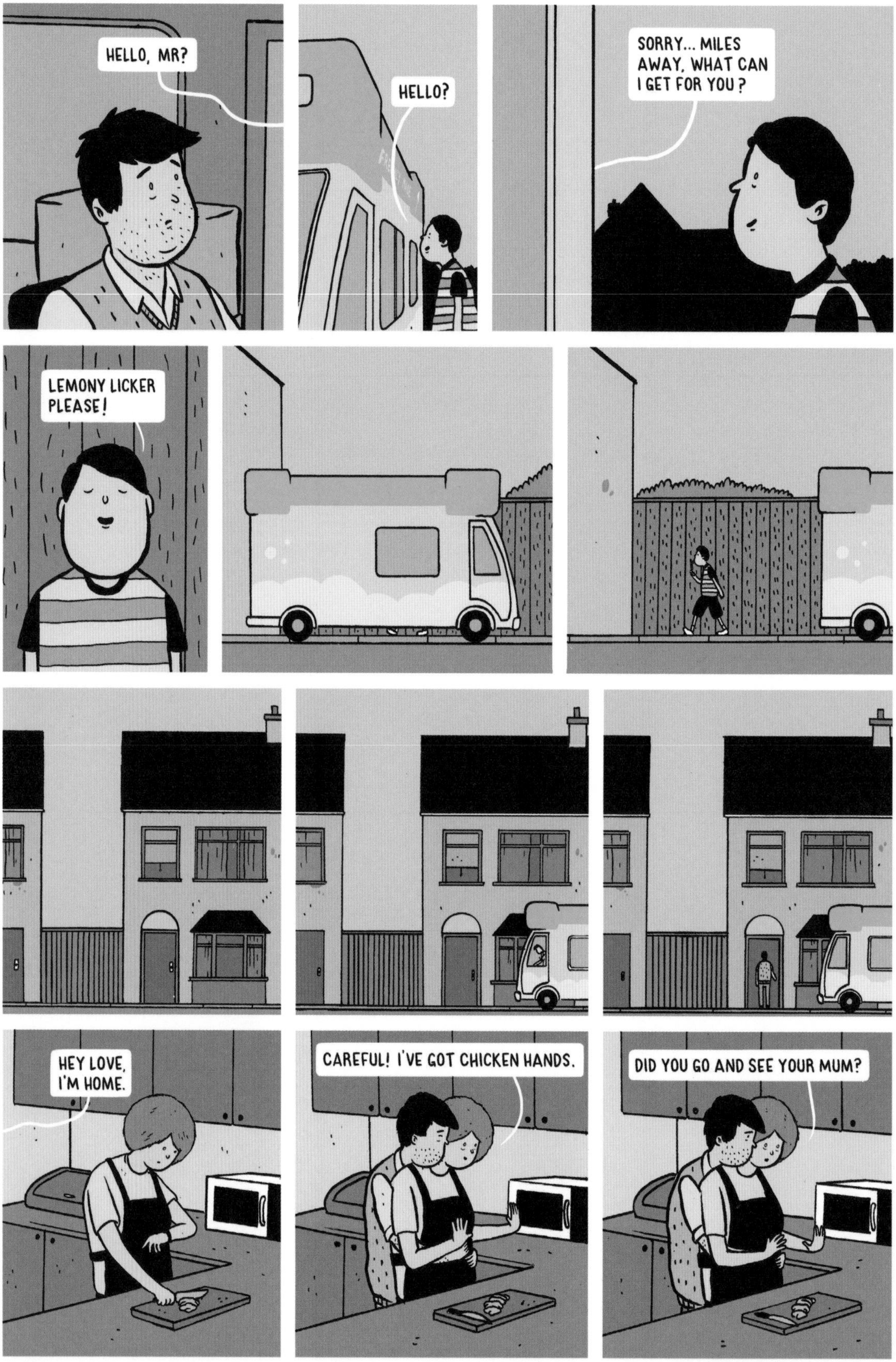
HELLO, MR?
HELLO?
SORRY... MILES AWAY, WHAT CAN I GET FOR YOU?
LEMONY LICKER PLEASE!
HEY LOVE, I'M HOME.
CAREFUL! I'VE GOT CHICKEN HANDS.
DID YOU GO AND SEE YOUR MUM?

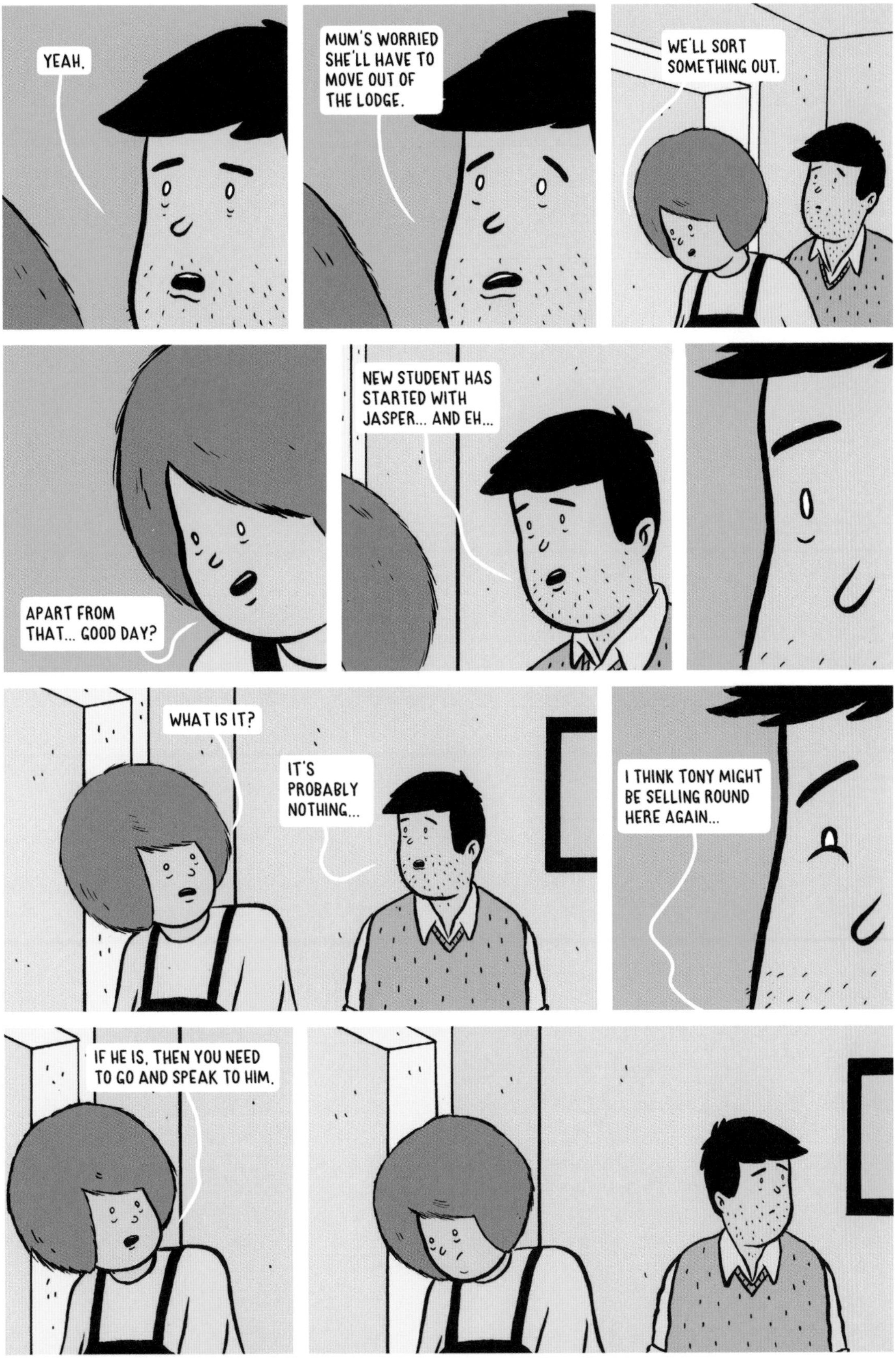
YEAH.
MUM'S WORRIED SHE'LL HAVE TO MOVE OUT OF THE LODGE.
WE'LL SORT SOMETHING OUT.
APART FROM THAT... GOOD DAY?
NEW STUDENT HAS STARTED WITH JASPER... AND EH...
WHAT IS IT?
IT'S PROBABLY NOTHING...
I THINK TONY MIGHT BE SELLING ROUND HERE AGAIN...
IF HE IS, THEN YOU NEED TO GO AND SPEAK TO HIM.

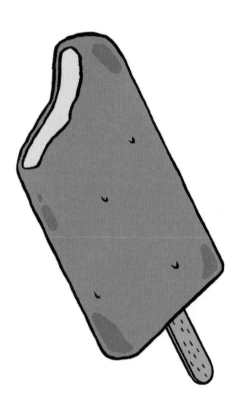

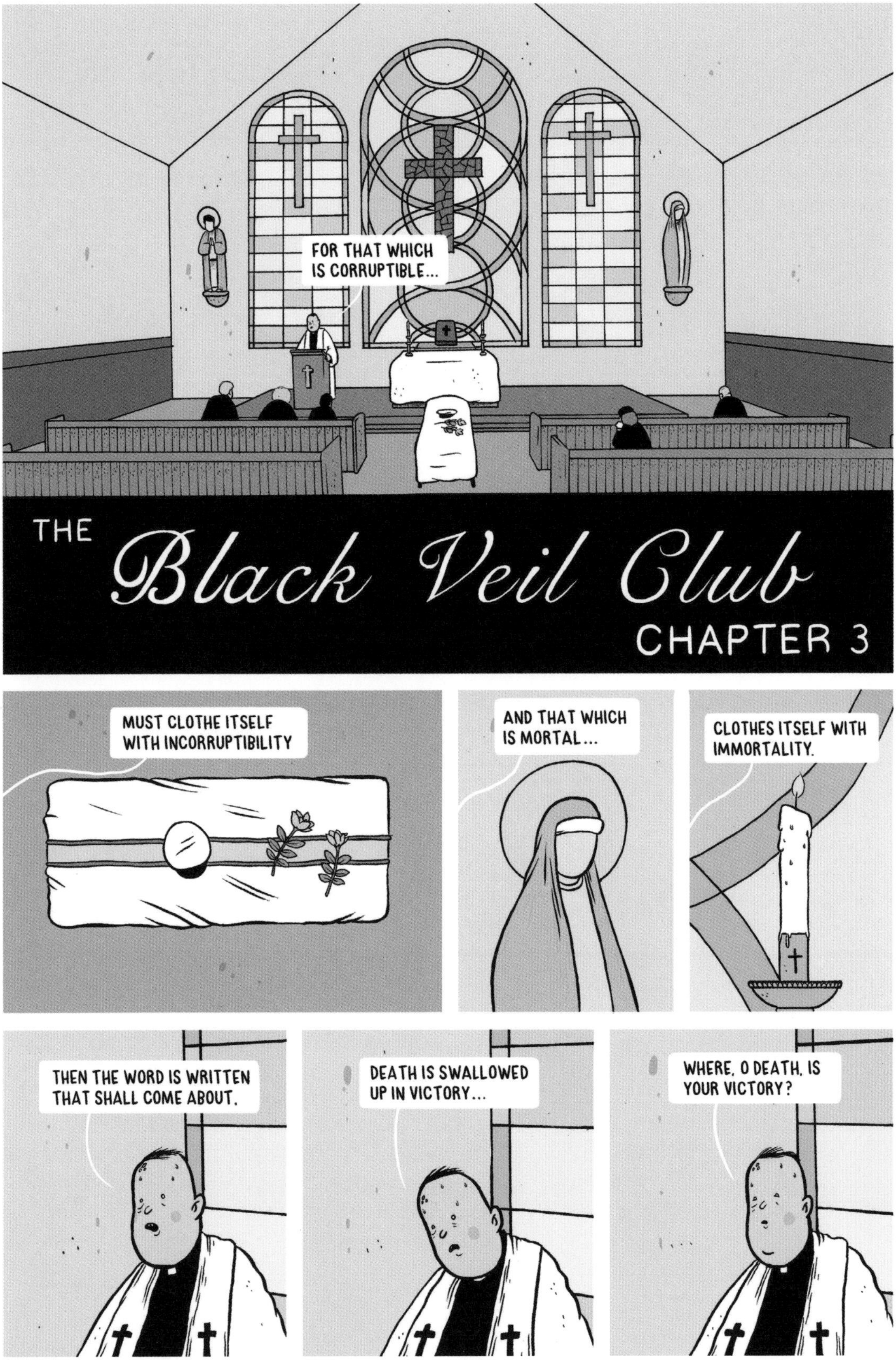
FOR THAT WHICH IS CORRUPTIBLE...
THE Black Veil Club
CHAPTER 3
MUST CLOTHE ITSELF WITH INCORRUPTIBILITY
AND THAT WHICH IS MORTAL...
CLOTHES ITSELF WITH IMMORTALITY.
THEN THE WORD IS WRITTEN THAT SHALL COME ABOUT.
DEATH IS SWALLOWED UP IN VICTORY...
WHERE, O DEATH, IS YOUR VICTORY?

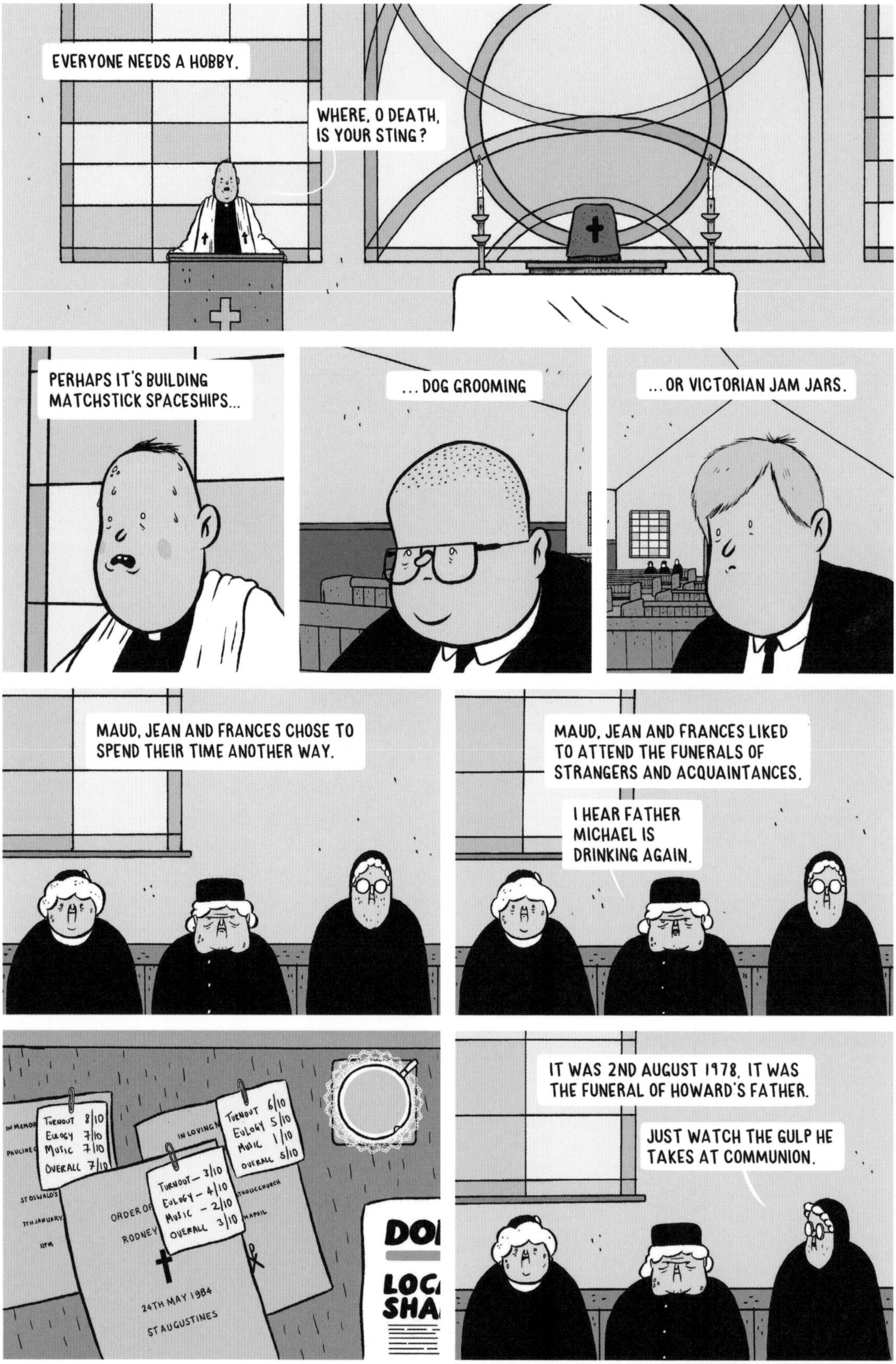

EVERYONE NEEDS A HOBBY.
WHERE, O DEATH, IS YOUR STING?
PERHAPS IT'S BUILDING MATCHSTICK SPACESHIPS...
... DOG GROOMING
... OR VICTORIAN JAM JARS.
MAUD, JEAN AND FRANCES CHOSE TO SPEND THEIR TIME ANOTHER WAY.
MAUD, JEAN AND FRANCES LIKED TO ATTEND THE FUNERALS OF STRANGERS AND ACQUAINTANCES.
I HEAR FATHER MICHAEL IS DRINKING AGAIN.
TURNOUT 8/10
EULOGY 7/10
MUSIC 7/10
OVERALL 7/10
TURNOUT 6/10
EULOGY 5/10
MUSIC 1/10
OVERALL 5/10
TURNOUT – 3/10
EULOGY – 4/10
MUSIC – 2/10
OVERALL 3/10
ORDER OF
RODNEY
24TH MAY 1984
ST AUGUSTINES
IT WAS 2ND AUGUST 1978, IT WAS THE FUNERAL OF HOWARD'S FATHER.
JUST WATCH THE GULP HE TAKES AT COMMUNION.

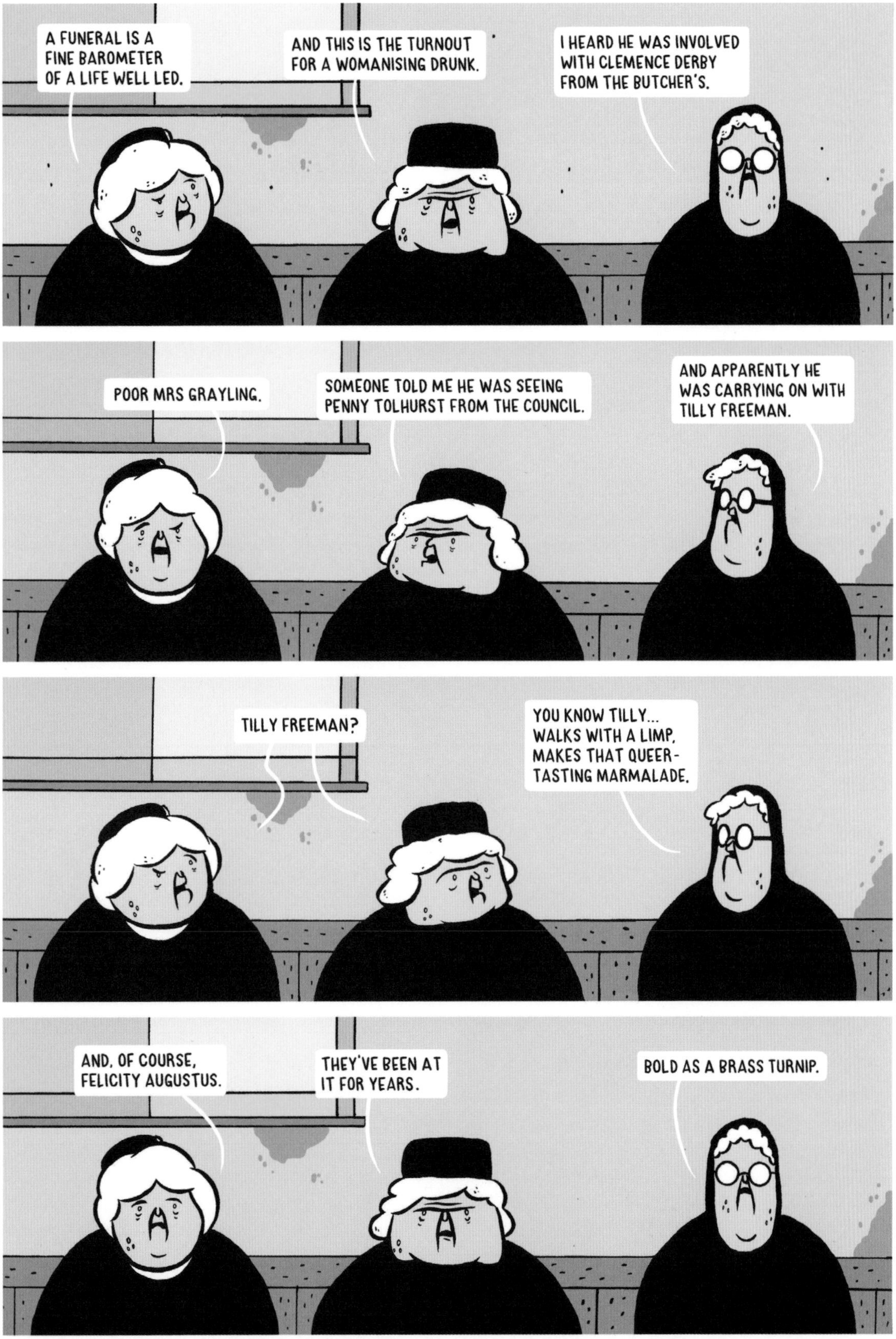
A FUNERAL IS A FINE BAROMETER OF A LIFE WELL LED.
AND THIS IS THE TURNOUT FOR A WOMANISING DRUNK.
I HEARD HE WAS INVOLVED WITH CLEMENCE DERBY FROM THE BUTCHER'S.
POOR MRS GRAYLING.
SOMEONE TOLD ME HE WAS SEEING PENNY TOLHURST FROM THE COUNCIL.
AND APPARENTLY HE WAS CARRYING ON WITH TILLY FREEMAN.
TILLY FREEMAN?
YOU KNOW TILLY... WALKS WITH A LIMP, MAKES THAT QUEER-TASTING MARMALADE.
AND, OF COURSE, FELICITY AUGUSTUS.
THEY'VE BEEN AT IT FOR YEARS.
BOLD AS A BRASS TURNIP.

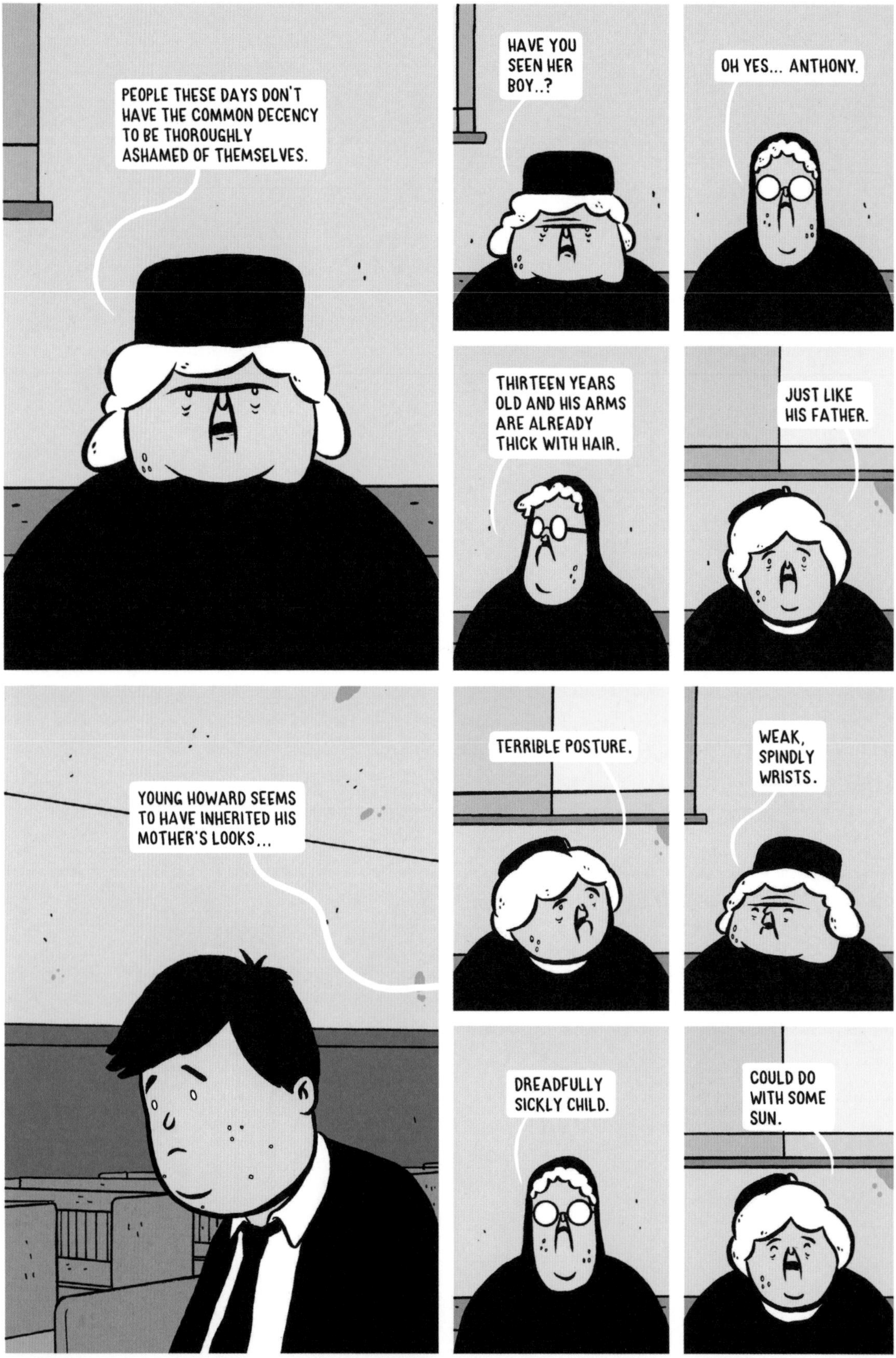
PEOPLE THESE DAYS DON'T HAVE THE COMMON DECENCY TO BE THOROUGHLY ASHAMED OF THEMSELVES.
HAVE YOU SEEN HER BOY..?
OH YES... ANTHONY.
THIRTEEN YEARS OLD AND HIS ARMS ARE ALREADY THICK WITH HAIR.
JUST LIKE HIS FATHER.
YOUNG HOWARD SEEMS TO HAVE INHERITED HIS MOTHER'S LOOKS...
TERRIBLE POSTURE.
WEAK, SPINDLY WRISTS.
DREADFULLY SICKLY CHILD.
COULD DO WITH SOME SUN.

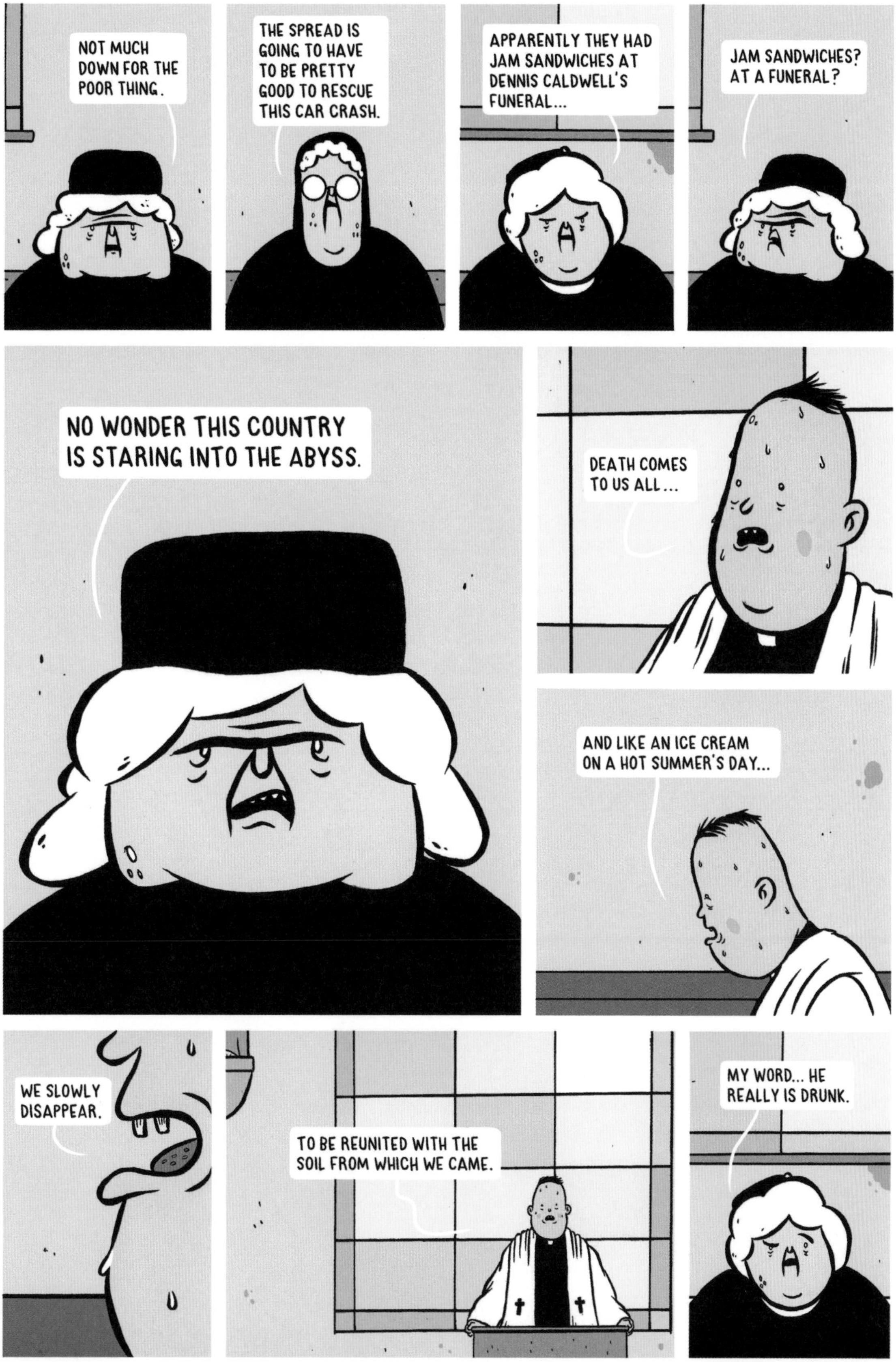
NOT MUCH DOWN FOR THE POOR THING.
THE SPREAD IS GOING TO HAVE TO BE PRETTY GOOD TO RESCUE THIS CAR CRASH.
APPARENTLY THEY HAD JAM SANDWICHES AT DENNIS CALDWELL'S FUNERAL...
JAM SANDWICHES? AT A FUNERAL?
NO WONDER THIS COUNTRY IS STARING INTO THE ABYSS.
DEATH COMES TO US ALL...
AND LIKE AN ICE CREAM ON A HOT SUMMER'S DAY...
WE SLOWLY DISAPPEAR.
TO BE REUNITED WITH THE SOIL FROM WHICH WE CAME.
MY WORD... HE REALLY IS DRUNK.

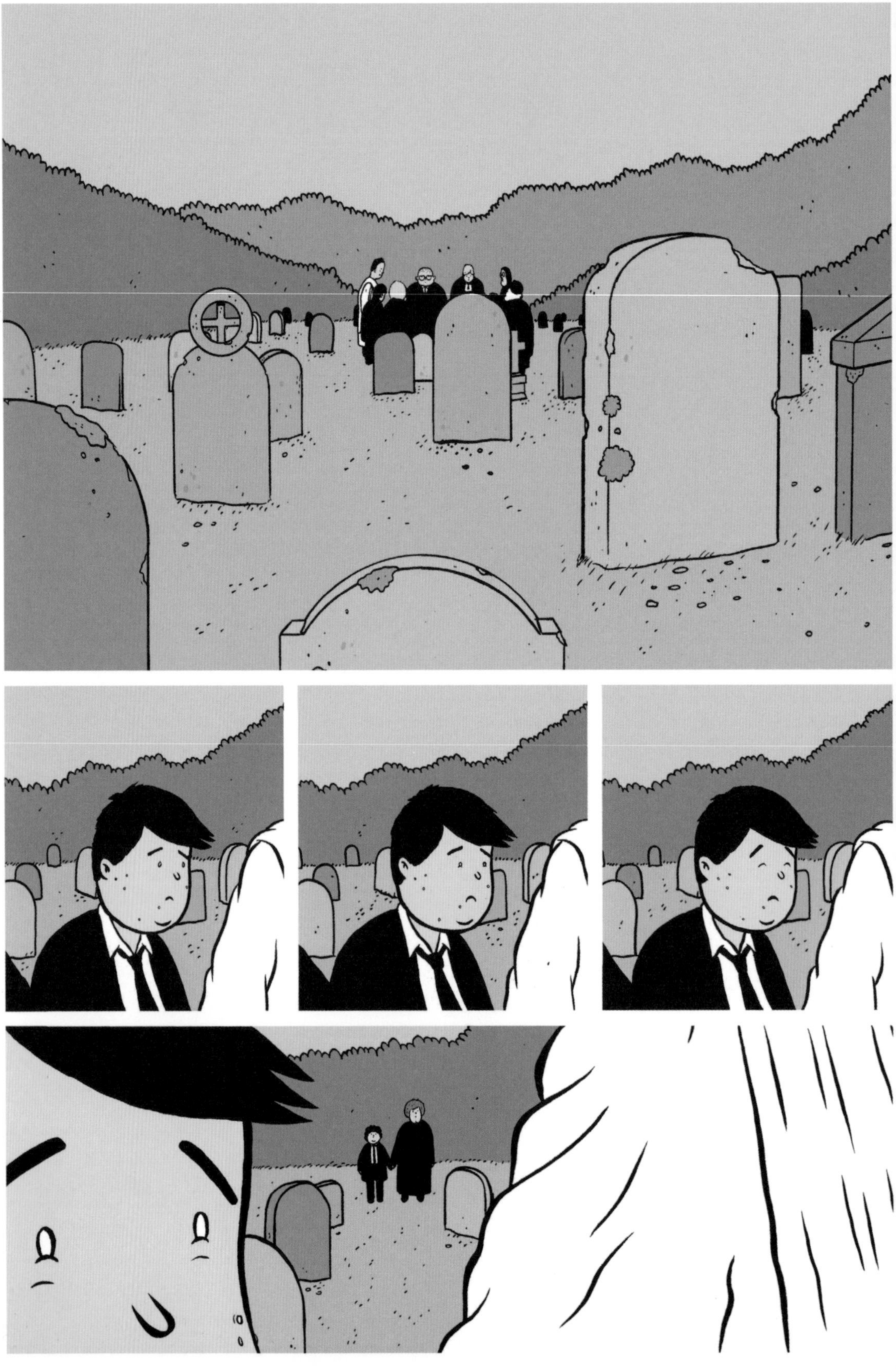

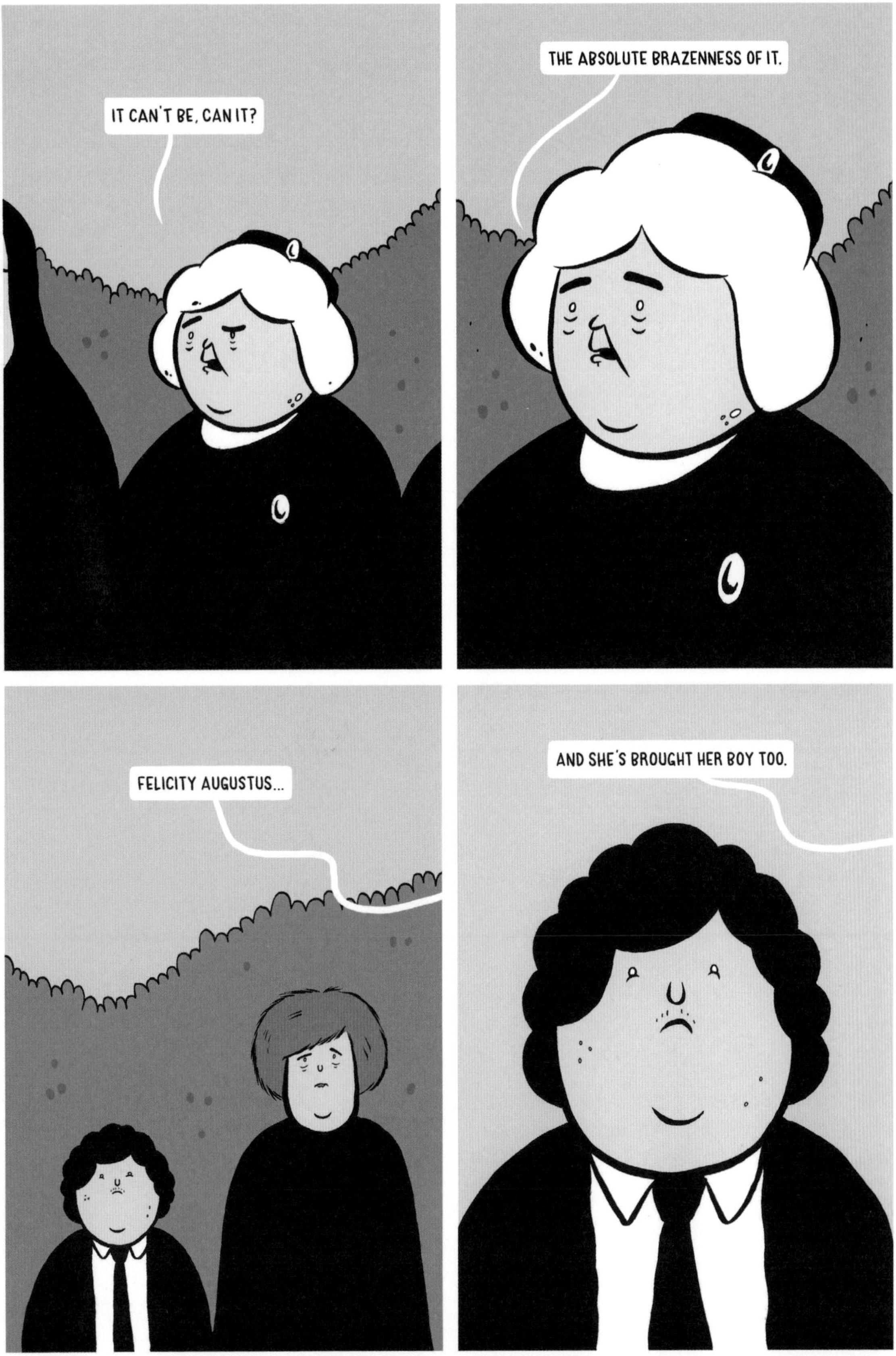
IT CAN'T BE, CAN IT?
THE ABSOLUTE BRAZENNESS OF IT.
FELICITY AUGUSTUS...
AND SHE'S BROUGHT HER BOY TOO.

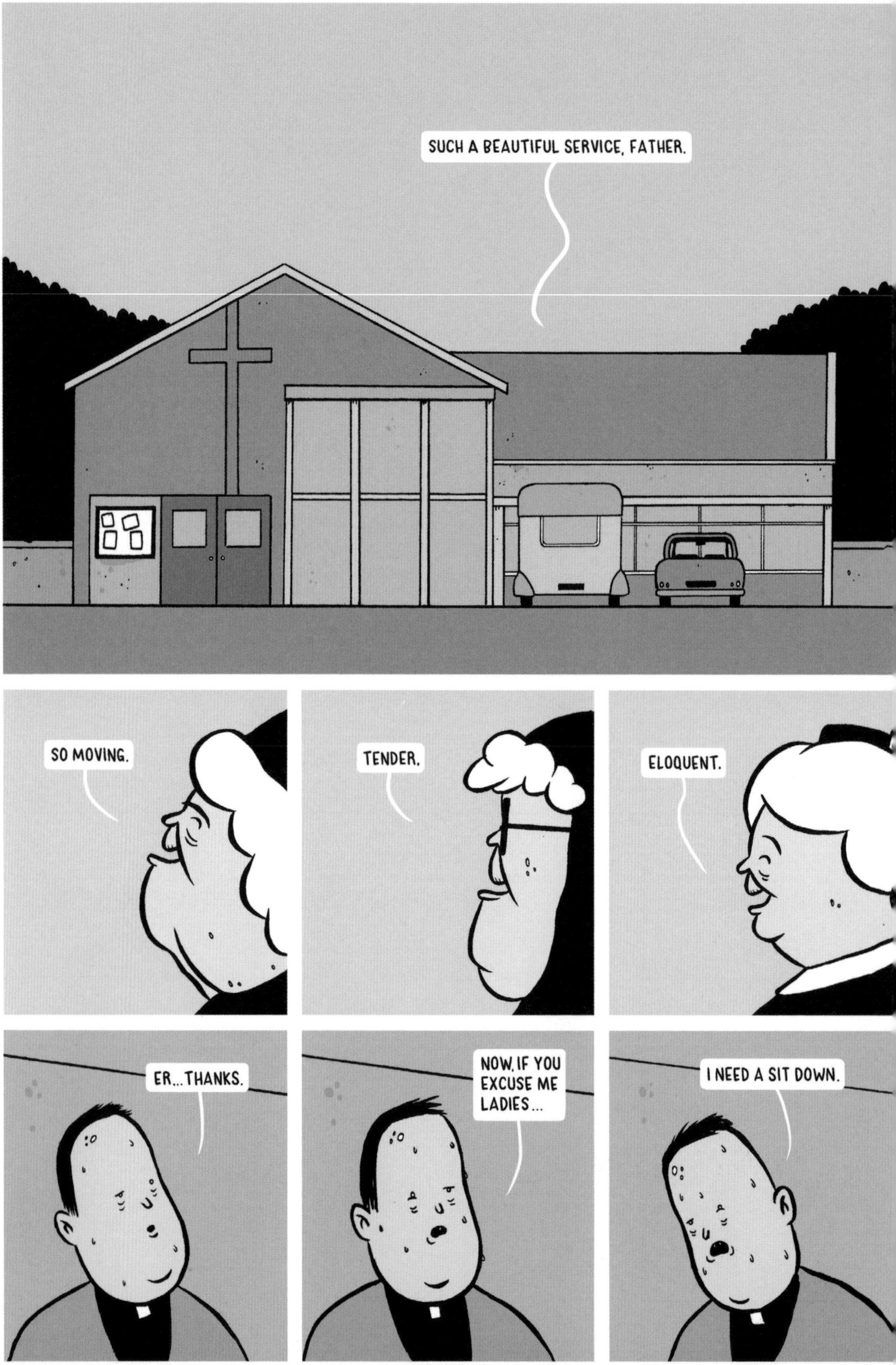
SUCH A BEAUTIFUL SERVICE, FATHER.
SO MOVING.
TENDER.
ELOQUENT.
ER... THANKS.
NOW, IF YOU EXCUSE ME LADIES...
I NEED A SIT DOWN.

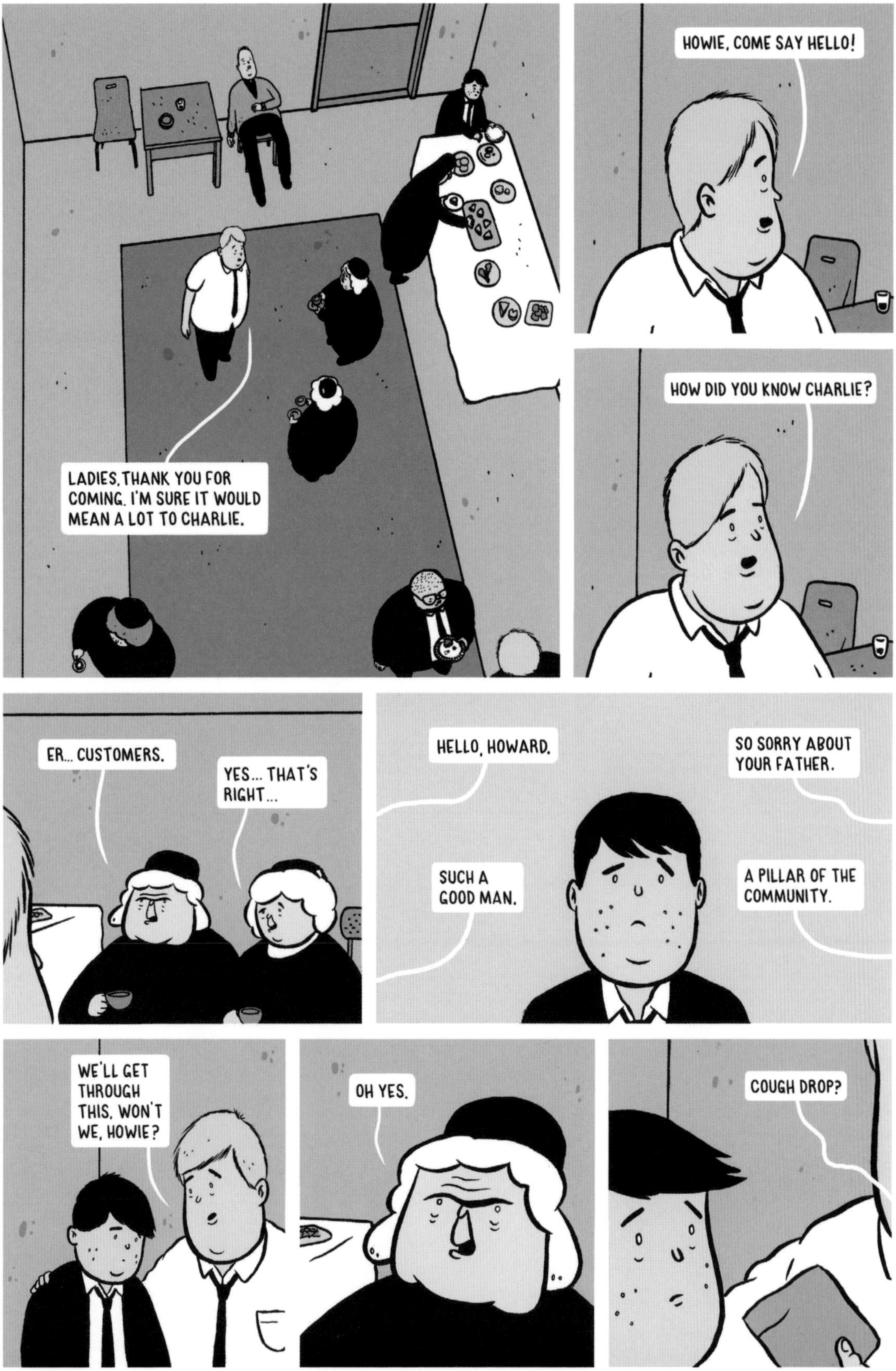
LADIES, THANK YOU FOR COMING. I'M SURE IT WOULD MEAN A LOT TO CHARLIE.
HOWIE, COME SAY HELLO!
HOW DID YOU KNOW CHARLIE?
ER... CUSTOMERS.
YES... THAT'S RIGHT...
HELLO, HOWARD.
SO SORRY ABOUT YOUR FATHER.
SUCH A GOOD MAN.
A PILLAR OF THE COMMUNITY.
WE'LL GET THROUGH THIS, WON'T WE, HOWIE?
OH YES.
COUGH DROP?

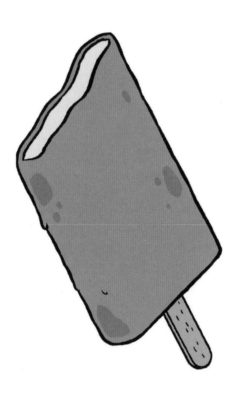

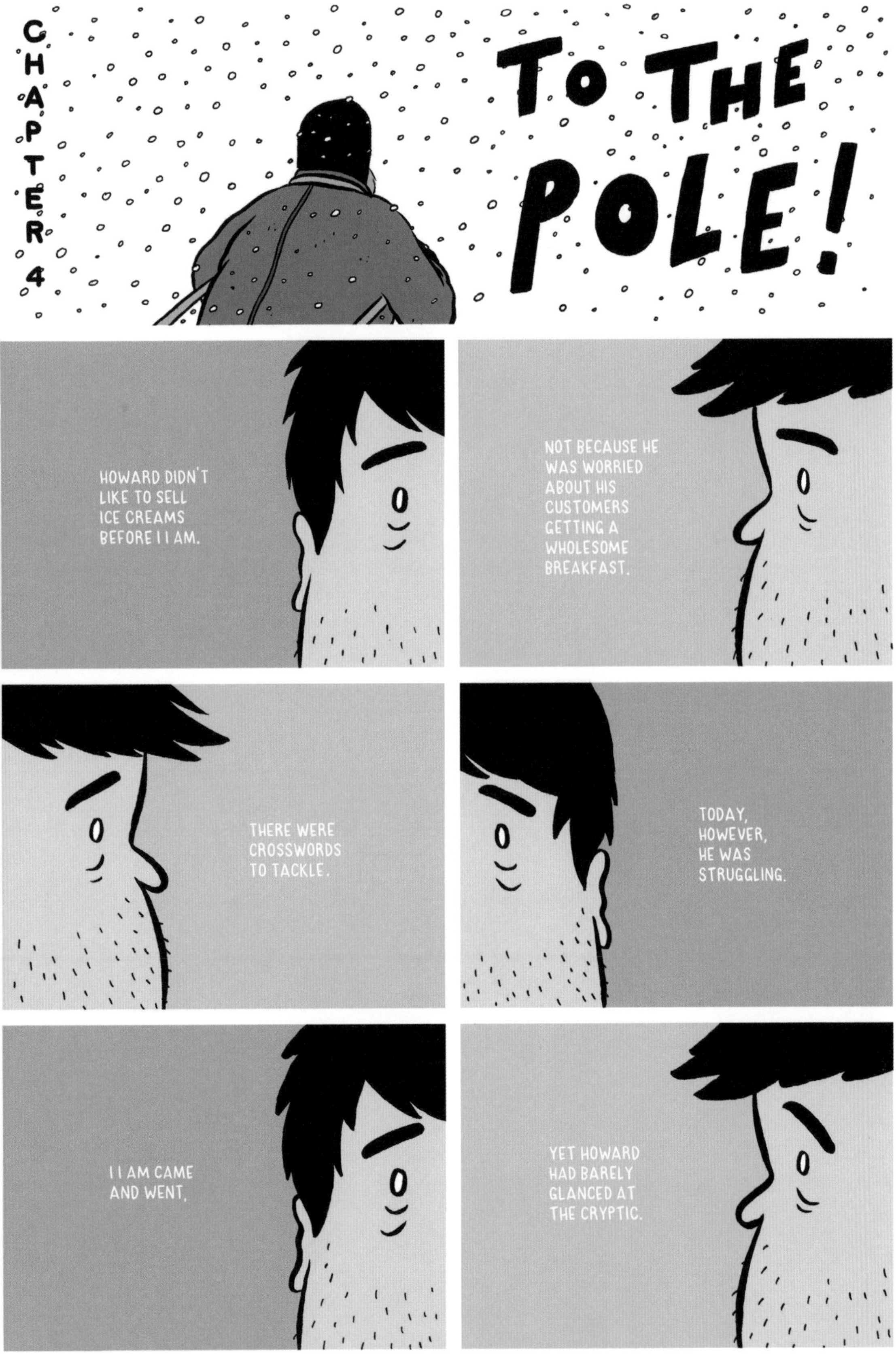
CHAPTER 4
TO THE POLE!
HOWARD DIDN'T LIKE TO SELL ICE CREAMS BEFORE 11 AM.
NOT BECAUSE HE WAS WORRIED ABOUT HIS CUSTOMERS GETTING A WHOLESOME BREAKFAST.
THERE WERE CROSSWORDS TO TACKLE.
TODAY, HOWEVER, HE WAS STRUGGLING.
11 AM CAME AND WENT,
YET HOWARD HAD BARELY GLANCED AT THE CRYPTIC.

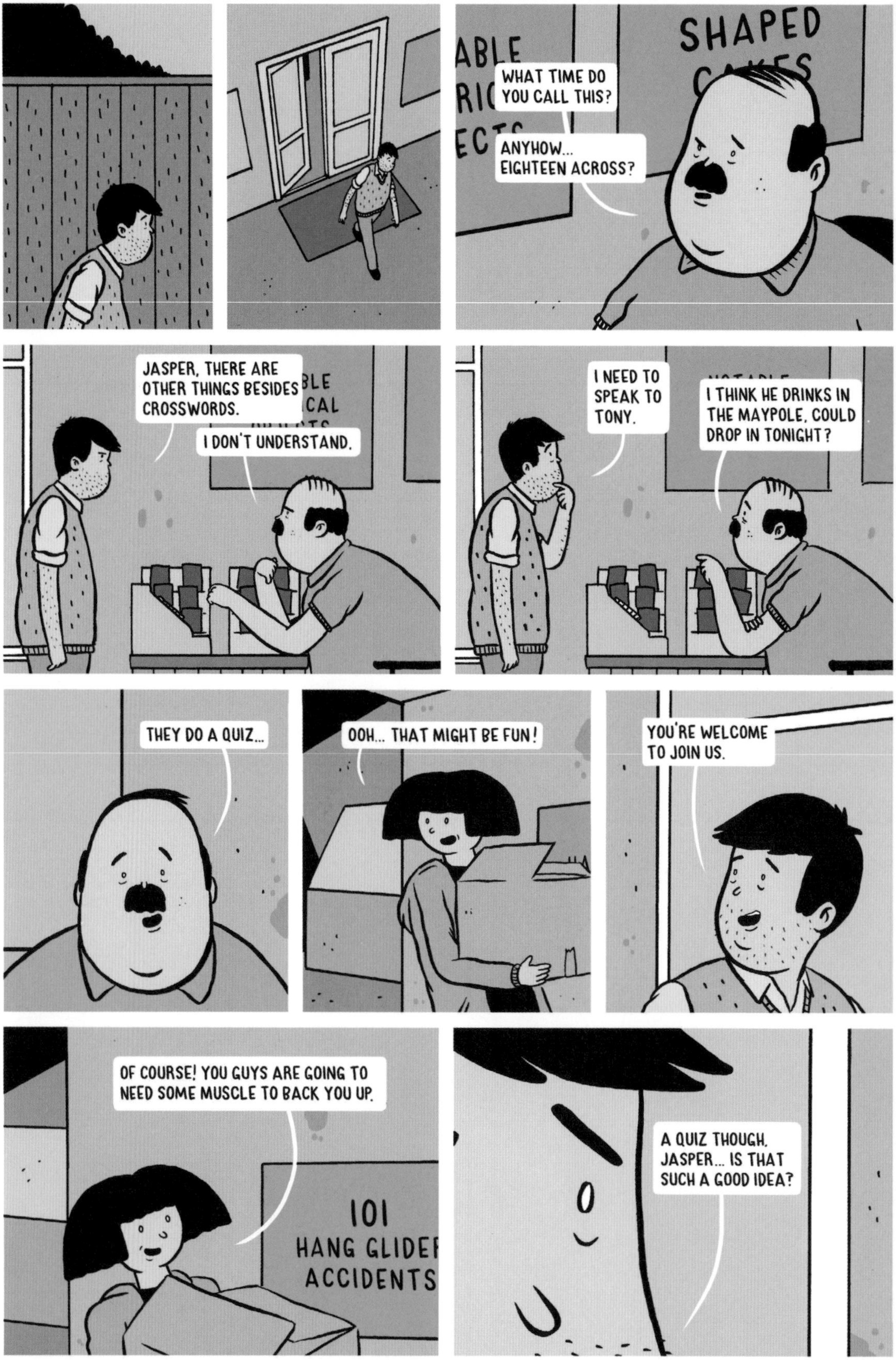
SHAPED
WHAT TIME DO YOU CALL THIS?
ANYHOW... EIGHTEEN ACROSS?
JASPER, THERE ARE OTHER THINGS BESIDES CROSSWORDS.
I DON'T UNDERSTAND.
I NEED TO SPEAK TO TONY.
I THINK HE DRINKS IN THE MAYPOLE, COULD DROP IN TONIGHT?
THEY DO A QUIZ...
OOH... THAT MIGHT BE FUN!
YOU'RE WELCOME TO JOIN US.
OF COURSE! YOU GUYS ARE GOING TO NEED SOME MUSCLE TO BACK YOU UP.
101
ACCIDENTS
A QUIZ THOUGH, JASPER... IS THAT SUCH A GOOD IDEA?

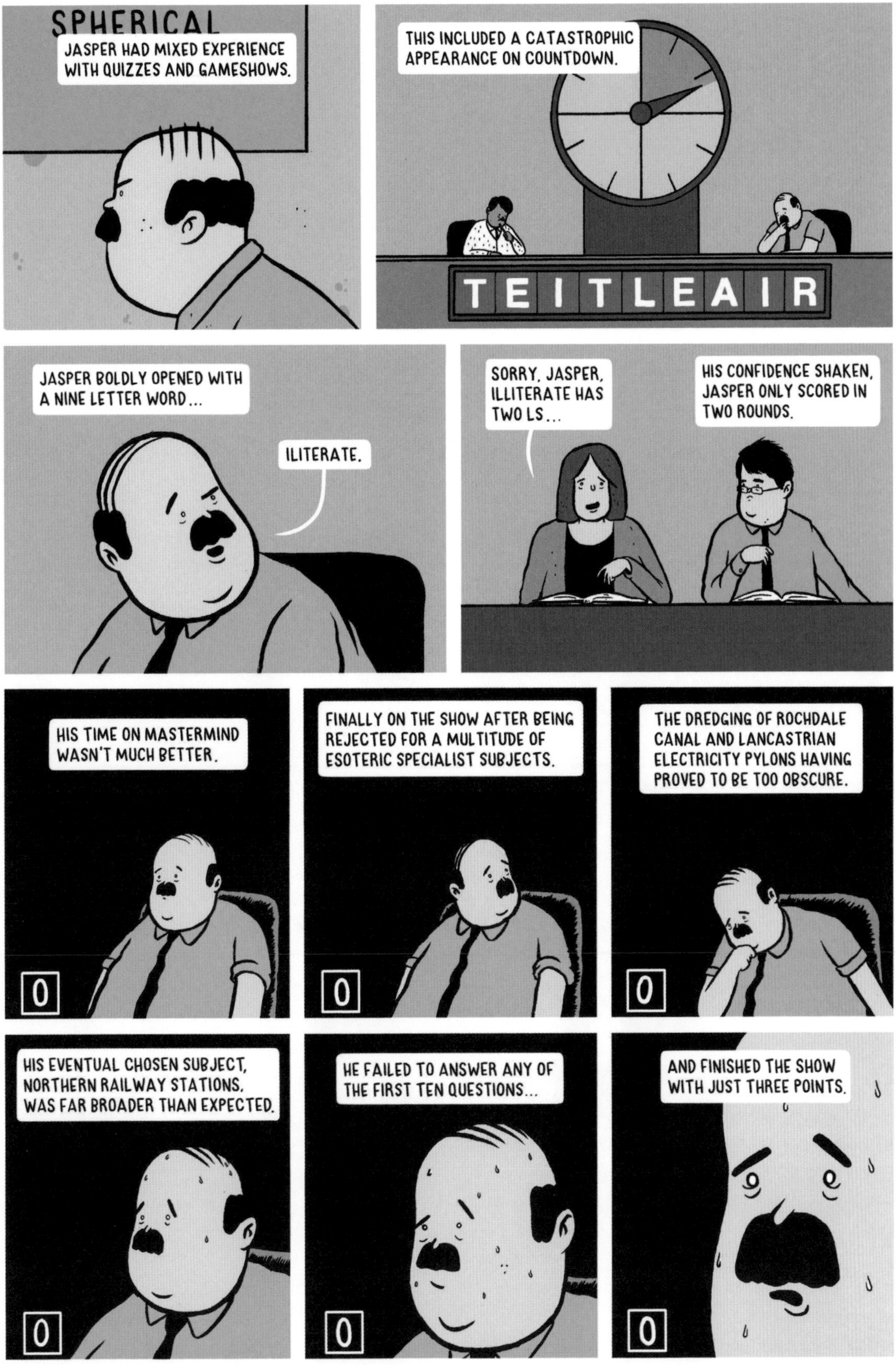
SPHERICAL
JASPER HAD MIXED EXPERIENCE WITH QUIZZES AND GAMESHOWS.
THIS INCLUDED A CATASTROPHIC APPEARANCE ON COUNTDOWN.
TEITLEAIR
JASPER BOLDLY OPENED WITH A NINE LETTER WORD...
ILITERATE.
SORRY, JASPER, ILLITERATE HAS TWO LS...
HIS CONFIDENCE SHAKEN, JASPER ONLY SCORED IN TWO ROUNDS.
HIS TIME ON MASTERMIND WASN'T MUCH BETTER.
0
FINALLY ON THE SHOW AFTER BEING REJECTED FOR A MULTITUDE OF ESOTERIC SPECIALIST SUBJECTS.
0
THE DREDGING OF ROCHDALE CANAL AND LANCASTRIAN ELECTRICITY PYLONS HAVING PROVED TO BE TOO OBSCURE.
0
HIS EVENTUAL CHOSEN SUBJECT, NORTHERN RAILWAY STATIONS, WAS FAR BROADER THAN EXPECTED.
0
HE FAILED TO ANSWER ANY OF THE FIRST TEN QUESTIONS...
0
AND FINISHED THE SHOW WITH JUST THREE POINTS.
0

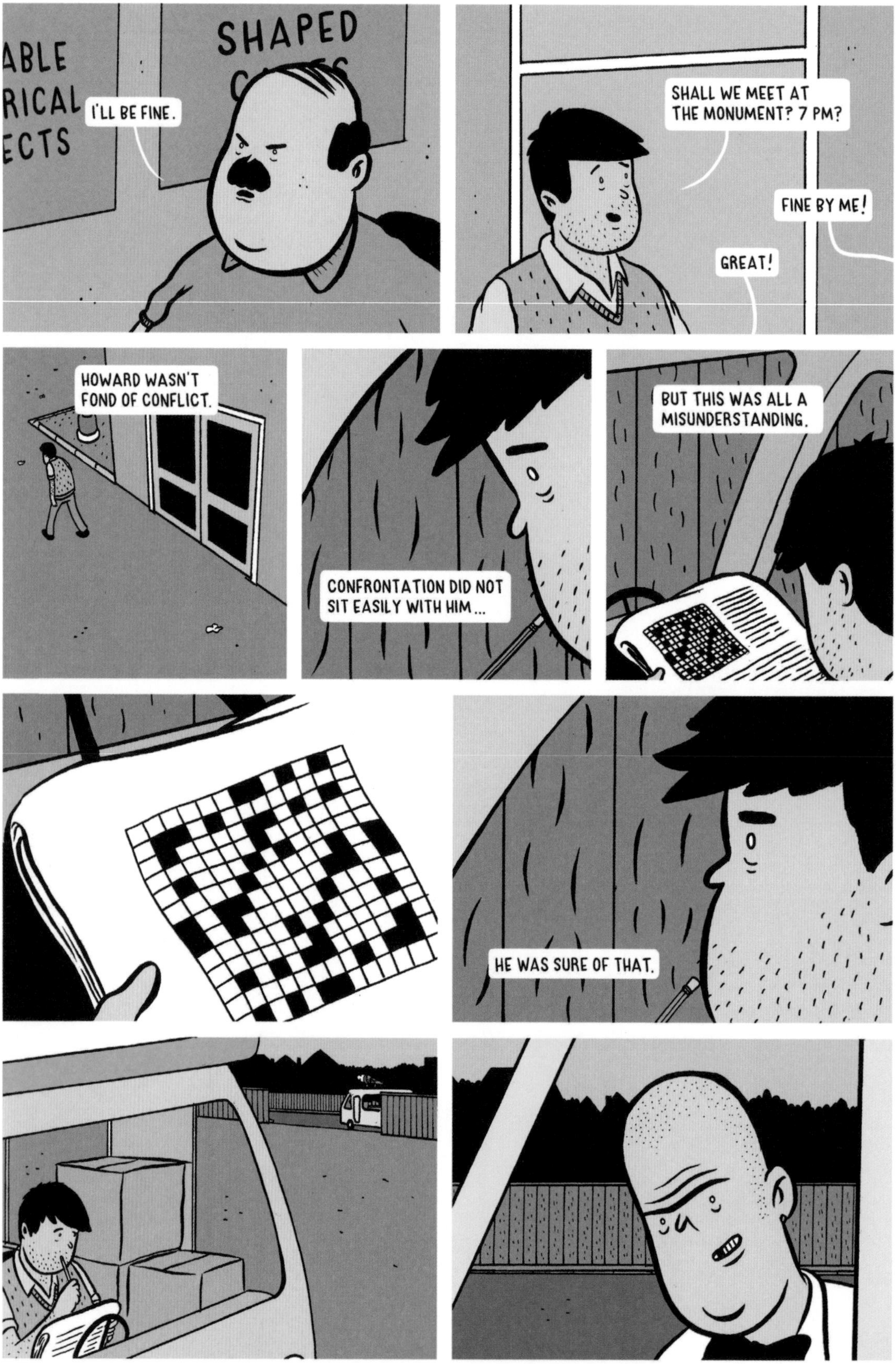
ABLE
RICAL
ECTS
SHAPED
I'LL BE FINE.
SHALL WE MEET AT THE MONUMENT? 7 PM?
FINE BY ME!
GREAT!
HOWARD WASN'T FOND OF CONFLICT.
CONFRONTATION DID NOT SIT EASILY WITH HIM...
BUT THIS WAS ALL A MISUNDERSTANDING.
HE WAS SURE OF THAT.

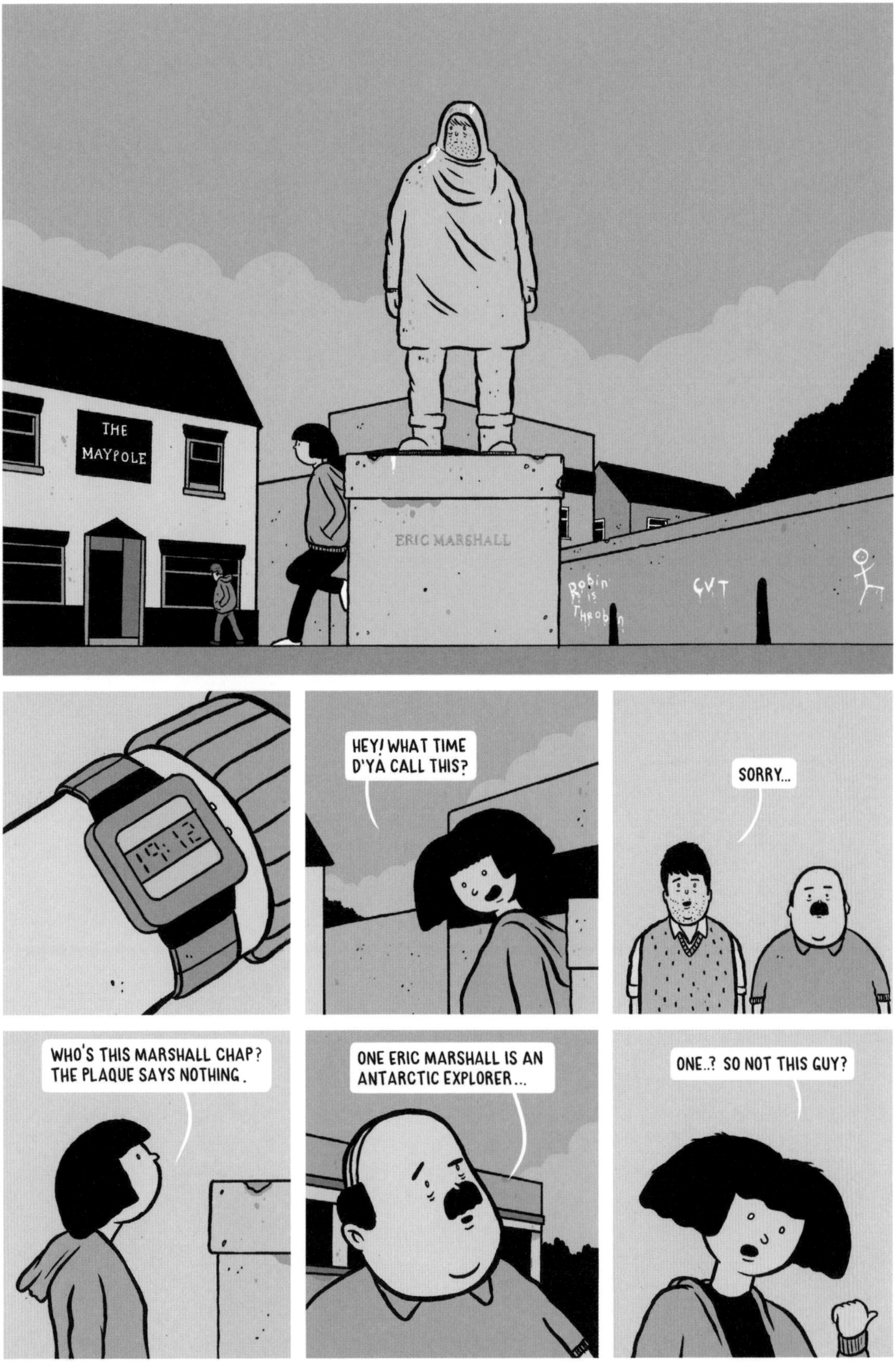
THE MAYPOLE
ERIC MARSHALL
19:12
HEY! WHAT TIME D'YA CALL THIS?
SORRY...
WHO'S THIS MARSHALL CHAP? THE PLAQUE SAYS NOTHING.
ONE ERIC MARSHALL IS AN ANTARCTIC EXPLORER...
ONE..? SO NOT THIS GUY?

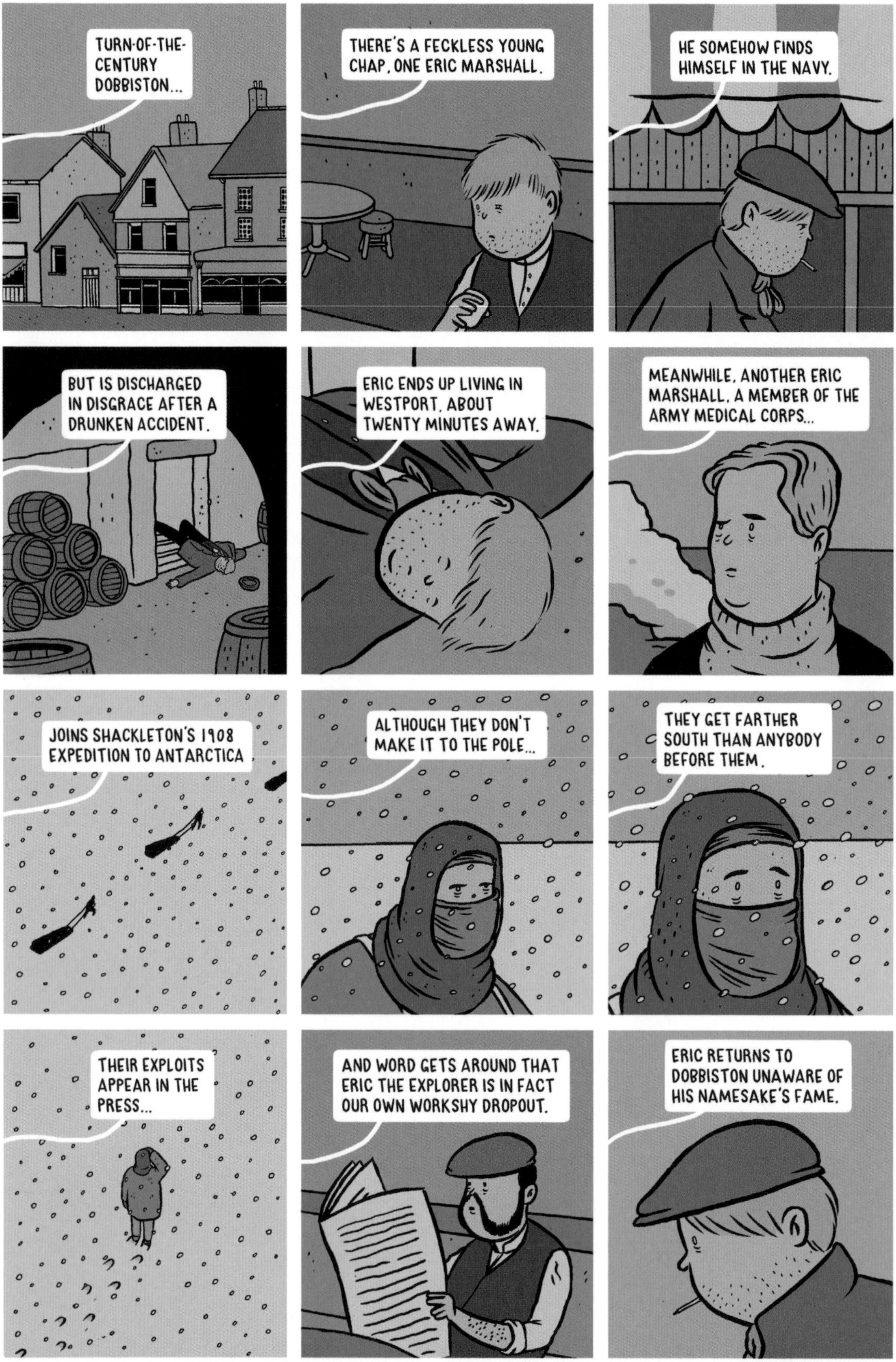
TURN-OF-THE-CENTURY DOBBISTON...
THERE'S A FECKLESS YOUNG CHAP, ONE ERIC MARSHALL.
HE SOMEHOW FINDS HIMSELF IN THE NAVY.
BUT IS DISCHARGED IN DISGRACE AFTER A DRUNKEN ACCIDENT.
ERIC ENDS UP LIVING IN WESTPORT, ABOUT TWENTY MINUTES AWAY.
MEANWHILE, ANOTHER ERIC MARSHALL, A MEMBER OF THE ARMY MEDICAL CORPS...
JOINS SHACKLETON'S 1908 EXPEDITION TO ANTARCTICA
ALTHOUGH THEY DON'T MAKE IT TO THE POLE...
THEY GET FARTHER SOUTH THAN ANYBODY BEFORE THEM.
THEIR EXPLOITS APPEAR IN THE PRESS...
AND WORD GETS AROUND THAT ERIC THE EXPLORER IS IN FACT OUR OWN WORKSHY DROPOUT.
ERIC RETURNS TO DOBBISTON UNAWARE OF HIS NAMESAKE'S FAME.

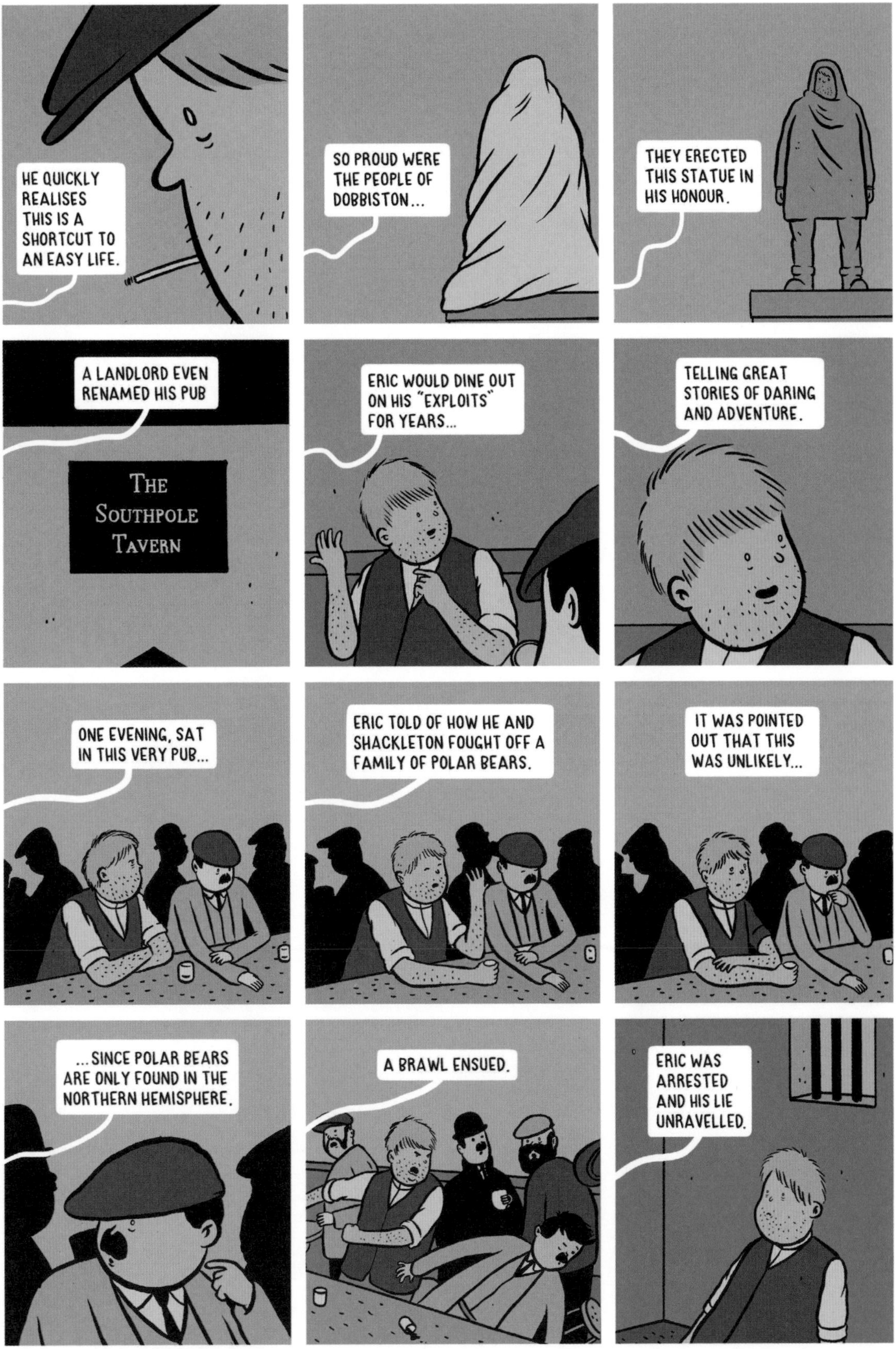
HE QUICKLY REALISES THIS IS A SHORTCUT TO AN EASY LIFE.
SO PROUD WERE THE PEOPLE OF DOBBISTON...
THEY ERECTED THIS STATUE IN HIS HONOUR.
A LANDLORD EVEN RENAMED HIS PUB
THE SOUTHPOLE TAVERN
ERIC WOULD DINE OUT ON HIS "EXPLOITS" FOR YEARS...
TELLING GREAT STORIES OF DARING AND ADVENTURE.
ONE EVENING, SAT IN THIS VERY PUB...
ERIC TOLD OF HOW HE AND SHACKLETON FOUGHT OFF A FAMILY OF POLAR BEARS.
IT WAS POINTED OUT THAT THIS WAS UNLIKELY...
...SINCE POLAR BEARS ARE ONLY FOUND IN THE NORTHERN HEMISPHERE.
A BRAWL ENSUED.
ERIC WAS ARRESTED AND HIS LIE UNRAVELLED.

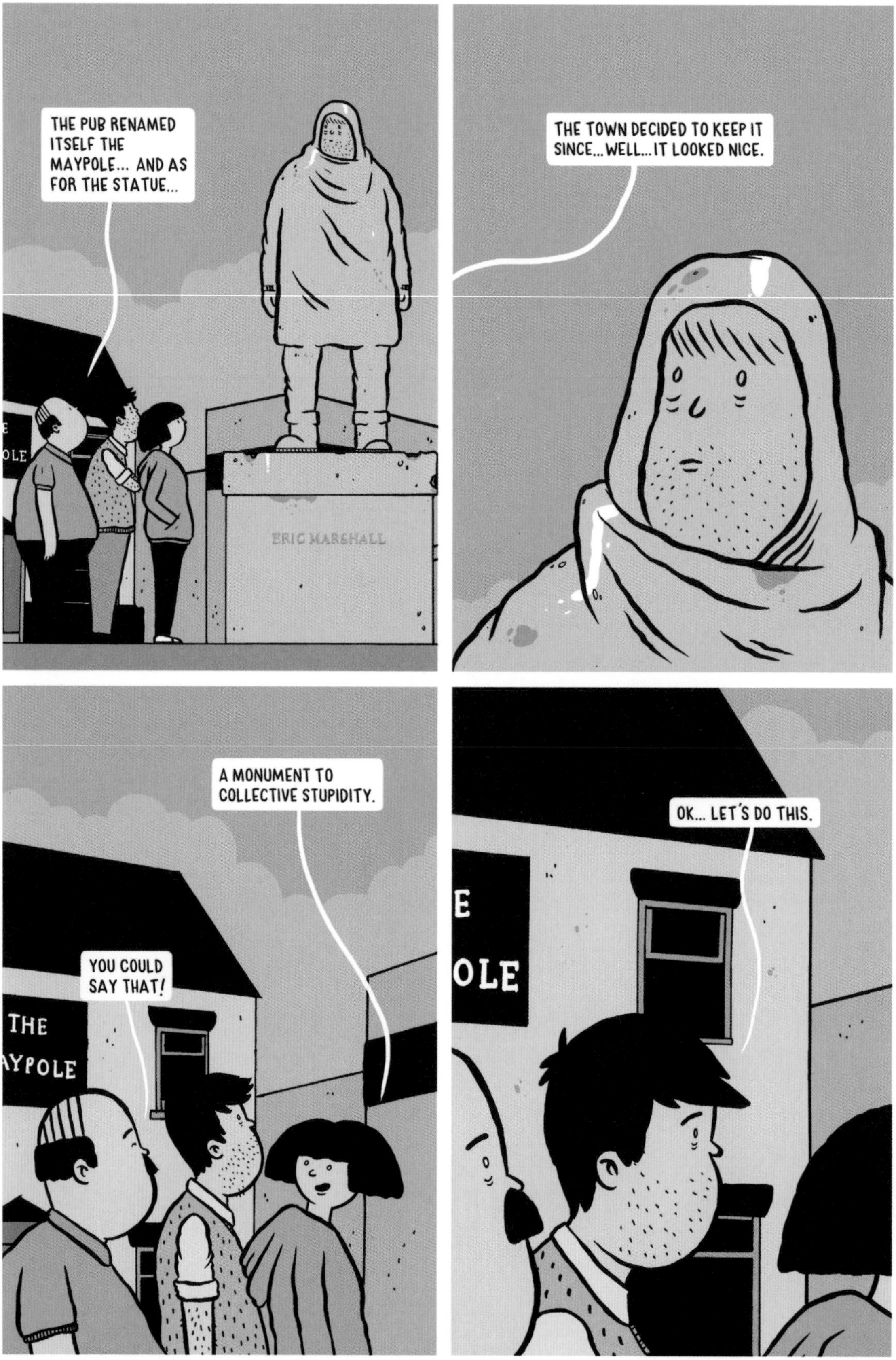
THE PUB RENAMED ITSELF THE MAYPOLE... AND AS FOR THE STATUE...
E
OLE
ERIC MARSHALL
THE TOWN DECIDED TO KEEP IT SINCE... WELL... IT LOOKED NICE.
A MONUMENT TO COLLECTIVE STUPIDITY.
YOU COULD SAY THAT!
THE
AYPOLE
OK... LET'S DO THIS.
E
OLE

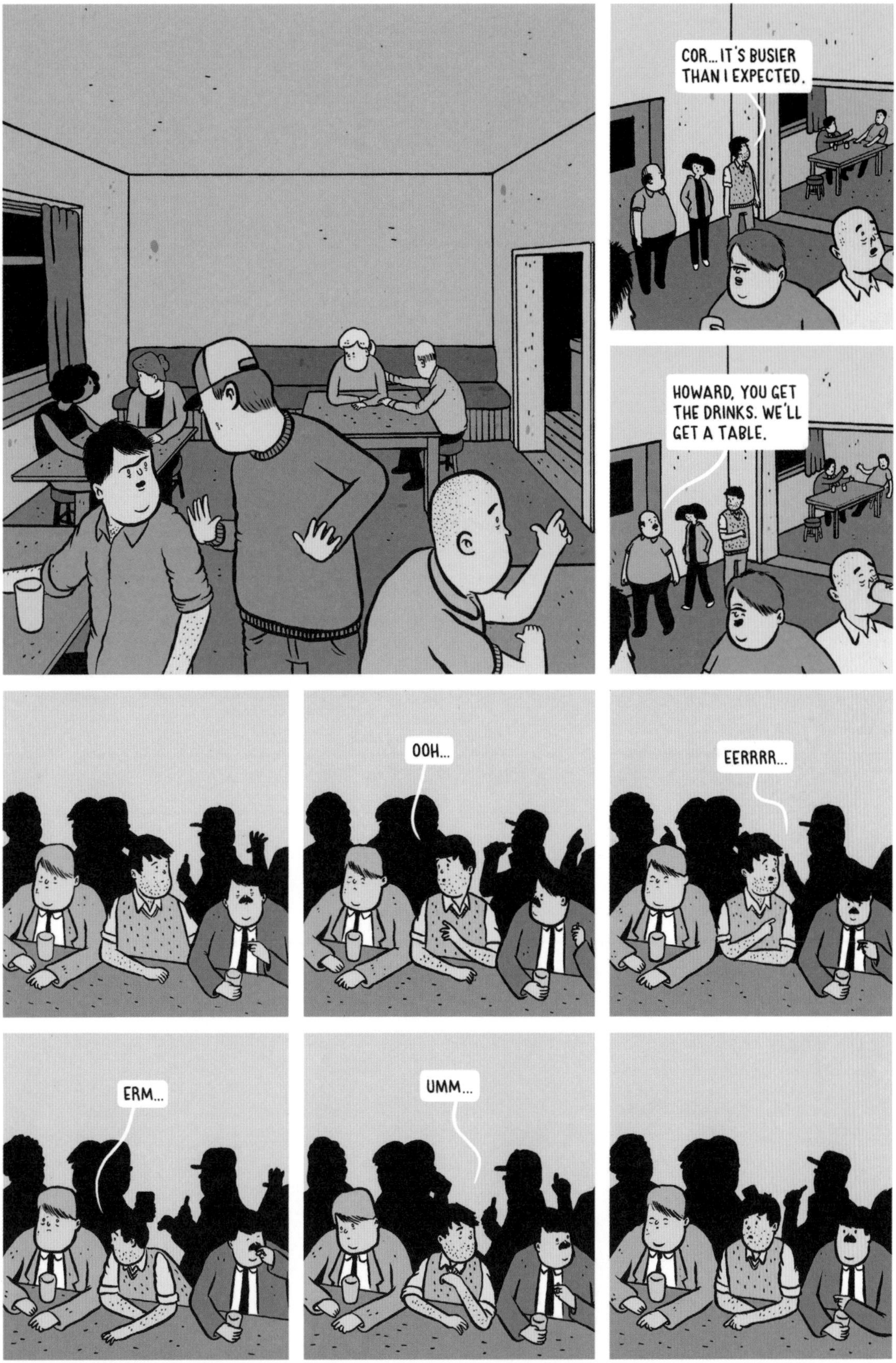
COR... IT'S BUSIER THAN I EXPECTED.
HOWARD, YOU GET THE DRINKS. WE'LL GET A TABLE.
OOH...
EERRRR...
ERM...
UMM...

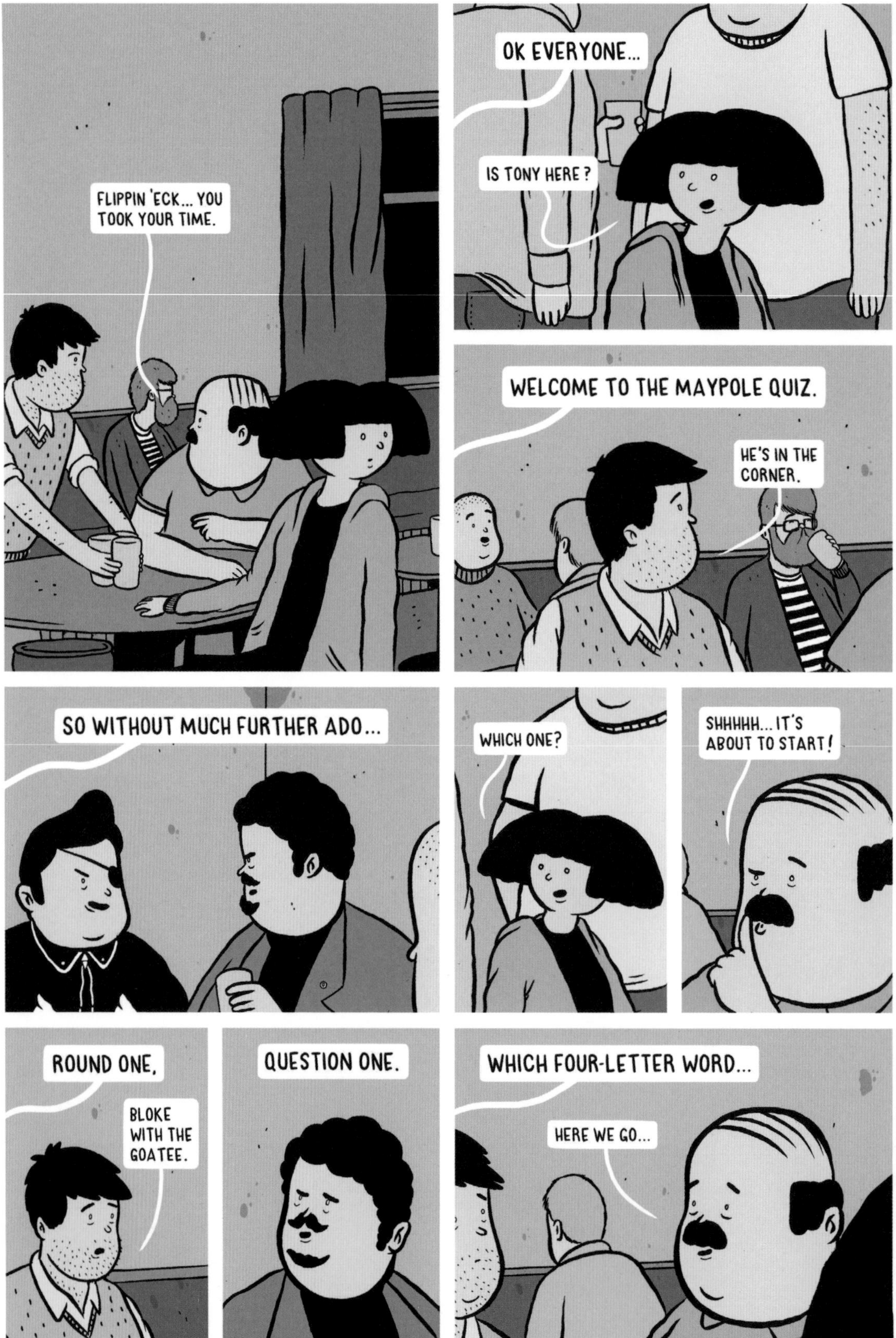
FLIPPIN 'ECK... YOU TOOK YOUR TIME.
OK EVERYONE...
IS TONY HERE ?
WELCOME TO THE MAYPOLE QUIZ.
HE'S IN THE CORNER.
SO WITHOUT MUCH FURTHER ADO...
WHICH ONE?
SHHHHH... IT'S ABOUT TO START!
ROUND ONE,
BLOKE WITH THE GOATEE.
QUESTION ONE.
WHICH FOUR-LETTER WORD...
HERE WE GO...

TWENTY QUESTIONS...

ANOTHER PINT...

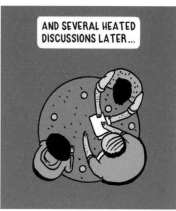

AND SEVERAL HEATED DISCUSSIONS LATER...

ARE WE PUTTING CASABLANCA?

JUST PUT SOMETHING!

I GUESS IT'S TIME TO SPEAK TO TONY.

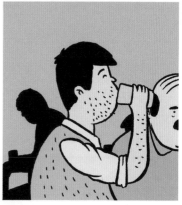

OK GUYS...

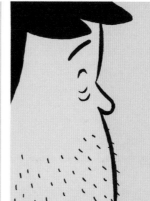

WISH ME LUCK!

TONY & HIS

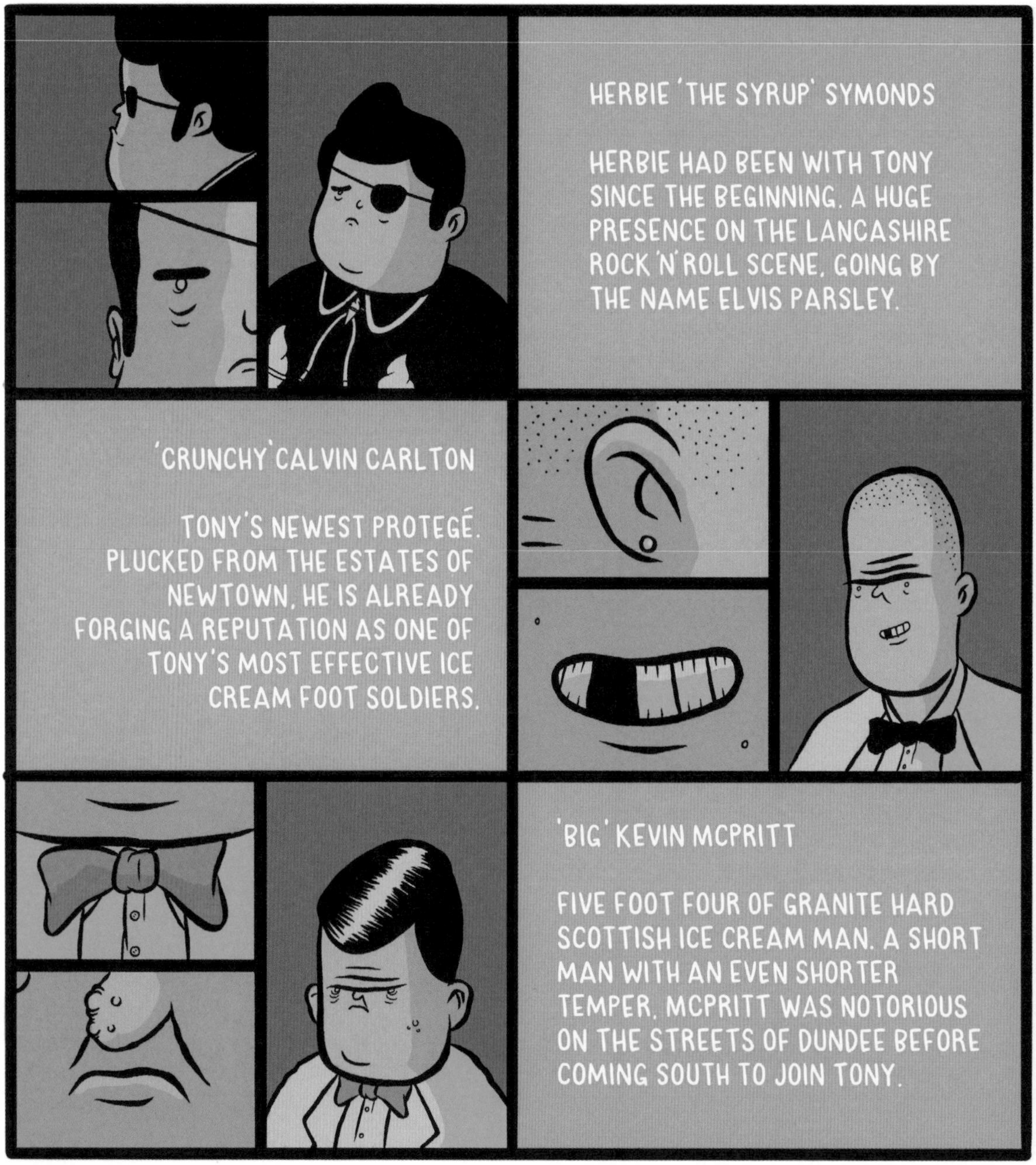
HERBIE 'THE SYRUP' SYMONDS
HERBIE HAD BEEN WITH TONY SINCE THE BEGINNING. A HUGE PRESENCE ON THE LANCASHIRE ROCK 'N' ROLL SCENE, GOING BY THE NAME ELVIS PARSLEY.
'CRUNCHY' CALVIN CARLTON
TONY'S NEWEST PROTEGÉ. PLUCKED FROM THE ESTATES OF NEWTOWN, HE IS ALREADY FORGING A REPUTATION AS ONE OF TONY'S MOST EFFECTIVE ICE CREAM FOOT SOLDIERS.
'BIG' KEVIN MCPRITT
FIVE FOOT FOUR OF GRANITE HARD SCOTTISH ICE CREAM MAN. A SHORT MAN WITH AN EVEN SHORTER TEMPER. MCPRITT WAS NOTORIOUS ON THE STREETS OF DUNDEE BEFORE COMING SOUTH TO JOIN TONY.

ENTOURAGE

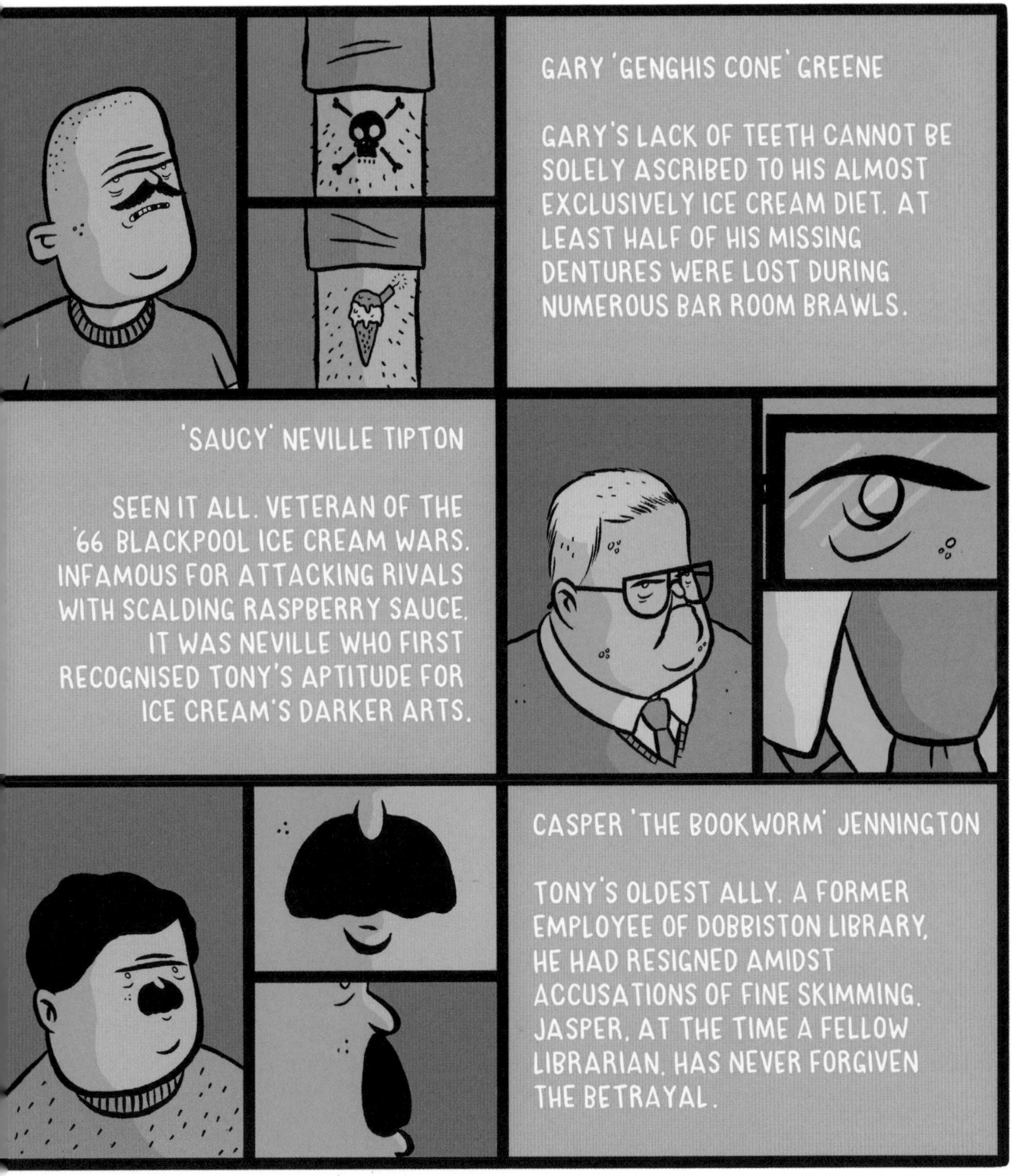
GARY 'GENGHIS CONE' GREENE
GARY'S LACK OF TEETH CANNOT BE SOLELY ASCRIBED TO HIS ALMOST EXCLUSIVELY ICE CREAM DIET. AT LEAST HALF OF HIS MISSING DENTURES WERE LOST DURING NUMEROUS BAR ROOM BRAWLS.
'SAUCY' NEVILLE TIPTON
SEEN IT ALL. VETERAN OF THE '66 BLACKPOOL ICE CREAM WARS. INFAMOUS FOR ATTACKING RIVALS WITH SCALDING RASPBERRY SAUCE. IT WAS NEVILLE WHO FIRST RECOGNISED TONY'S APTITUDE FOR ICE CREAM'S DARKER ARTS.
CASPER 'THE BOOKWORM' JENNINGTON
TONY'S OLDEST ALLY. A FORMER EMPLOYEE OF DOBBISTON LIBRARY, HE HAD RESIGNED AMIDST ACCUSATIONS OF FINE SKIMMING. JASPER, AT THE TIME A FELLOW LIBRARIAN, HAS NEVER FORGIVEN THE BETRAYAL.

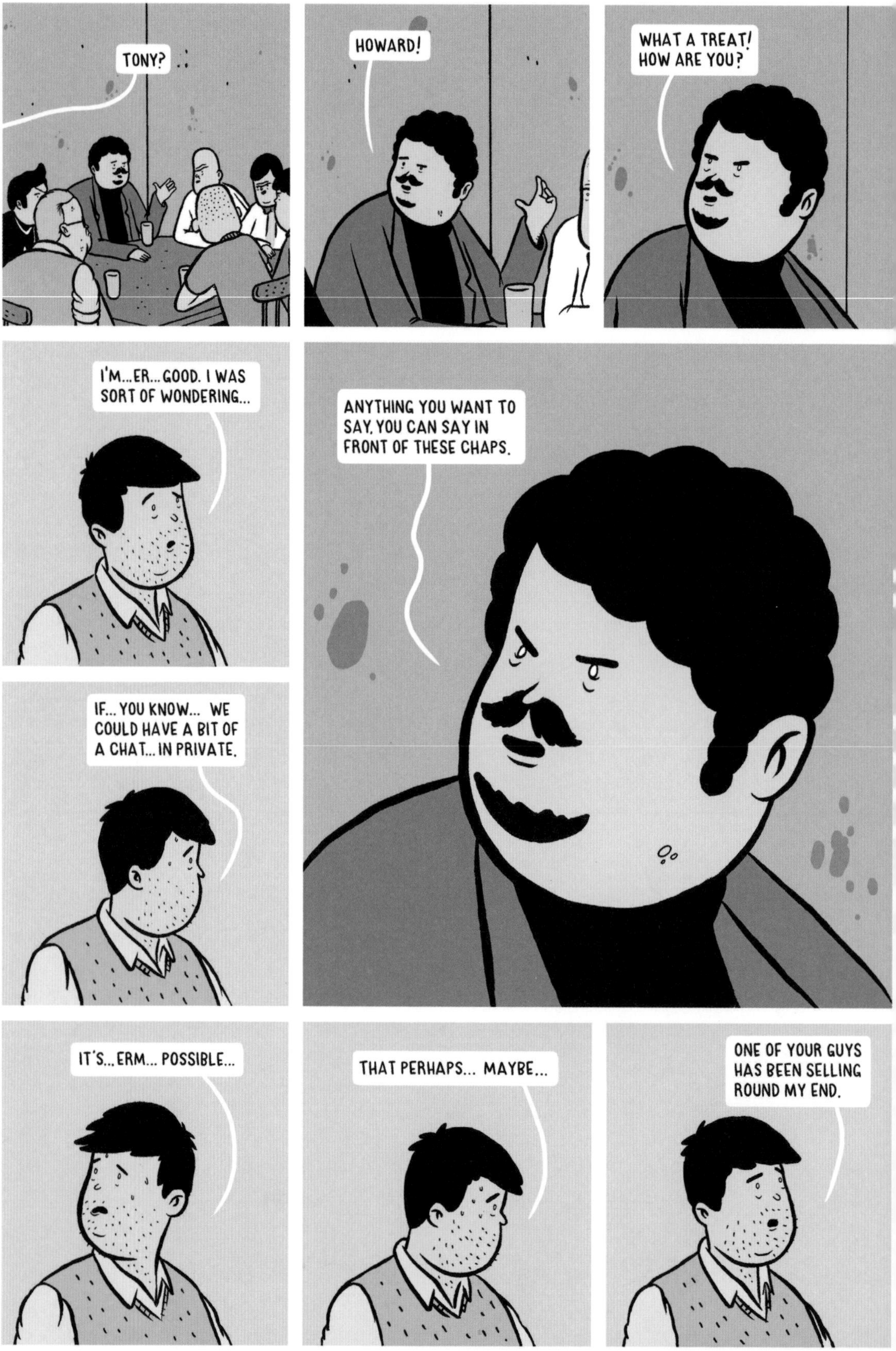
TONY?
HOWARD!
WHAT A TREAT! HOW ARE YOU?
I'M...ER...GOOD. I WAS SORT OF WONDERING...
IF... YOU KNOW... WE COULD HAVE A BIT OF A CHAT... IN PRIVATE.
ANYTHING YOU WANT TO SAY, YOU CAN SAY IN FRONT OF THESE CHAPS.
IT'S... ERM... POSSIBLE...
THAT PERHAPS... MAYBE...
ONE OF YOUR GUYS HAS BEEN SELLING ROUND MY END.

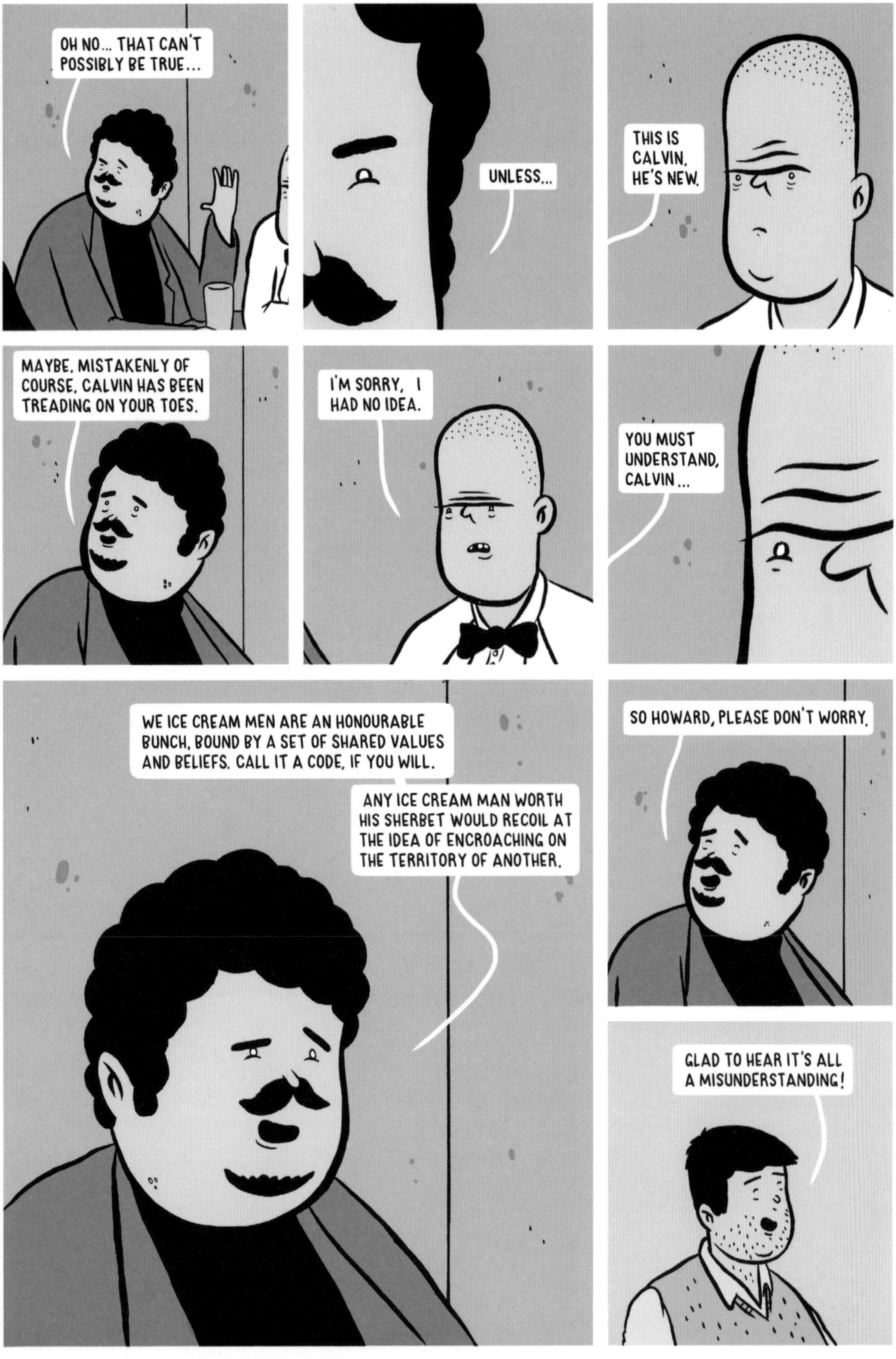
OH NO... THAT CAN'T POSSIBLY BE TRUE...
UNLESS...
THIS IS CALVIN, HE'S NEW.
MAYBE, MISTAKENLY OF COURSE, CALVIN HAS BEEN TREADING ON YOUR TOES.
I'M SORRY, I HAD NO IDEA.
YOU MUST UNDERSTAND, CALVIN...
WE ICE CREAM MEN ARE AN HONOURABLE BUNCH, BOUND BY A SET OF SHARED VALUES AND BELIEFS. CALL IT A CODE, IF YOU WILL.
ANY ICE CREAM MAN WORTH HIS SHERBET WOULD RECOIL AT THE IDEA OF ENCROACHING ON THE TERRITORY OF ANOTHER.
SO HOWARD, PLEASE DON'T WORRY.
GLAD TO HEAR IT'S ALL A MISUNDERSTANDING!

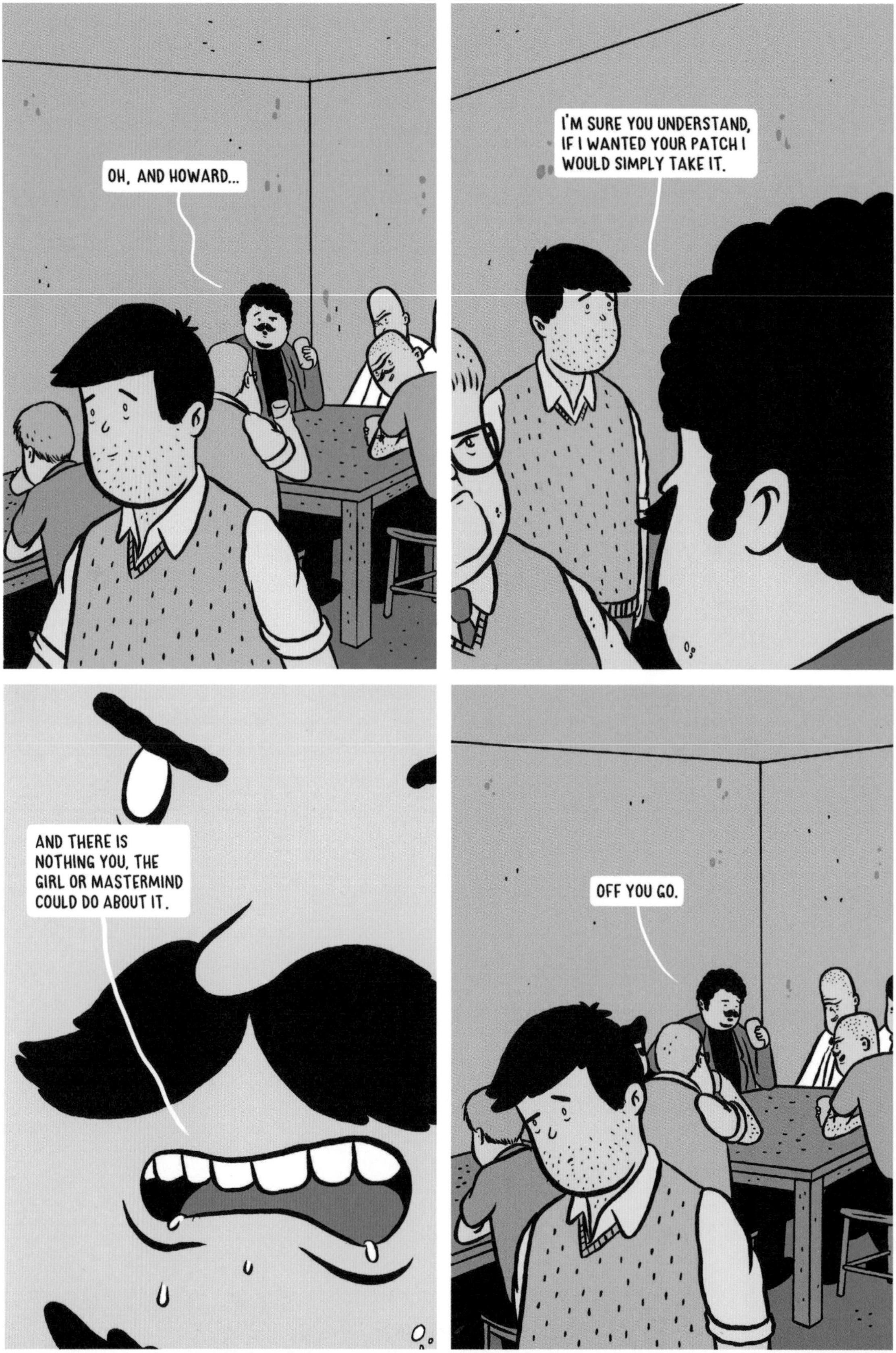
OH, AND HOWARD...
I'M SURE YOU UNDERSTAND, IF I WANTED YOUR PATCH I WOULD SIMPLY TAKE IT.
AND THERE IS NOTHING YOU, THE GIRL OR MASTERMIND COULD DO ABOUT IT.
OFF YOU GO.

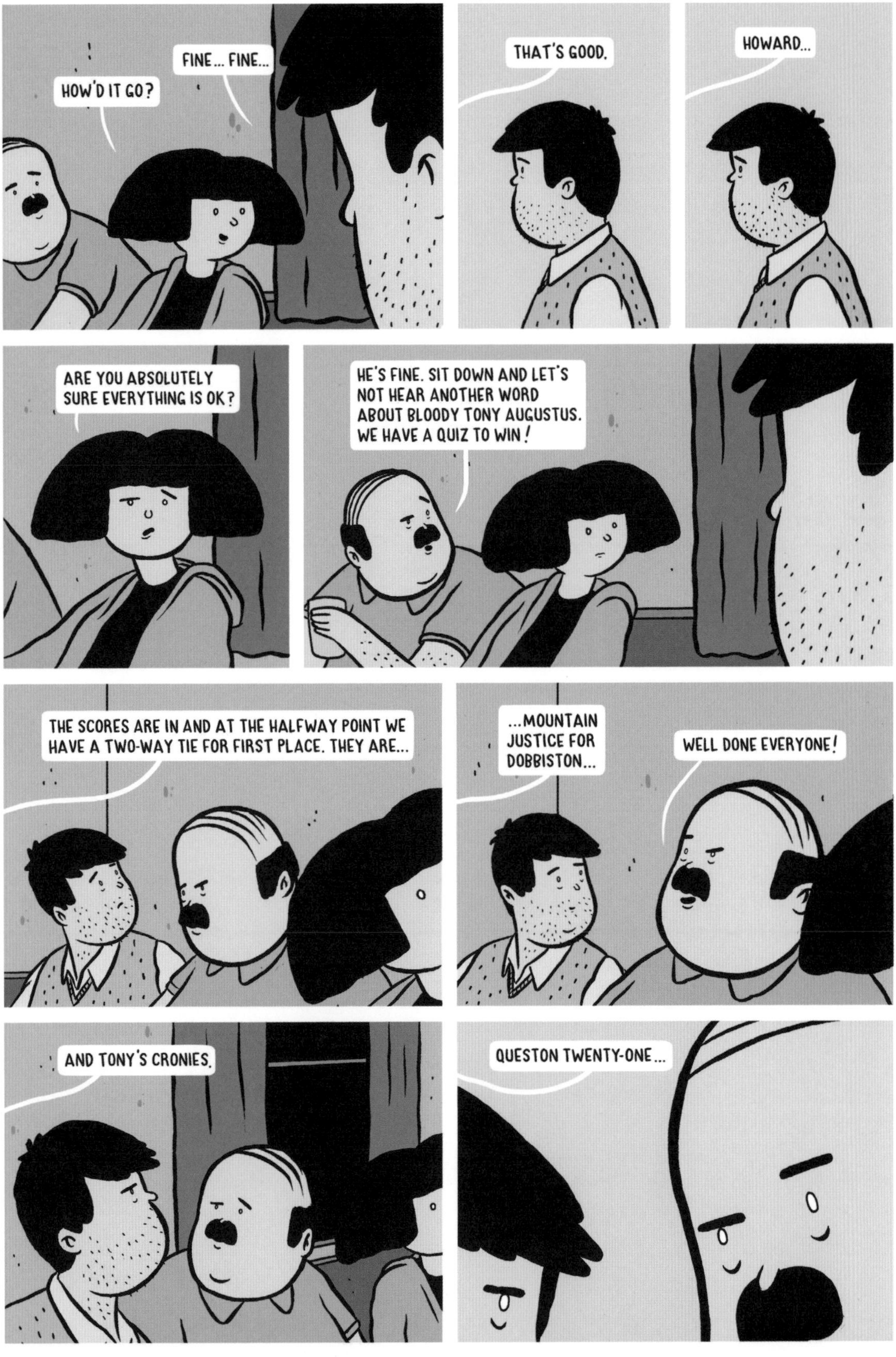
HOW'D IT GO?
FINE... FINE...
THAT'S GOOD.
HOWARD...
ARE YOU ABSOLUTELY SURE EVERYTHING IS OK?
HE'S FINE. SIT DOWN AND LET'S NOT HEAR ANOTHER WORD ABOUT BLOODY TONY AUGUSTUS. WE HAVE A QUIZ TO WIN!
THE SCORES ARE IN AND AT THE HALFWAY POINT WE HAVE A TWO-WAY TIE FOR FIRST PLACE. THEY ARE...
...MOUNTAIN JUSTICE FOR DOBBISTON...
WELL DONE EVERYONE!
AND TONY'S CRONIES.
QUESTON TWENTY-ONE...

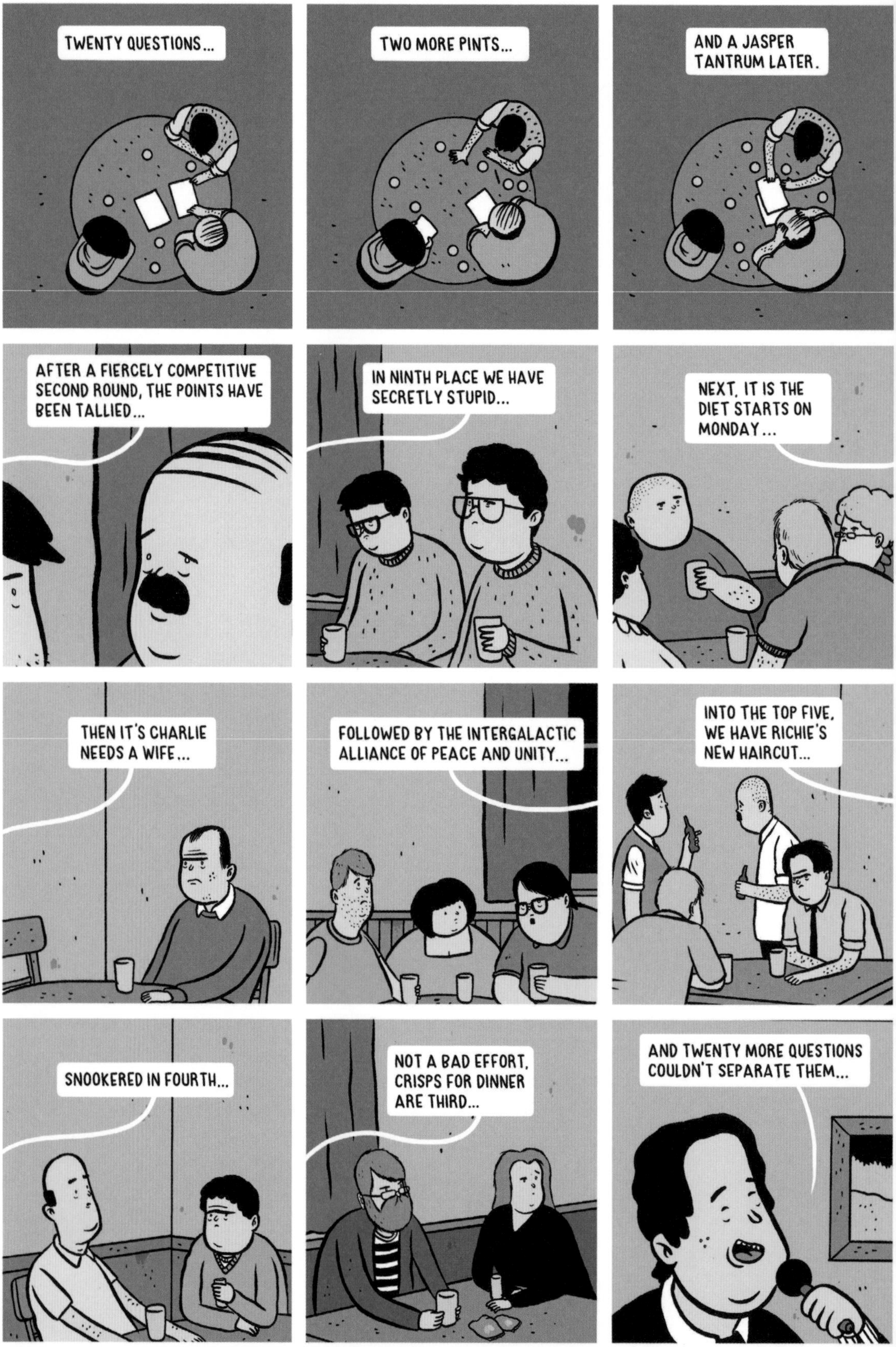
TWENTY QUESTIONS...
TWO MORE PINTS...
AND A JASPER TANTRUM LATER.
AFTER A FIERCELY COMPETITIVE SECOND ROUND, THE POINTS HAVE BEEN TALLIED...
IN NINTH PLACE WE HAVE SECRETLY STUPID...
NEXT, IT IS THE DIET STARTS ON MONDAY...
THEN IT'S CHARLIE NEEDS A WIFE...
FOLLOWED BY THE INTERGALACTIC ALLIANCE OF PEACE AND UNITY...
INTO THE TOP FIVE, WE HAVE RICHIE'S NEW HAIRCUT...
SNOOKERED IN FOURTH...
NOT A BAD EFFORT, CRISPS FOR DINNER ARE THIRD...
AND TWENTY MORE QUESTIONS COULDN'T SEPARATE THEM...

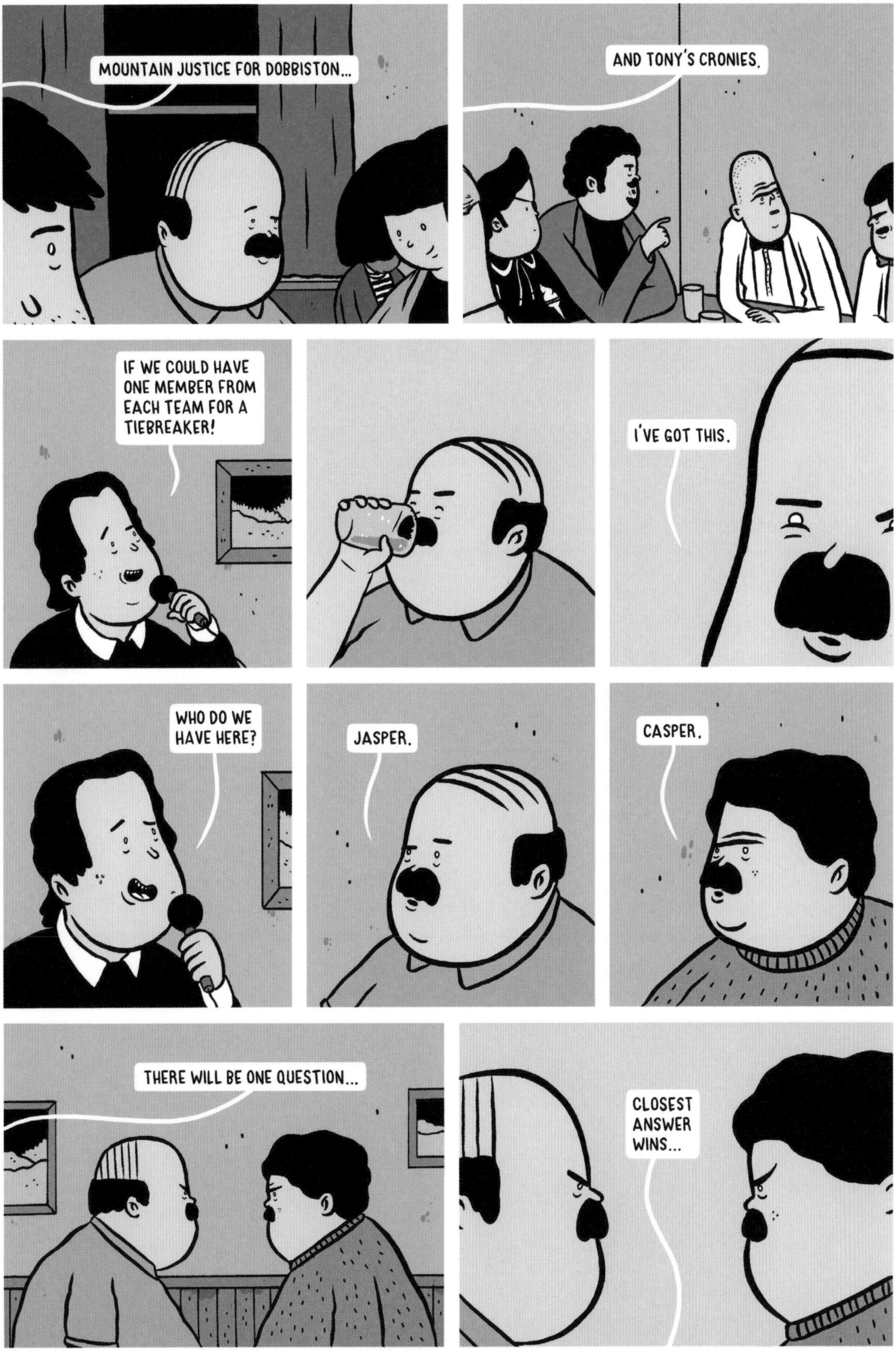
MOUNTAIN JUSTICE FOR DOBBISTON...
AND TONY'S CRONIES.
IF WE COULD HAVE ONE MEMBER FROM EACH TEAM FOR A TIEBREAKER!
I'VE GOT THIS.
WHO DO WE HAVE HERE?
JASPER.
CASPER.
THERE WILL BE ONE QUESTION...
CLOSEST ANSWER WINS...

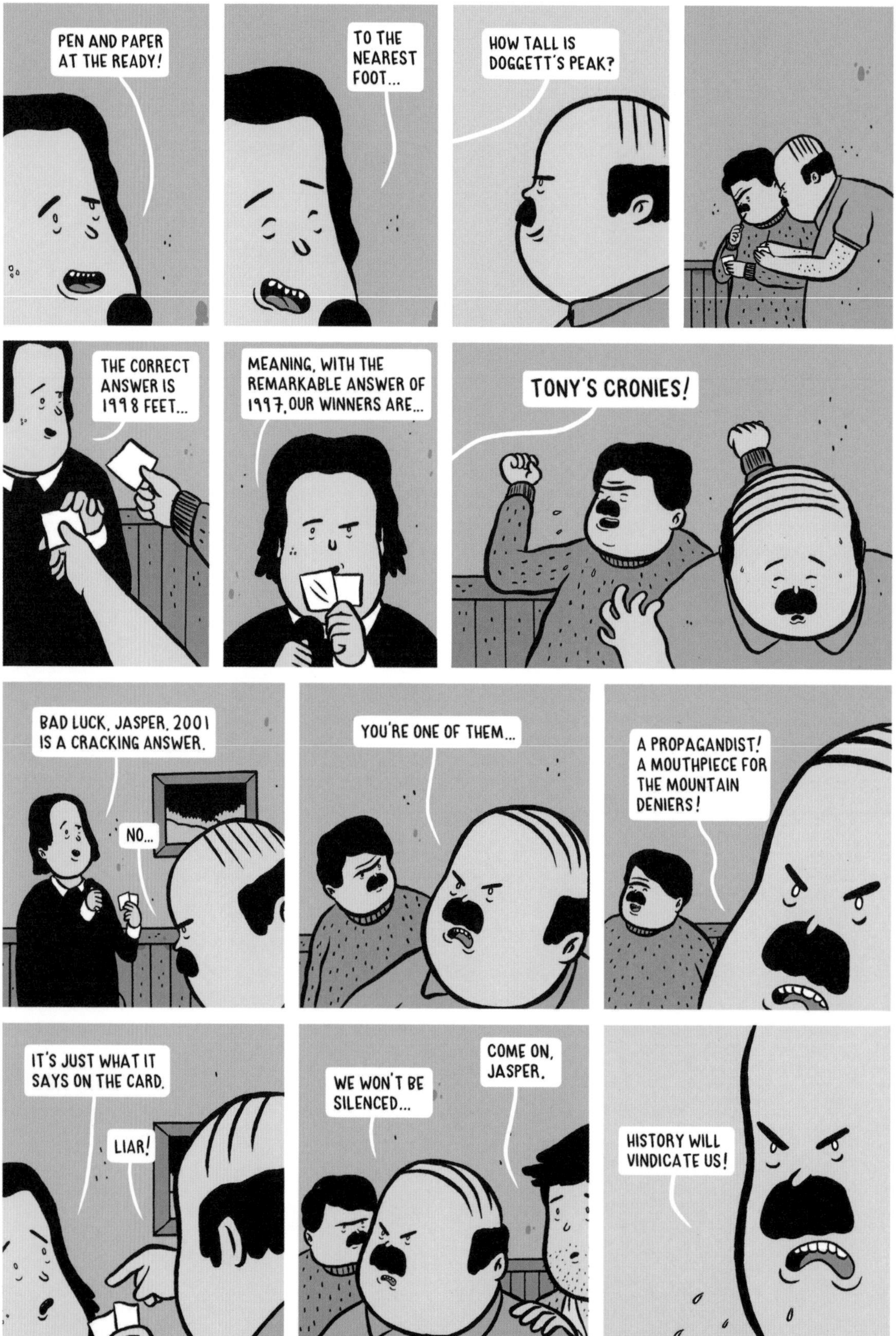
PEN AND PAPER AT THE READY!
TO THE NEAREST FOOT...
HOW TALL IS DOGGETT'S PEAK?
THE CORRECT ANSWER IS 1998 FEET...
MEANING, WITH THE REMARKABLE ANSWER OF 1997, OUR WINNERS ARE...
TONY'S CRONIES!
BAD LUCK, JASPER. 2001 IS A CRACKING ANSWER.
NO...
YOU'RE ONE OF THEM...
A PROPAGANDIST! A MOUTHPIECE FOR THE MOUNTAIN DENIERS!
IT'S JUST WHAT IT SAYS ON THE CARD.
LIAR!
WE WON'T BE SILENCED...
COME ON, JASPER.
HISTORY WILL VINDICATE US!

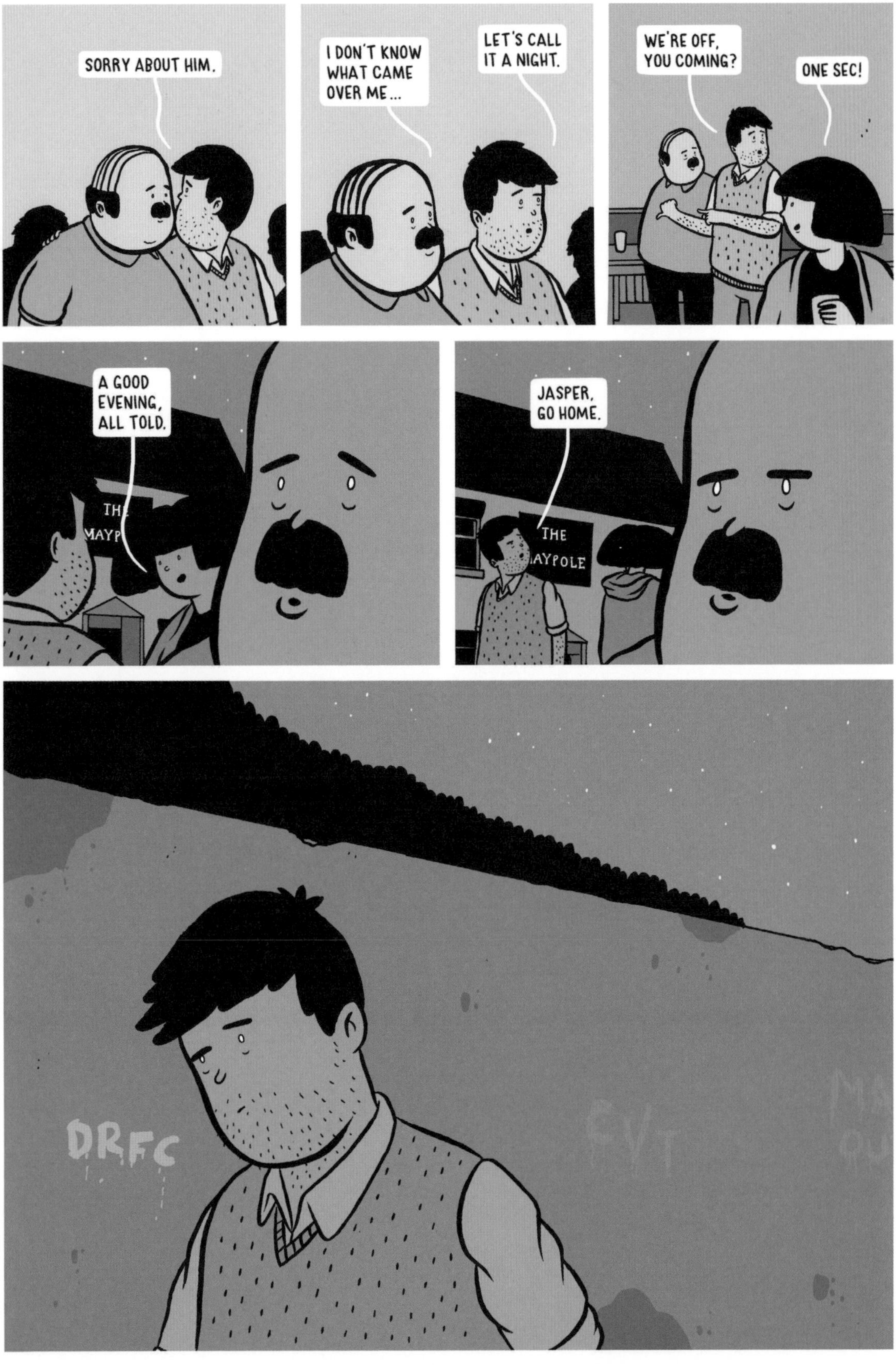
SORRY ABOUT HIM.
I DON'T KNOW WHAT CAME OVER ME...
LET'S CALL IT A NIGHT.
WE'RE OFF, YOU COMING?
ONE SEC!
A GOOD EVENING, ALL TOLD.
JASPER, GO HOME.
DRFC

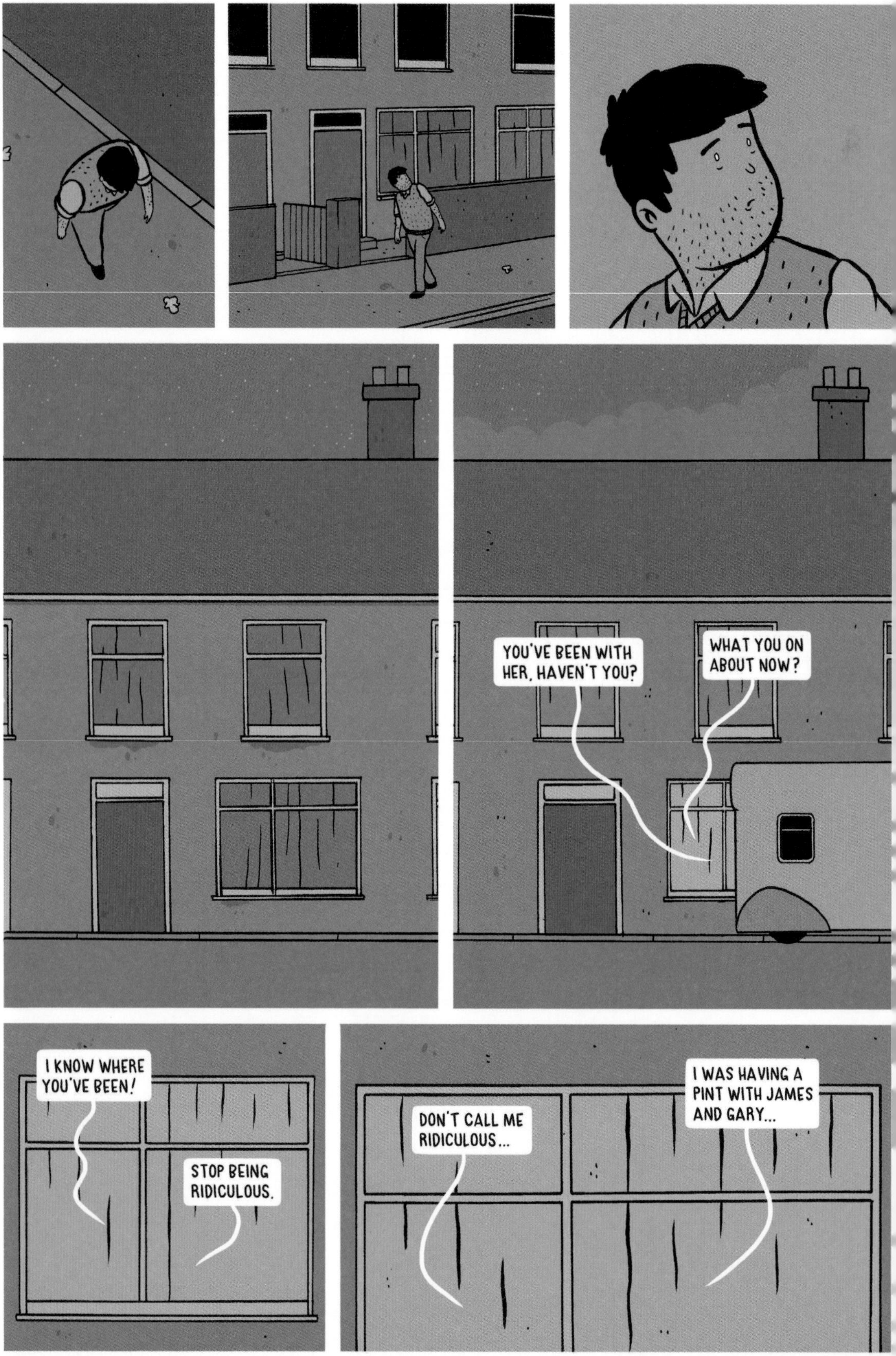
YOU'VE BEEN WITH HER, HAVEN'T YOU?
WHAT YOU ON ABOUT NOW?
I KNOW WHERE YOU'VE BEEN!
STOP BEING RIDICULOUS.
DON'T CALL ME RIDICULOUS...
I WAS HAVING A PINT WITH JAMES AND GARY...

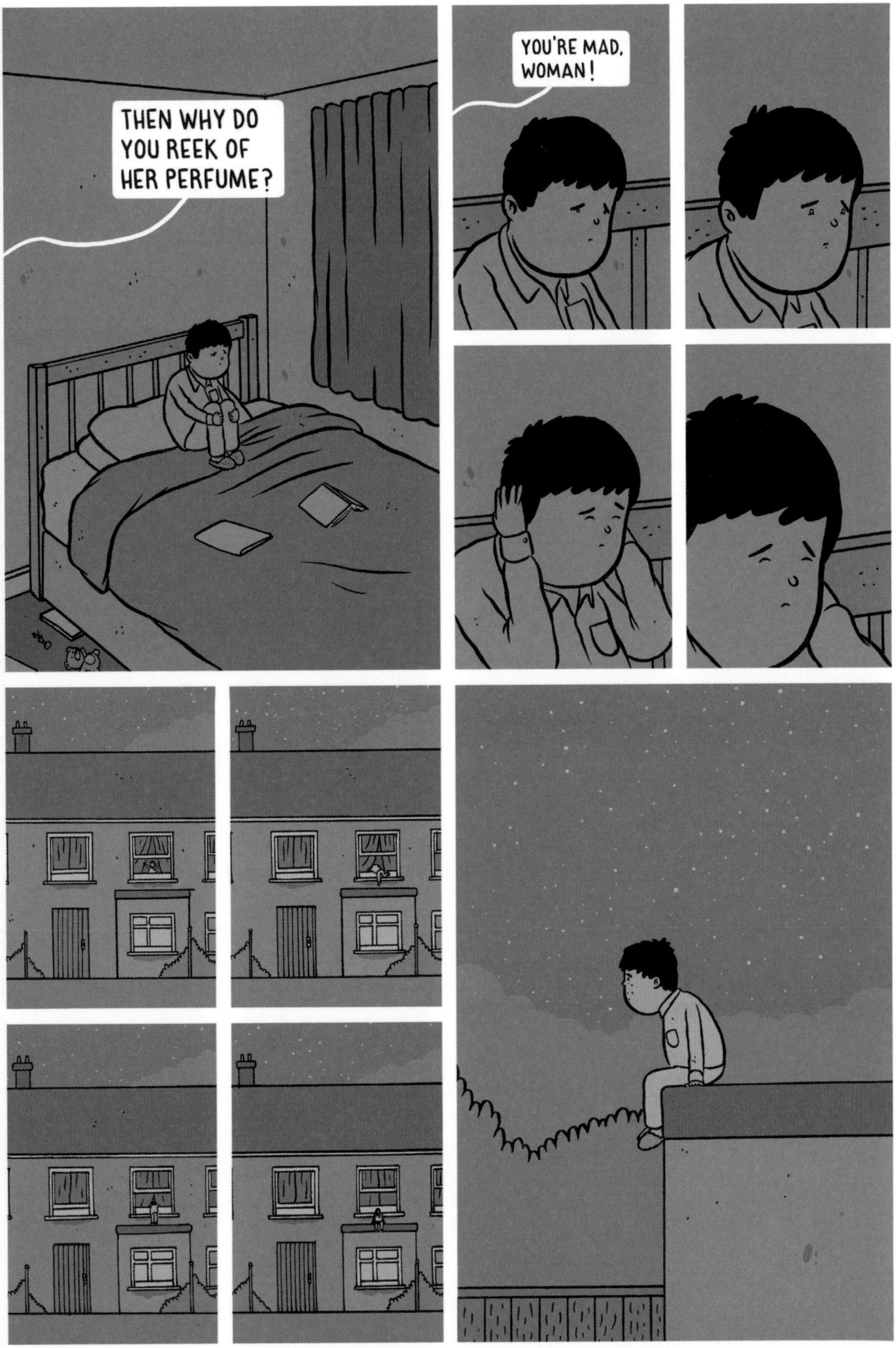
THEN WHY DO YOU REEK OF HER PERFUME?
YOU'RE MAD, WOMAN!

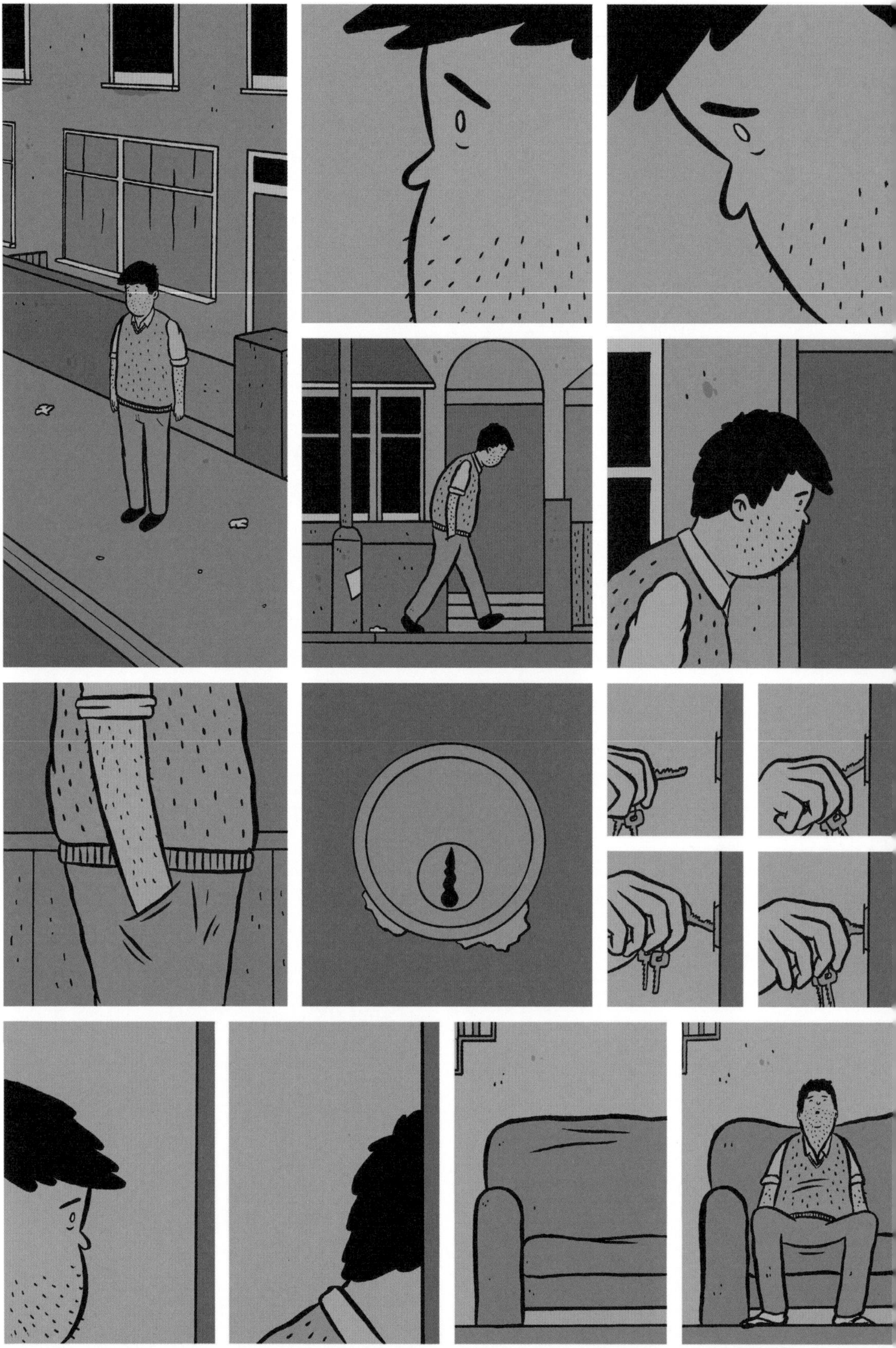

CHAPTER FIVE

HOWARD FALLS VICTIM TO THE GUTTER PRESS

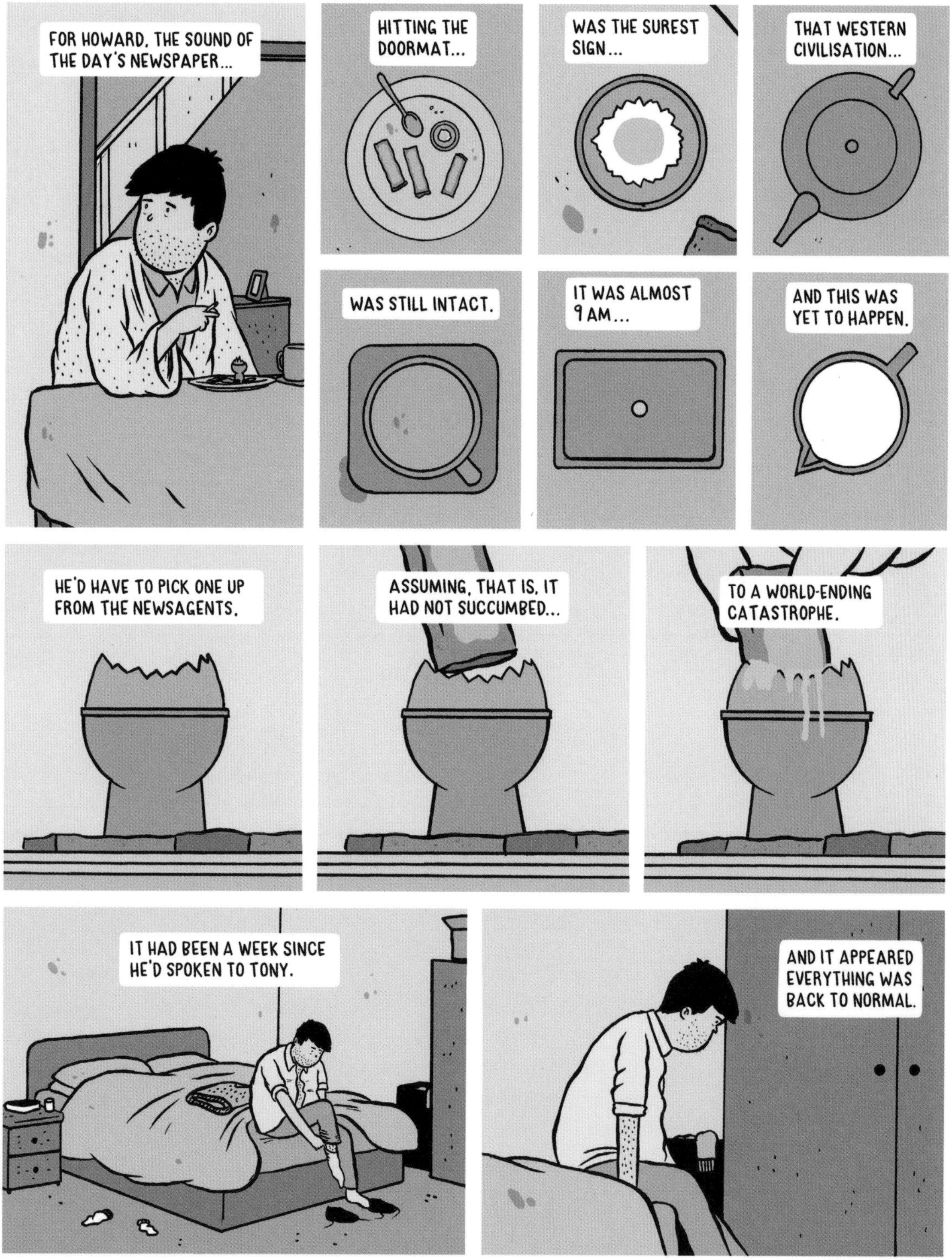
FOR HOWARD, THE SOUND OF THE DAY'S NEWSPAPER...
HITTING THE DOORMAT...
WAS THE SUREST SIGN...
THAT WESTERN CIVILISATION...
WAS STILL INTACT.
IT WAS ALMOST 9 AM...
AND THIS WAS YET TO HAPPEN.
HE'D HAVE TO PICK ONE UP FROM THE NEWSAGENTS.
ASSUMING, THAT IS, IT HAD NOT SUCCUMBED...
TO A WORLD-ENDING CATASTROPHE.
IT HAD BEEN A WEEK SINCE HE'D SPOKEN TO TONY.
AND IT APPEARED EVERYTHING WAS BACK TO NORMAL.

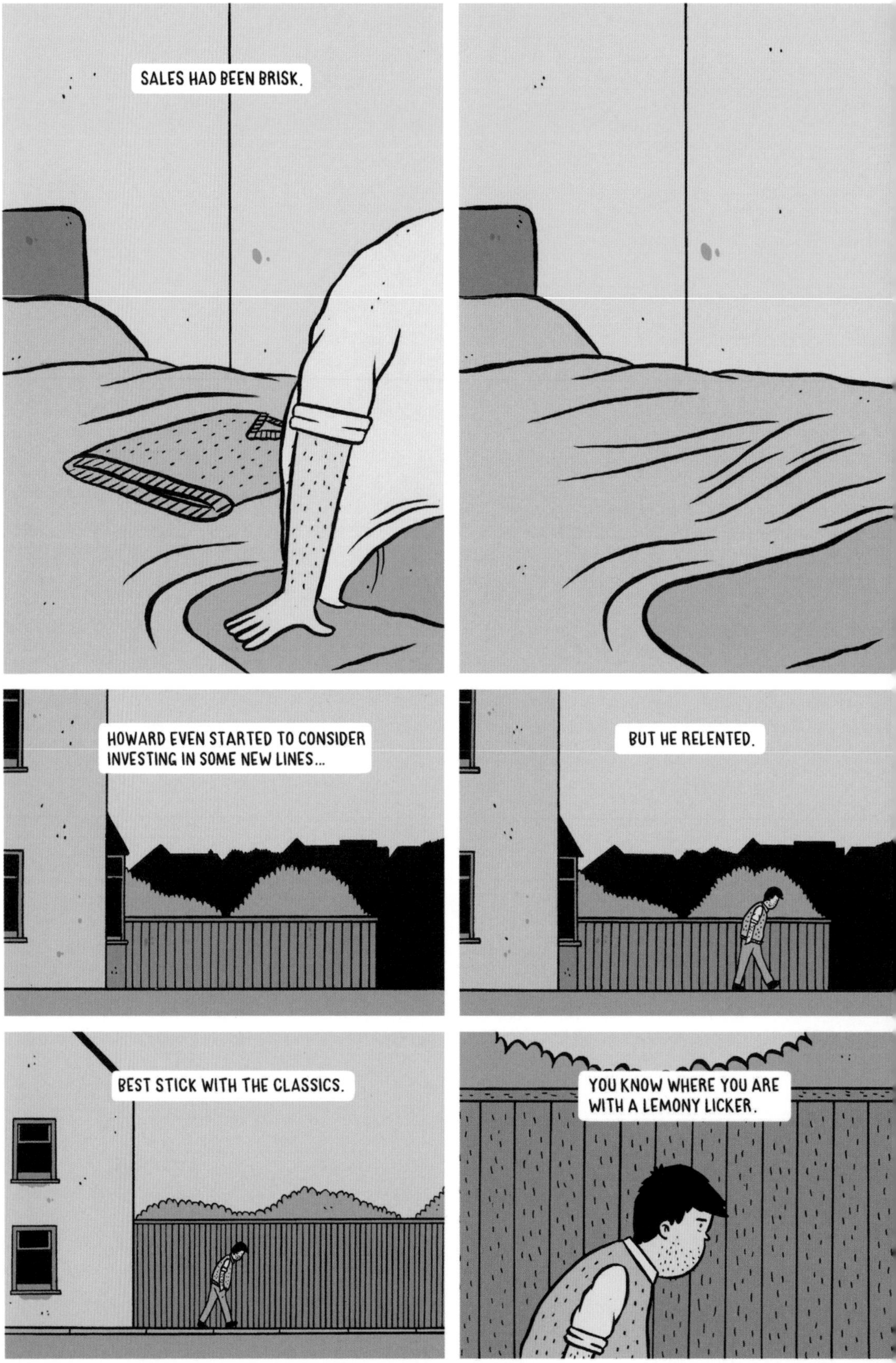
SALES HAD BEEN BRISK.
HOWARD EVEN STARTED TO CONSIDER INVESTING IN SOME NEW LINES...
BUT HE RELENTED.
BEST STICK WITH THE CLASSICS.
YOU KNOW WHERE YOU ARE WITH A LEMONY LICKER.

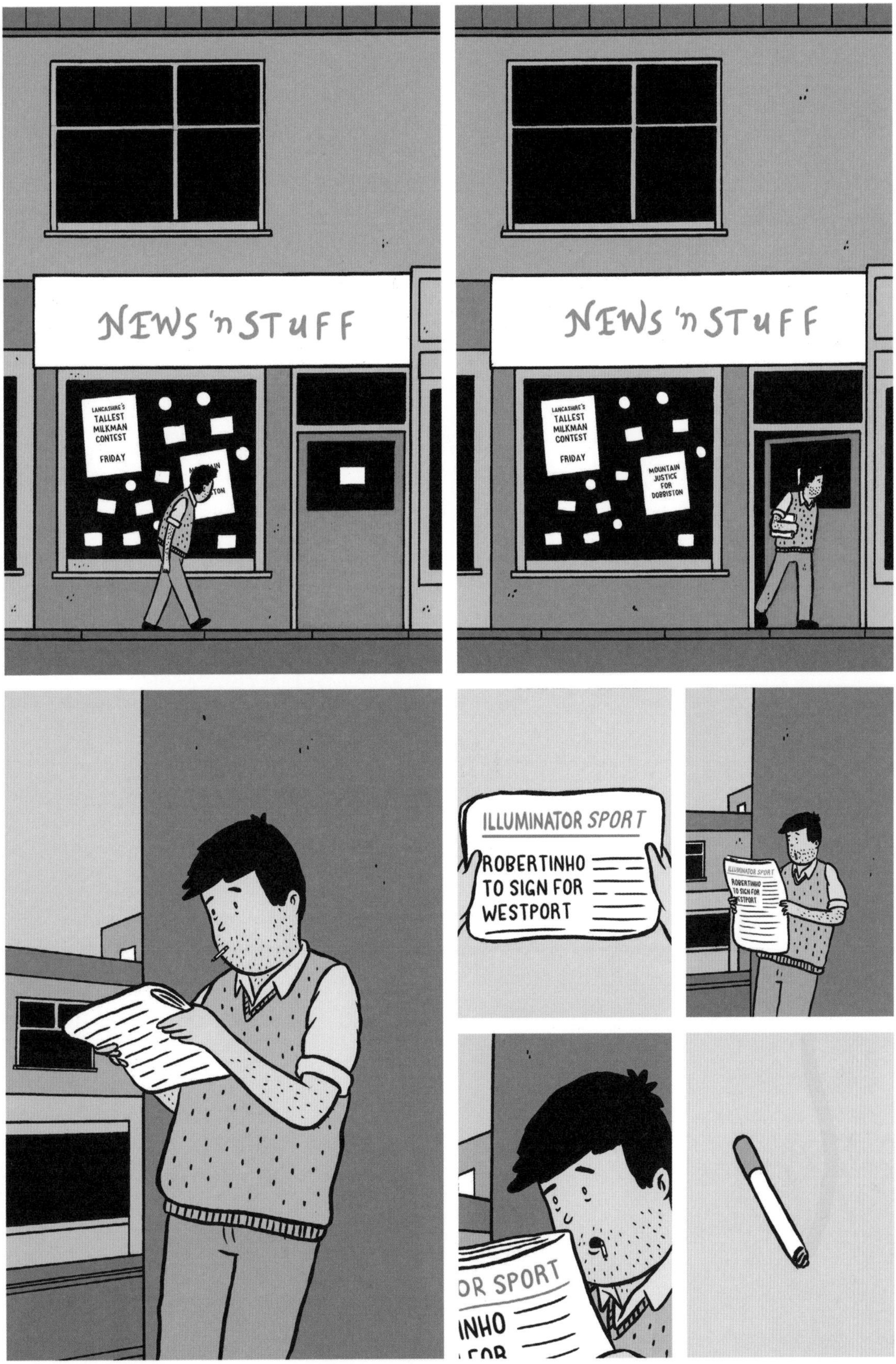
NEWS 'n STUFF
LANCASHIRE'S TALLEST MILKMAN CONTEST FRIDAY
NEWS 'n STUFF
LANCASHIRE'S TALLEST MILKMAN CONTEST FRIDAY
MOUNTAIN JUSTICE FOR DOBBISTON
ILLUMINATOR SPORT
ROBERTINHO TO SIGN FOR WESTPORT

DOBBISTON
ILLUMINATOR

19TH JULY, 1995

ICE CREAM VAN MADE ME SICK!

EXCLUSIVE BY SEAN TIBERIUS

LOCAL RESIDENT, AMANDA CRIPPS, CLAIMS TO HAVE GOT MORE THAN SHE BARGAINED FOR AFTER PURCHASING FOOD FROM LOCAL ICE CREAM MAN, HOWARD 'CAPTAIN CONE' GRAYLING. "AS I TUCKED INTO MY DOUBLE CONE I KNEW SOMETHING WAS WRONG. FAST FORWARD A FEW MINUTES AND I WAS BUSY SICKING MY GUTS UP..."

CONTINUED ON PAGE 3

BOWLS CLUB MYSTERY DEEPENS
BY CHRISTOPHER SLOPP

THE FUTURE OF DOBBISTON BOWLS CLUB WAS THROWN INTO QUESTION LAST NIGHT, AS IT WAS REVEALED THAT THREE MORE SETS OF BOWLS HAVE GONE MISSING. HAVING LOOKED SET TO WIN THE WEST LANCASHIRE LEAGUE FOR THE FIRST TIME SINCE THE SECOND WORLD WAR, THE CLUB ARE NOW IN DANGER OF NOT EVEN BEING ABLE TO COMPLETE THEIR REMAINING FIXTURES. CLUB PRESIDENT, MALCOLM HANSHAW, VOWED TO FIGHT ON ...

CONTINUED ON PAGE 16

SAMBA MAGICIAN SET FOR SANDPIPERS?

SEE BACK PAGE FOR DETAILS! PLUS TWENTY PAGES OF DOBBISTON SPORTS NEWS!

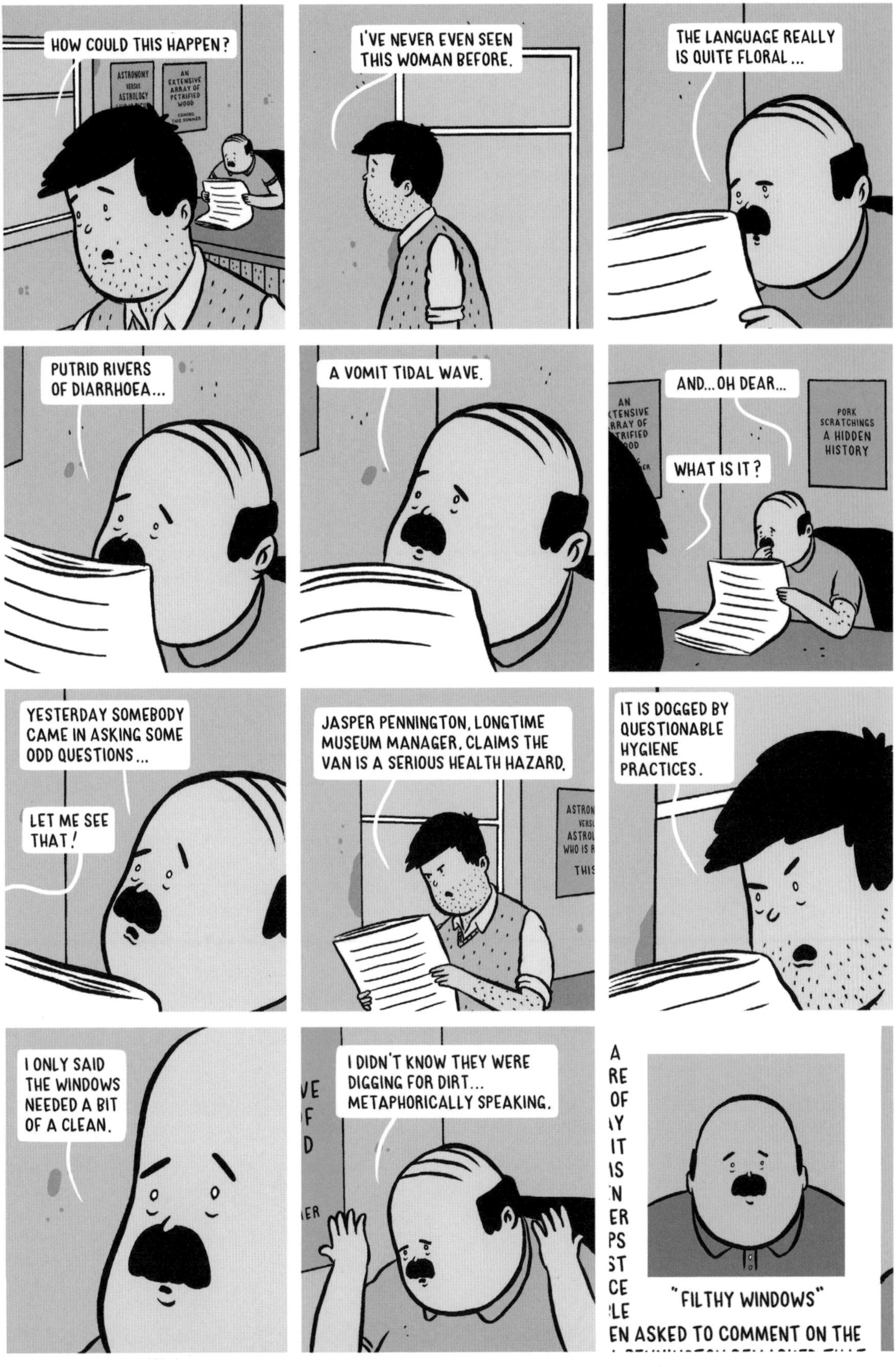
HOW COULD THIS HAPPEN?
ASTRONOMY VERSUS ASTROLOGY
AN EXTENSIVE ARRAY OF PETRIFIED WOOD
COMING THIS SUMMER
I'VE NEVER EVEN SEEN THIS WOMAN BEFORE.
THE LANGUAGE REALLY IS QUITE FLORAL ...
PUTRID RIVERS OF DIARRHOEA...
A VOMIT TIDAL WAVE.
AND... OH DEAR...
WHAT IS IT?
PORK SCRATCHINGS A HIDDEN HISTORY
YESTERDAY SOMEBODY CAME IN ASKING SOME ODD QUESTIONS...
LET ME SEE THAT!
JASPER PENNINGTON, LONGTIME MUSEUM MANAGER, CLAIMS THE VAN IS A SERIOUS HEALTH HAZARD.
IT IS DOGGED BY QUESTIONABLE HYGIENE PRACTICES.
I ONLY SAID THE WINDOWS NEEDED A BIT OF A CLEAN.
I DIDN'T KNOW THEY WERE DIGGING FOR DIRT... METAPHORICALLY SPEAKING.
"FILTHY WINDOWS"

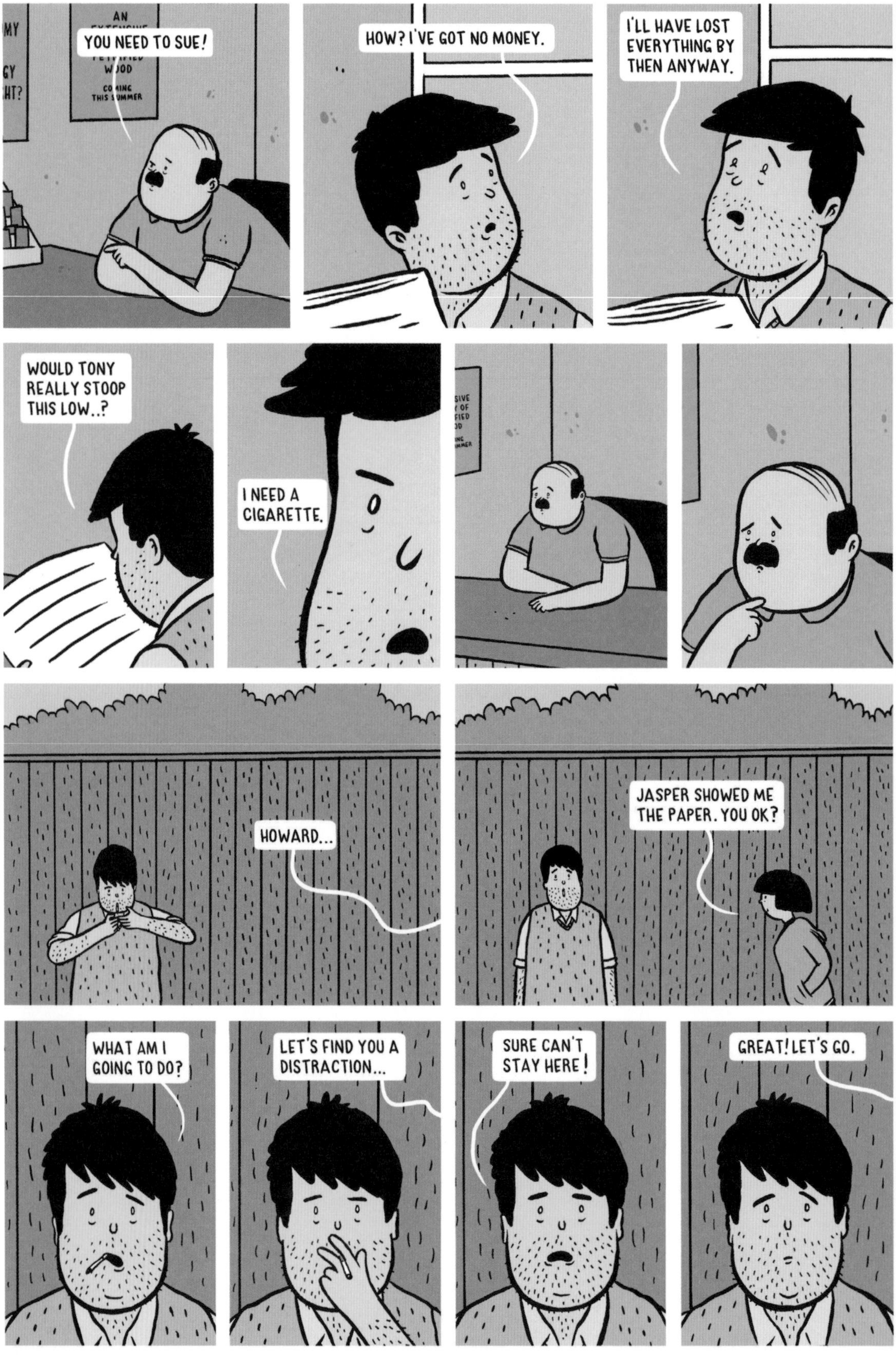
AN
EXTENSIVE
PETRIFIED
WOOD
COMING
THIS SUMMER
YOU NEED TO SUE!
HOW? I'VE GOT NO MONEY.
I'LL HAVE LOST EVERYTHING BY THEN ANYWAY.
WOULD TONY REALLY STOOP THIS LOW..?
I NEED A CIGARETTE.
HOWARD...
JASPER SHOWED ME THE PAPER. YOU OK?
WHAT AM I GOING TO DO?
LET'S FIND YOU A DISTRACTION...
SURE CAN'T STAY HERE!
GREAT! LET'S GO.

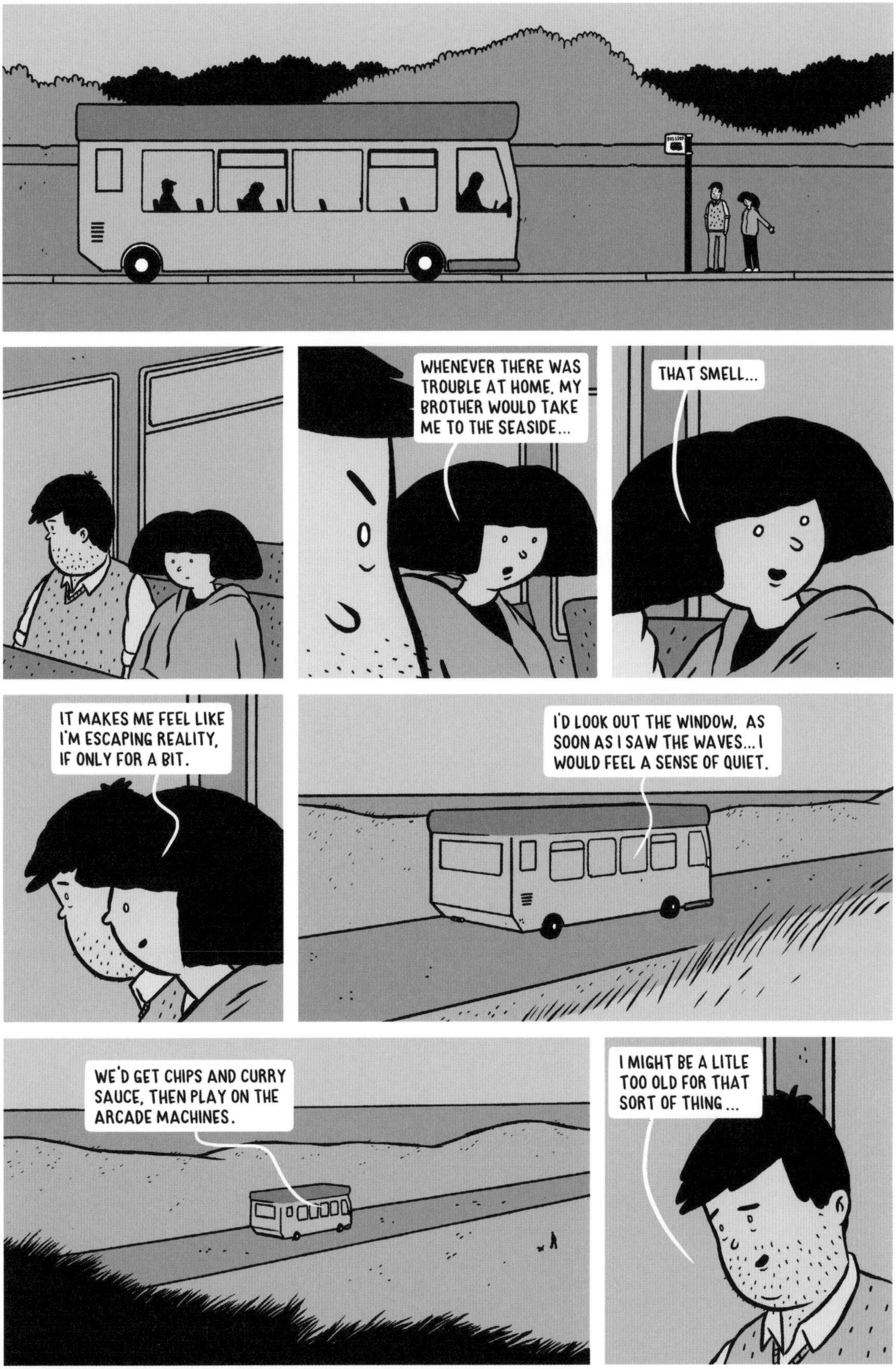
WHENEVER THERE WAS TROUBLE AT HOME, MY BROTHER WOULD TAKE ME TO THE SEASIDE...
THAT SMELL...
IT MAKES ME FEEL LIKE I'M ESCAPING REALITY, IF ONLY FOR A BIT.
I'D LOOK OUT THE WINDOW. AS SOON AS I SAW THE WAVES... I WOULD FEEL A SENSE OF QUIET.
WE'D GET CHIPS AND CURRY SAUCE, THEN PLAY ON THE ARCADE MACHINES.
I MIGHT BE A LITLE TOO OLD FOR THAT SORT OF THING...

YOU'VE GOT TO BE KIDDING ME!

LANCASHIRE HOT SLOT

HOW IS THAT EVEN POSSIBLE?

LOOK AT IT!

IT'S WELL ATTESTED...

THAT IN ARCADES...

CERTAIN LAWS OF PHYSICS CEASE TO APPLY.

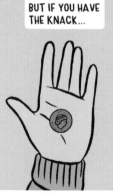

BUT IF YOU HAVE THE KNACK...

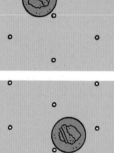

EVEN THESE IMPEDIMENTS TO NATURE...

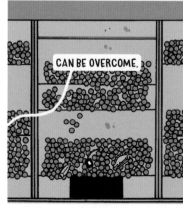

CAN BE OVERCOME.

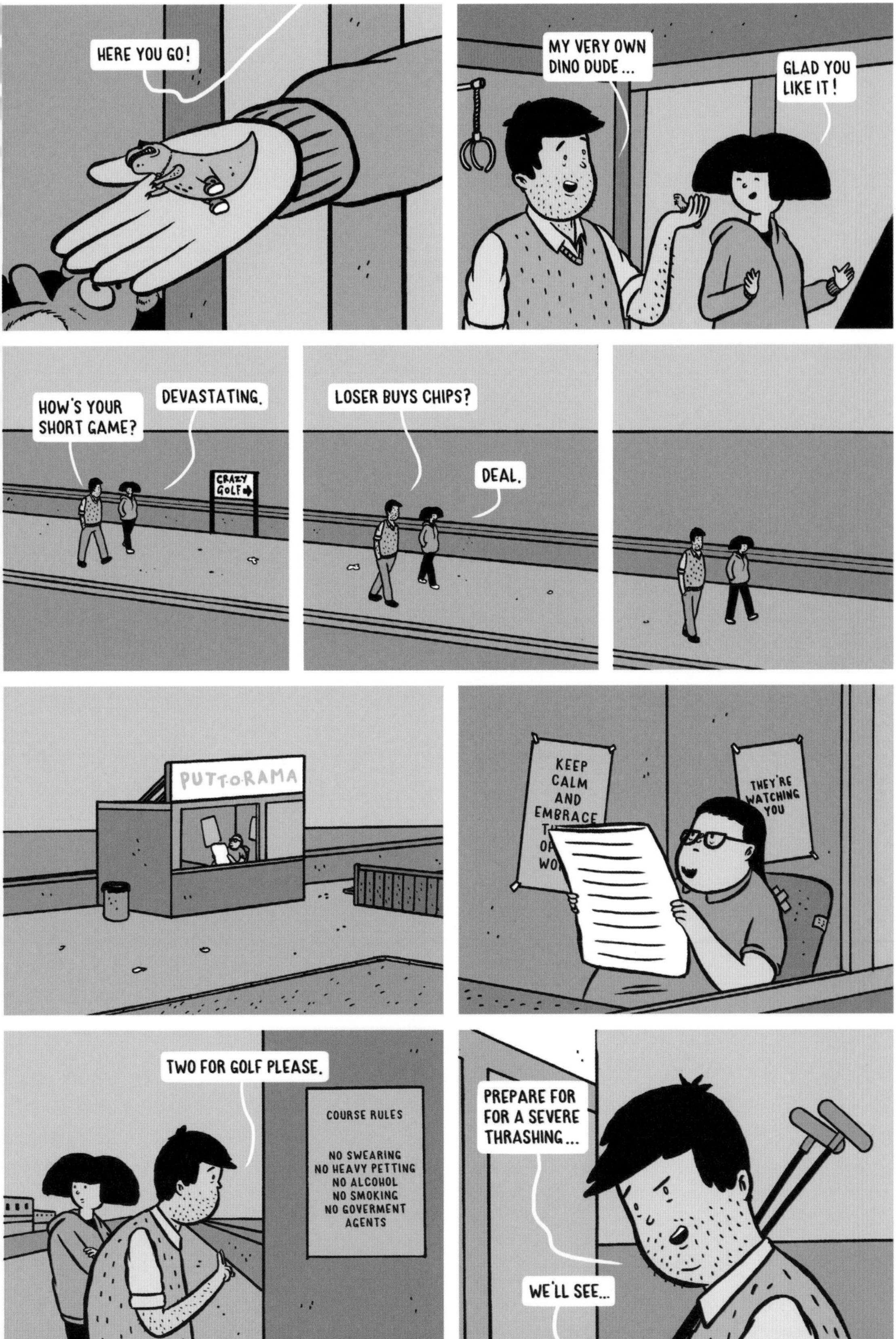
HERE YOU GO!
MY VERY OWN DINO DUDE...
GLAD YOU LIKE IT!
HOW'S YOUR SHORT GAME?
DEVASTATING.
CRAZY GOLF
LOSER BUYS CHIPS?
DEAL.
PUTT-O-RAMA
KEEP CALM AND EMBRACE
THEY'RE WATCHING YOU
TWO FOR GOLF PLEASE.
COURSE RULES
NO SWEARING
NO HEAVY PETTING
NO ALCOHOL
NO SMOKING
NO GOVERMENT AGENTS
PREPARE FOR FOR A SEVERE THRASHING...
WE'LL SEE...

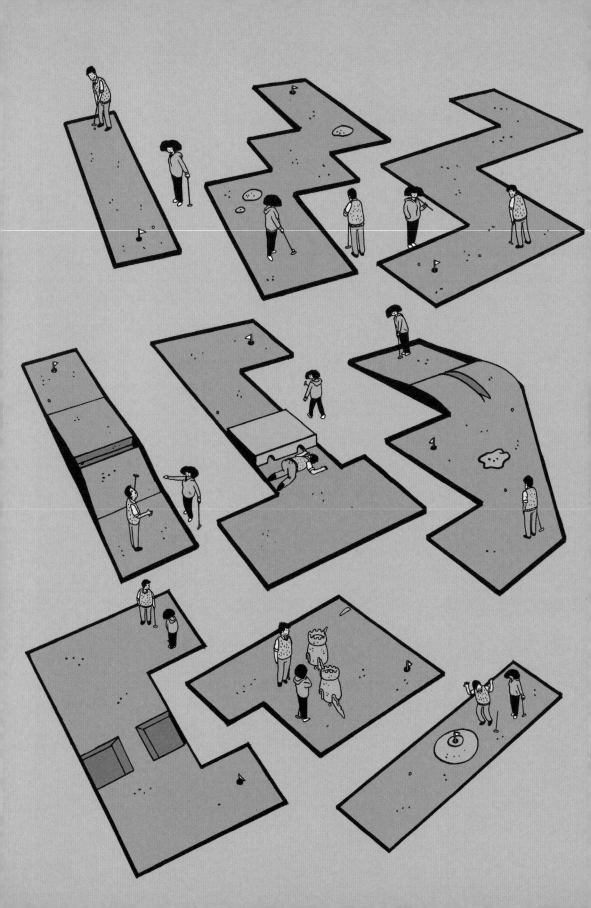

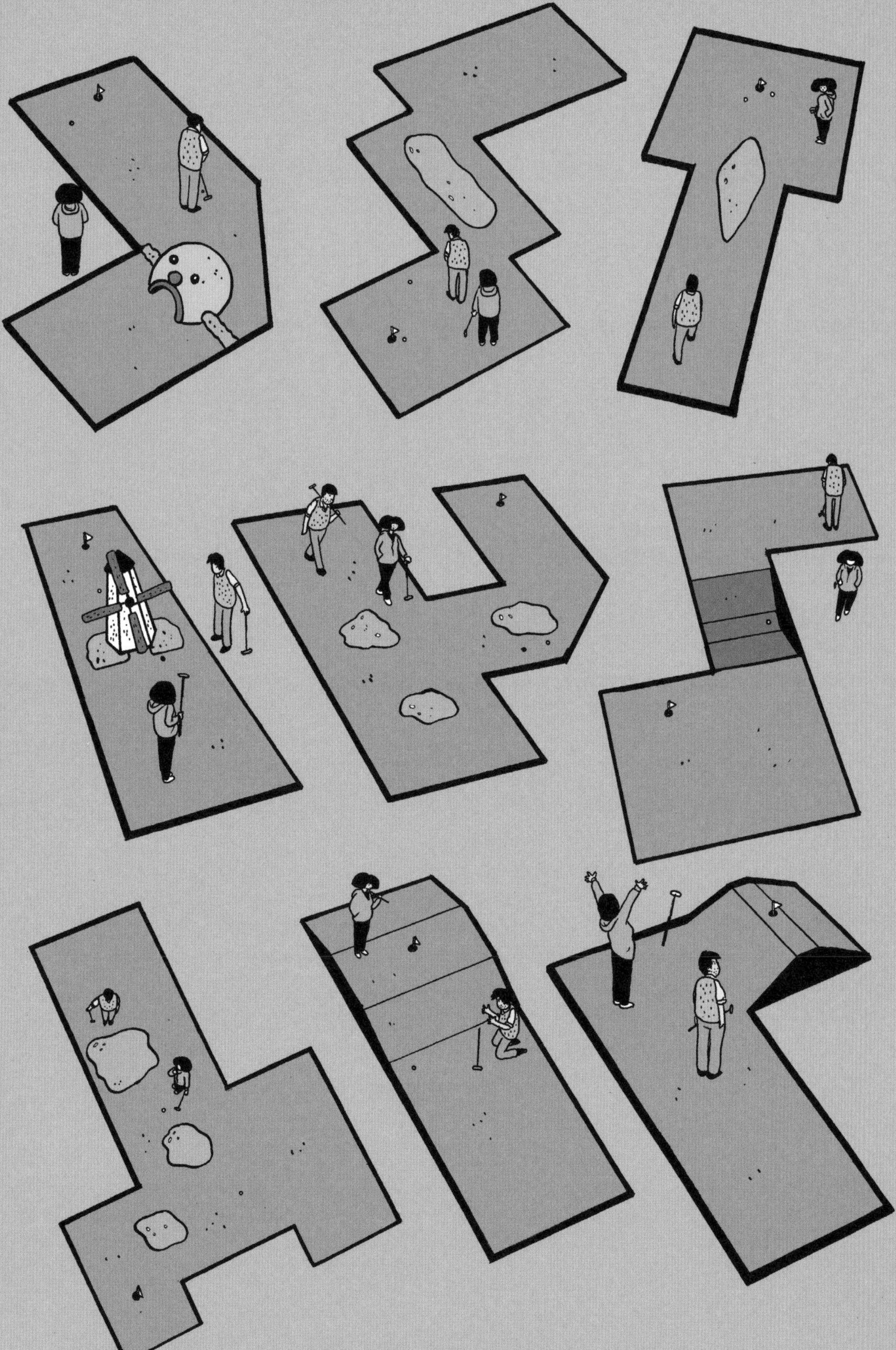

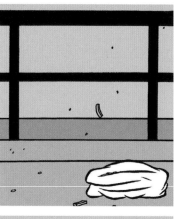

ME AND JENNY USED TO COME HERE A LOT IN THE EARLY DAYS.

WATCH THE WAVES, STUFF OUR FACES WITH CHIPS AND TALK ABOUT ALL THE PLACES WE WERE GOING TO VISIT...

NOT THAT WE'VE ACTUALLY BEEN TO ANY.

THERE'S STILL TIME, YOU'RE NOT THAT OLD...

THANKS.

HOW DID YOU AND YOUR WIFE MEET?

I'M NOT SURE I SHOULD TELL YOU...

YOU ABSOLUTELY HAVE TO NOW!

OK, IT MIGHT SURPRISE YOU... WE MET BALLROOM DANCING.

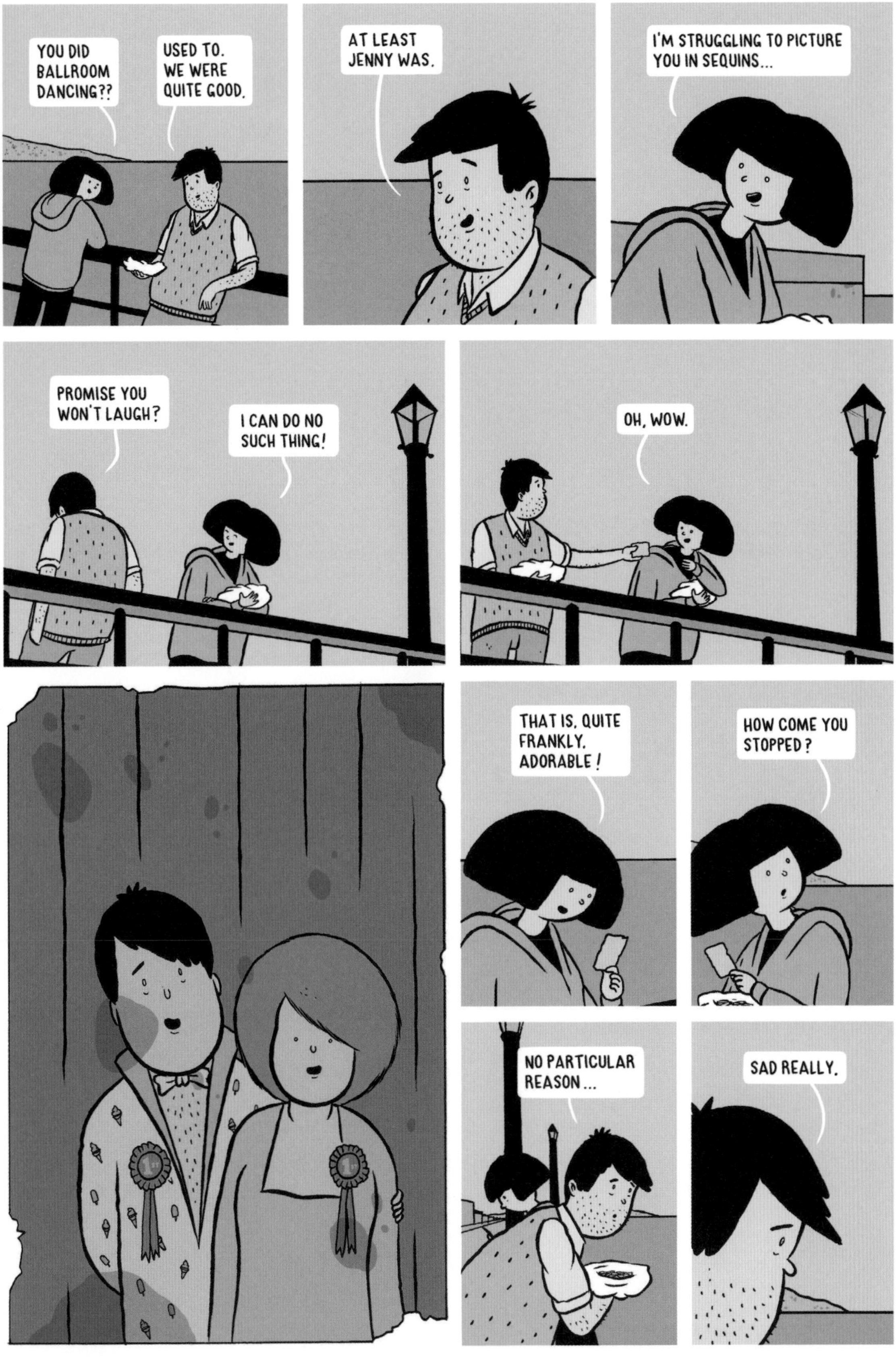
YOU DID BALLROOM DANCING??
USED TO. WE WERE QUITE GOOD.
AT LEAST JENNY WAS.
I'M STRUGGLING TO PICTURE YOU IN SEQUINS...
PROMISE YOU WON'T LAUGH?
I CAN DO NO SUCH THING!
OH, WOW.
THAT IS, QUITE FRANKLY, ADORABLE!
HOW COME YOU STOPPED?
NO PARTICULAR REASON...
SAD REALLY.

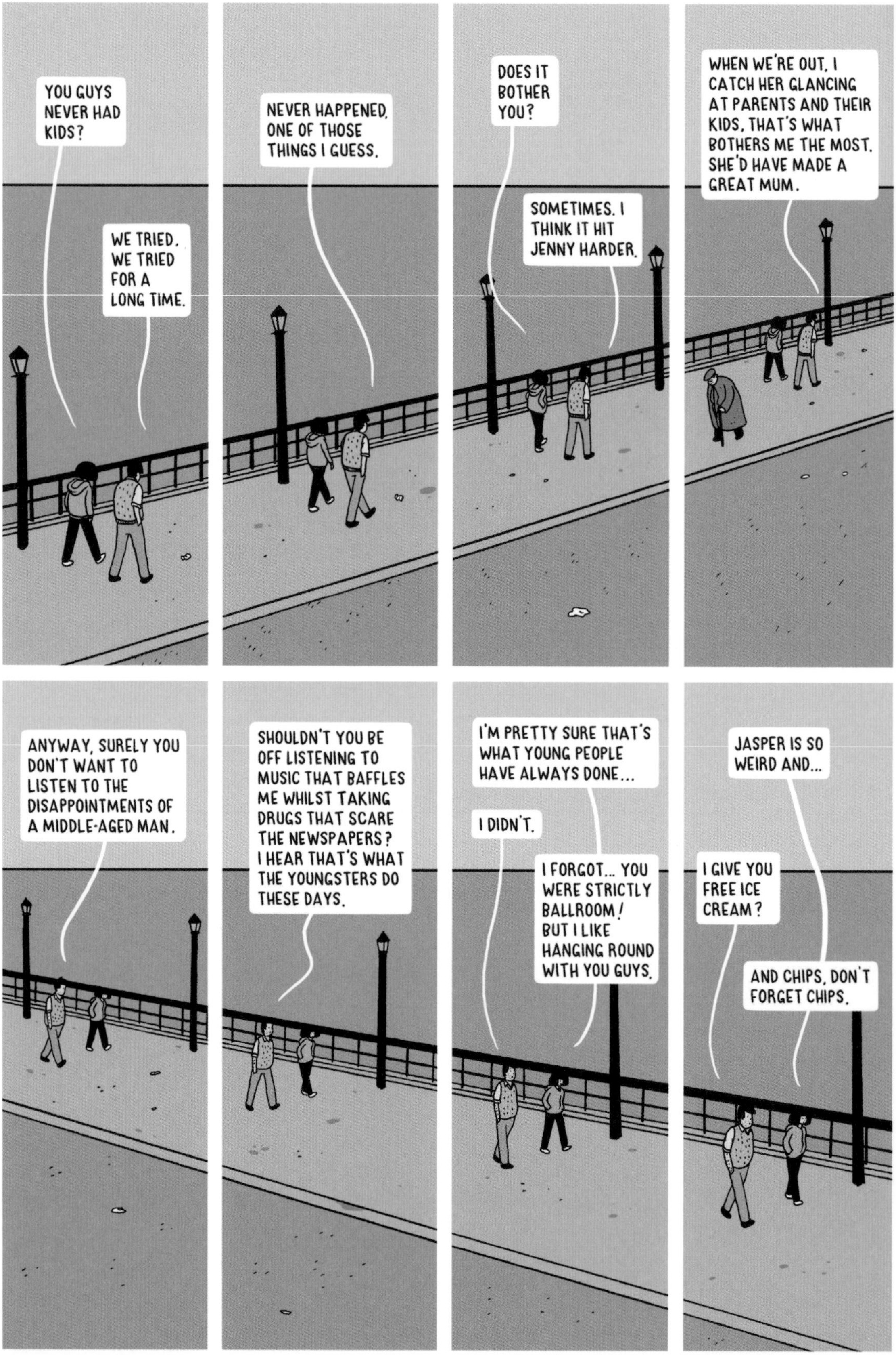
YOU GUYS NEVER HAD KIDS?
WE TRIED, WE TRIED FOR A LONG TIME.
NEVER HAPPENED, ONE OF THOSE THINGS I GUESS.
DOES IT BOTHER YOU?
SOMETIMES. I THINK IT HIT JENNY HARDER.
WHEN WE'RE OUT, I CATCH HER GLANCING AT PARENTS AND THEIR KIDS, THAT'S WHAT BOTHERS ME THE MOST. SHE'D HAVE MADE A GREAT MUM.
ANYWAY, SURELY YOU DON'T WANT TO LISTEN TO THE DISAPPOINTMENTS OF A MIDDLE-AGED MAN.
SHOULDN'T YOU BE OFF LISTENING TO MUSIC THAT BAFFLES ME WHILST TAKING DRUGS THAT SCARE THE NEWSPAPERS? I HEAR THAT'S WHAT THE YOUNGSTERS DO THESE DAYS.
I'M PRETTY SURE THAT'S WHAT YOUNG PEOPLE HAVE ALWAYS DONE...
I DIDN'T.
I FORGOT... YOU WERE STRICTLY BALLROOM! BUT I LIKE HANGING ROUND WITH YOU GUYS.
JASPER IS SO WEIRD AND...
I GIVE YOU FREE ICE CREAM?
AND CHIPS, DON'T FORGET CHIPS.

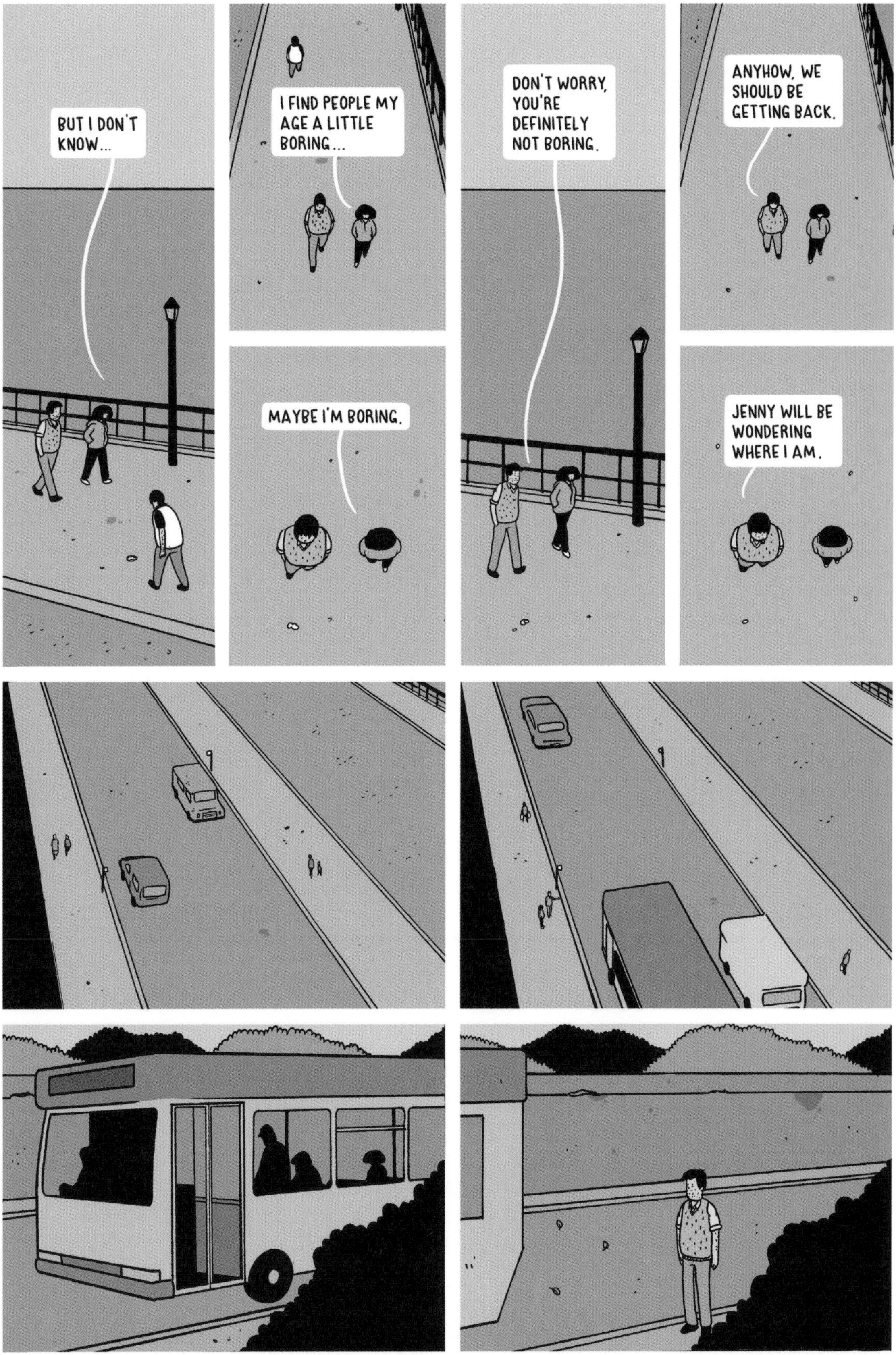
BUT I DON'T KNOW...
I FIND PEOPLE MY AGE A LITTLE BORING...
MAYBE I'M BORING.
DON'T WORRY, YOU'RE DEFINITELY NOT BORING.
ANYHOW, WE SHOULD BE GETTING BACK.
JENNY WILL BE WONDERING WHERE I AM.

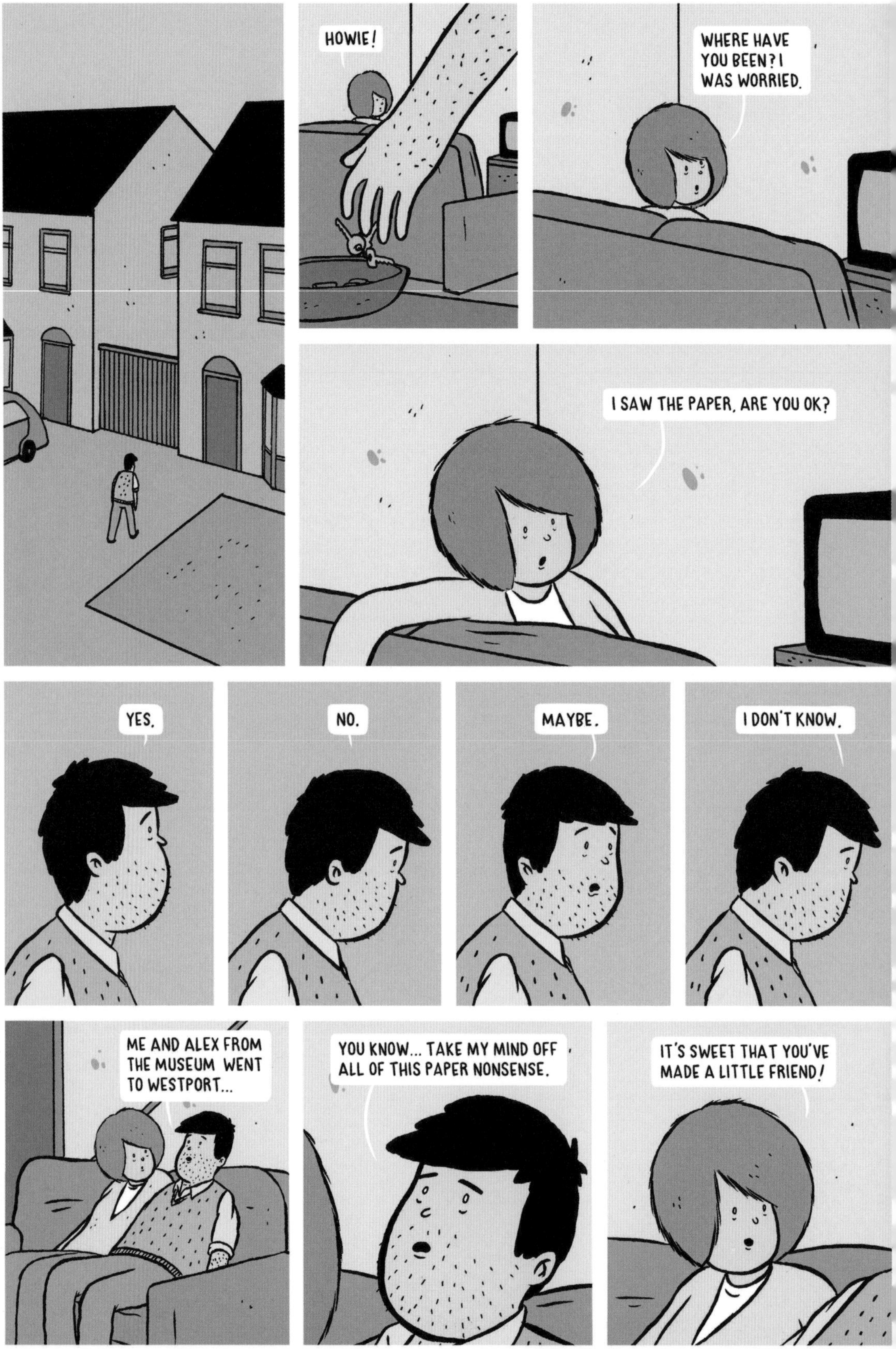
HOWIE!
WHERE HAVE YOU BEEN? I WAS WORRIED.
I SAW THE PAPER, ARE YOU OK?
YES.
NO.
MAYBE.
I DON'T KNOW.
ME AND ALEX FROM THE MUSEUM WENT TO WESTPORT...
YOU KNOW... TAKE MY MIND OFF ALL OF THIS PAPER NONSENSE.
IT'S SWEET THAT YOU'VE MADE A LITTLE FRIEND!

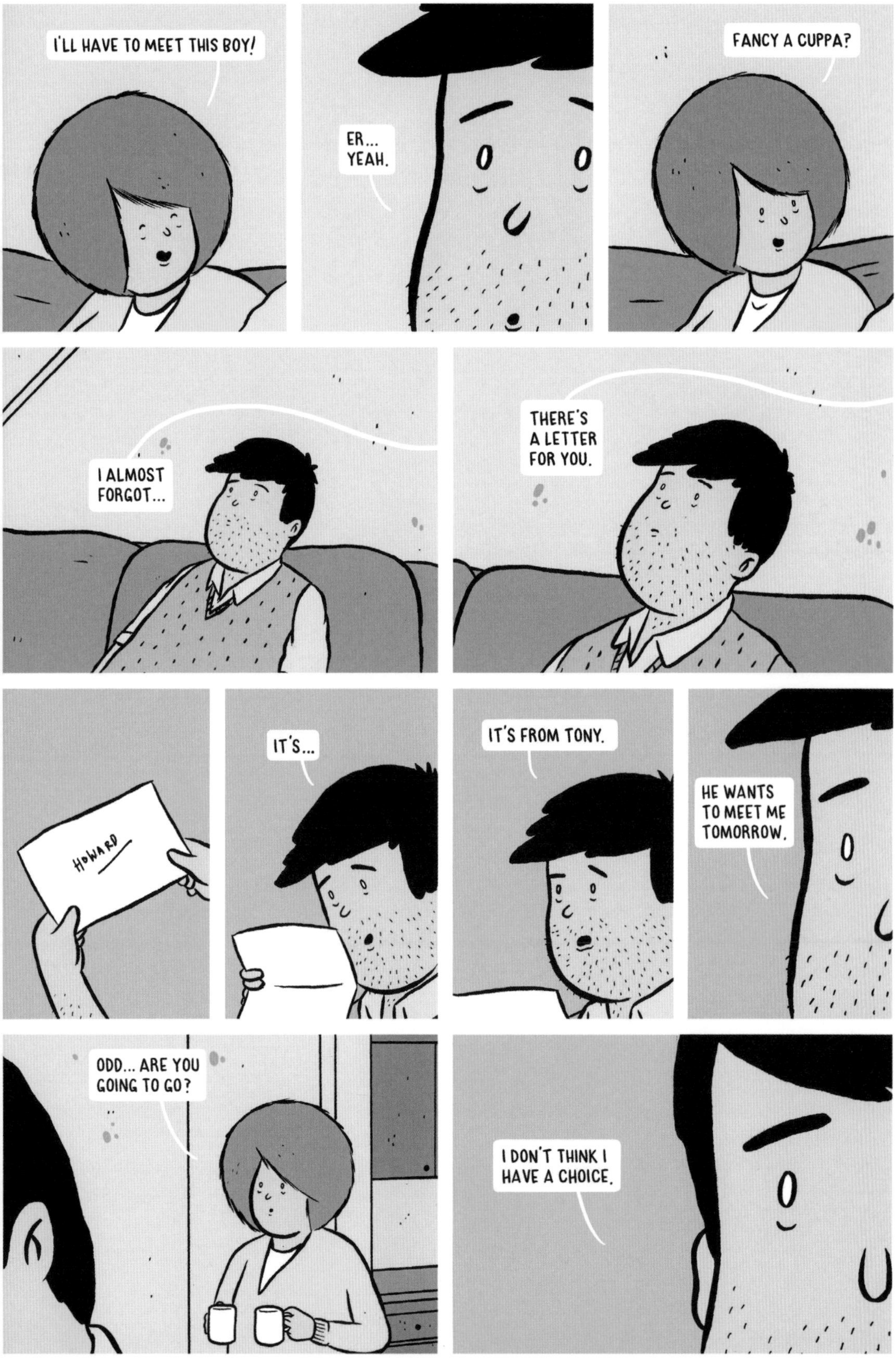
I'LL HAVE TO MEET THIS BOY!
ER... YEAH.
FANCY A CUPPA?
I ALMOST FORGOT...
THERE'S A LETTER FOR YOU.
HOWARD
IT'S...
IT'S FROM TONY.
HE WANTS TO MEET ME TOMORROW.
ODD... ARE YOU GOING TO GO?
I DON'T THINK I HAVE A CHOICE.

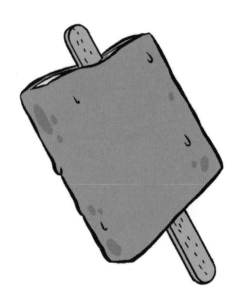

CHAPTER SIX

THE CLOCK THAT SAT ON HOWARD'S BEDSIDE TABLE HAD BEEN HIS SINCE CHILDHOOD.

THE ORMOCHRON TRAVEL CHIME ALARM CLOCK WAS A DESIGN CLASSIC.

FOR MANY, ITS ELEGANT AND SIMPLE LINES PLACED IT AT THE APEX OF FORM AND UTILITY.

IT WAS SET TO STIR ITS OWNER AT 7 AM.

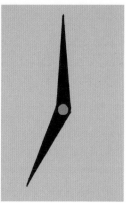

AS ON EVERY OTHER DAY FOR AS LONG AS HOWARD COULD REMEMBER, IT RANG OUT AT ITS ALLOTTED TIME.

BUT HOWARD WAS ALREADY AWAKE.

HE HAD BEEN FOR A COUPLE OF HOURS.

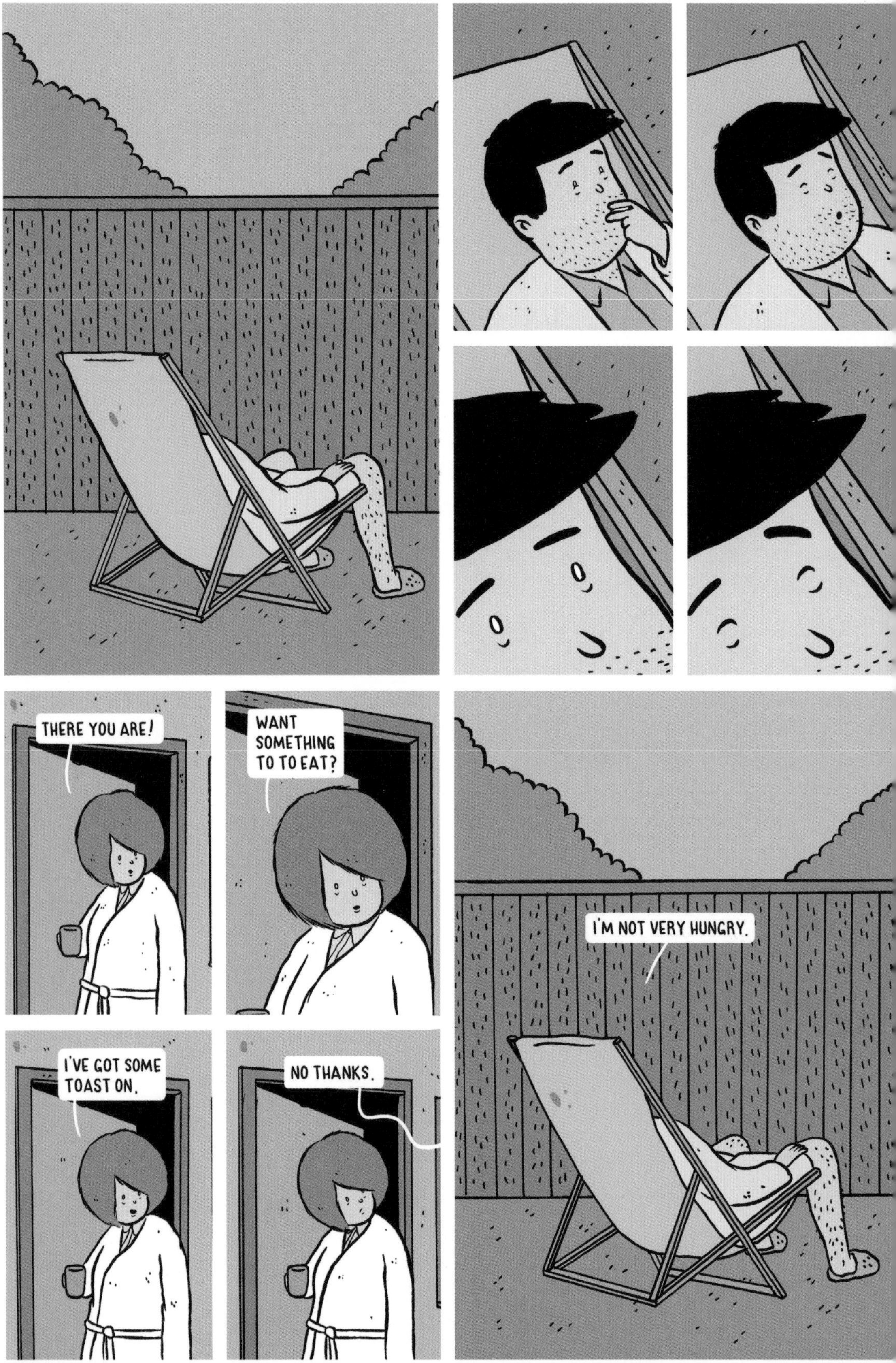
THERE YOU ARE!
WANT SOMETHING TO TO EAT?
I'VE GOT SOME TOAST ON.
NO THANKS.
I'M NOT VERY HUNGRY.

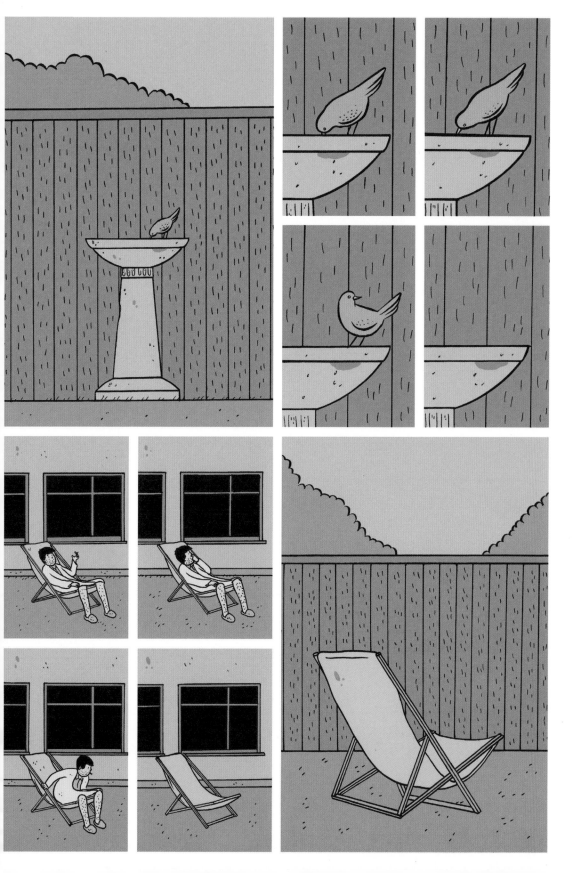

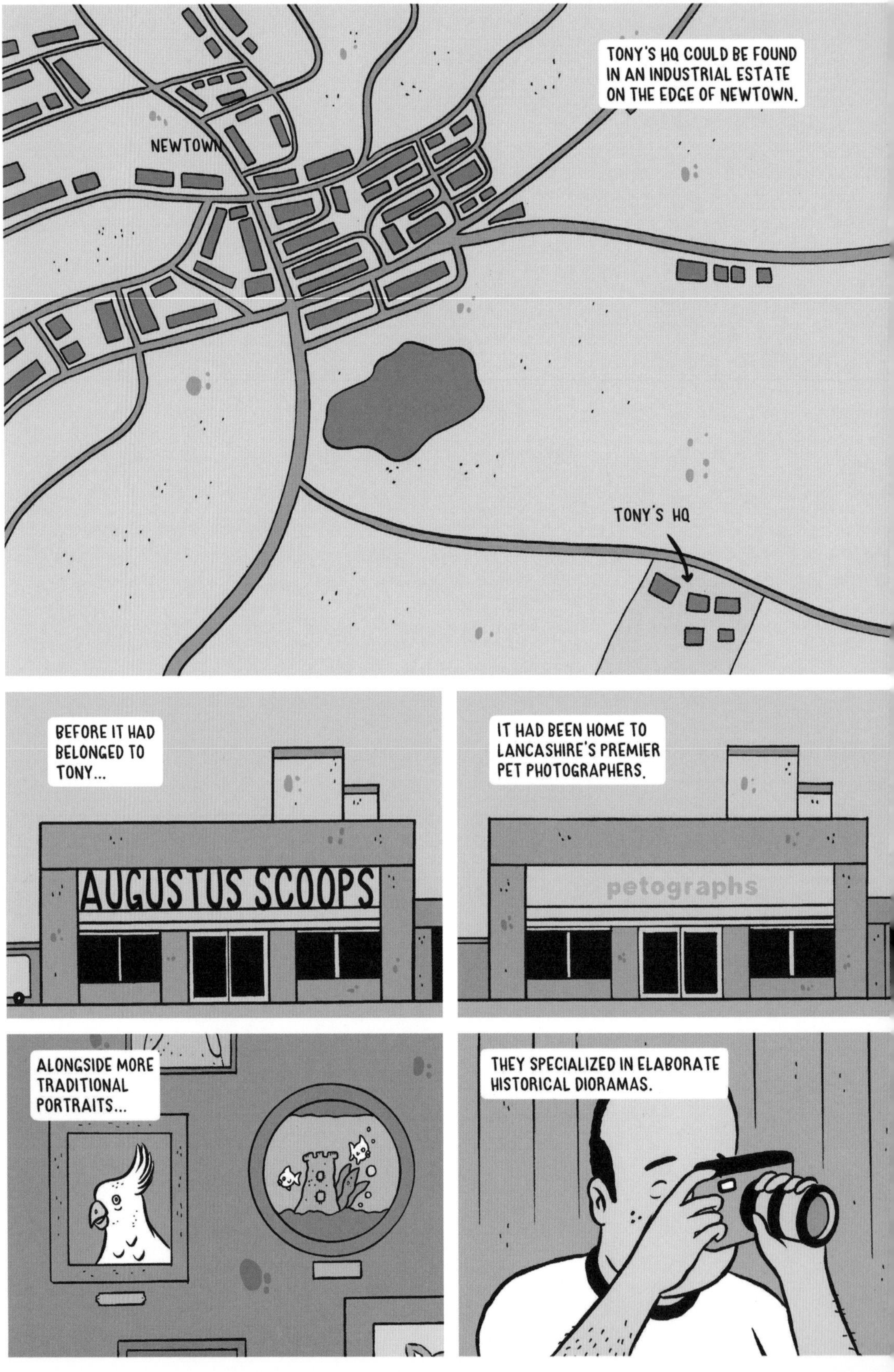
TONY'S HQ COULD BE FOUND IN AN INDUSTRIAL ESTATE ON THE EDGE OF NEWTOWN.
NEWTOWN
TONY'S HQ
BEFORE IT HAD BELONGED TO TONY...
AUGUSTUS SCOOPS
IT HAD BEEN HOME TO LANCASHIRE'S PREMIER PET PHOTOGRAPHERS.
petographs
ALONGSIDE MORE TRADITIONAL PORTRAITS...
THEY SPECIALIZED IN ELABORATE HISTORICAL DIORAMAS.

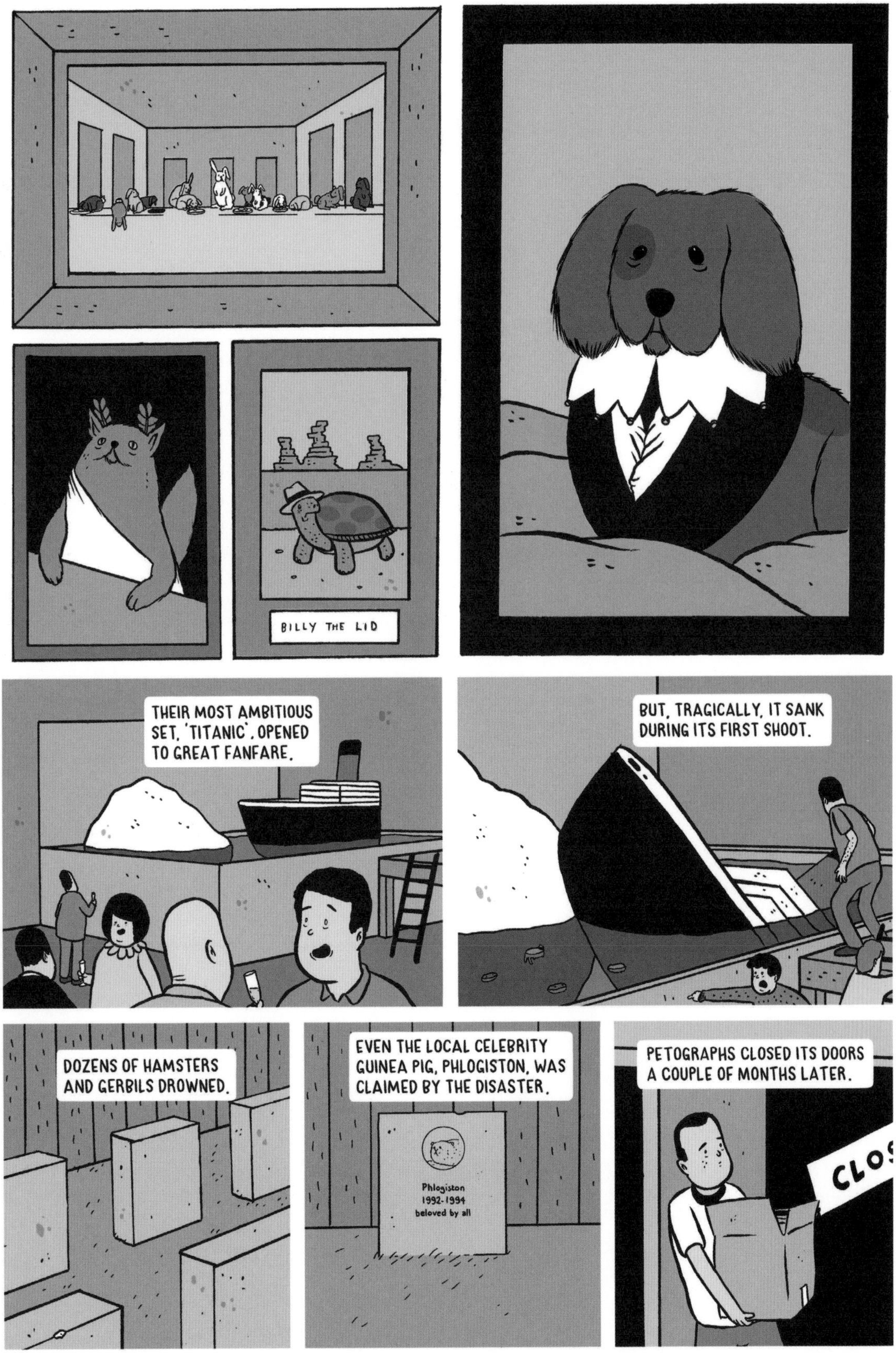
BILLY THE LID
THEIR MOST AMBITIOUS SET, 'TITANIC', OPENED TO GREAT FANFARE.
BUT, TRAGICALLY, IT SANK DURING ITS FIRST SHOOT.
DOZENS OF HAMSTERS AND GERBILS DROWNED.
EVEN THE LOCAL CELEBRITY GUINEA PIG, PHLOGISTON, WAS CLAIMED BY THE DISASTER.
Phlogiston
1992-1994
beloved by all
PETOGRAPHS CLOSED ITS DOORS A COUPLE OF MONTHS LATER.
CLOS

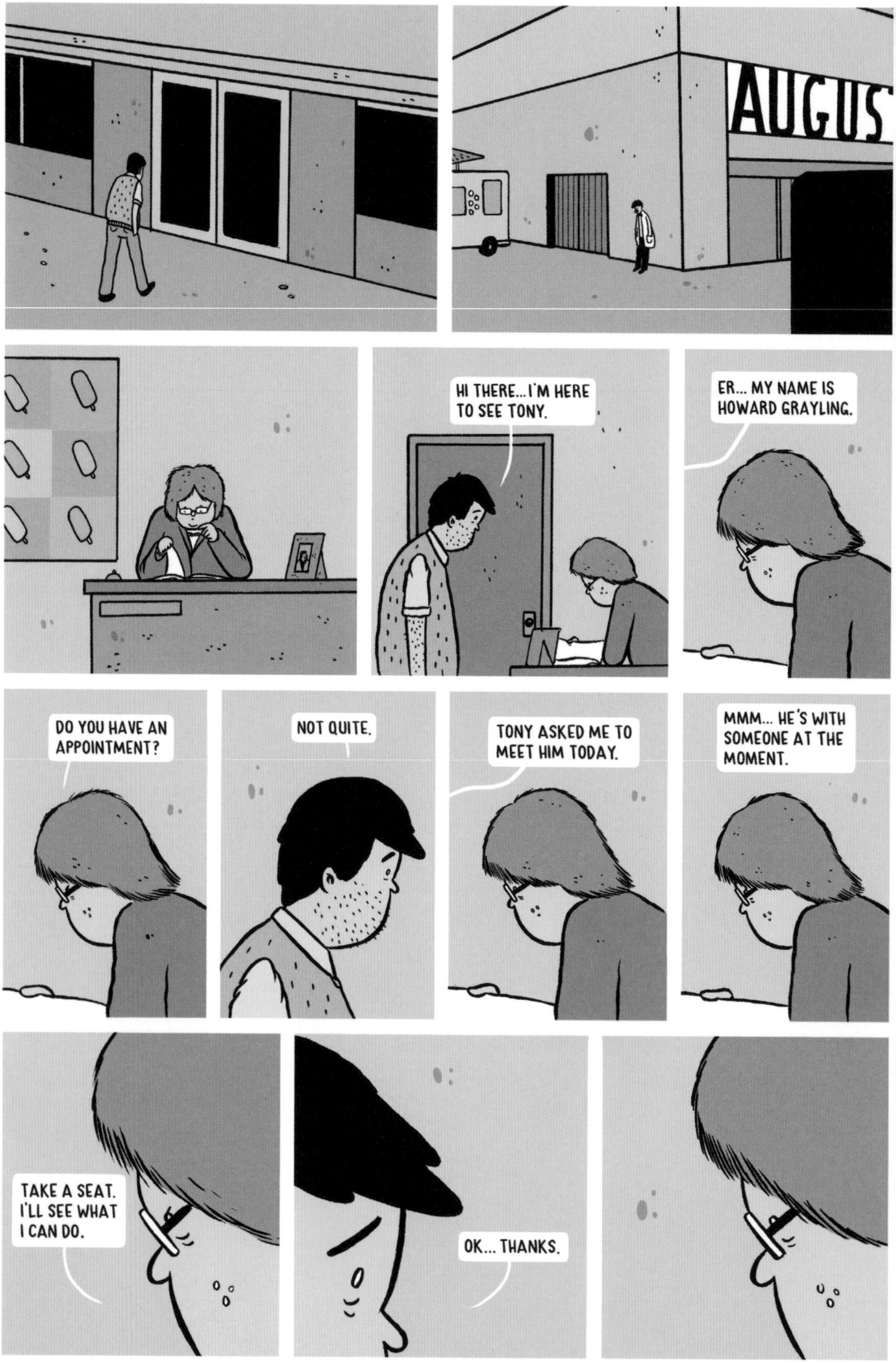
AUGUS
HI THERE... I'M HERE TO SEE TONY.
ER... MY NAME IS HOWARD GRAYLING.
DO YOU HAVE AN APPOINTMENT?
NOT QUITE.
TONY ASKED ME TO MEET HIM TODAY.
MMM... HE'S WITH SOMEONE AT THE MOMENT.
TAKE A SEAT. I'LL SEE WHAT I CAN DO.
OK... THANKS.

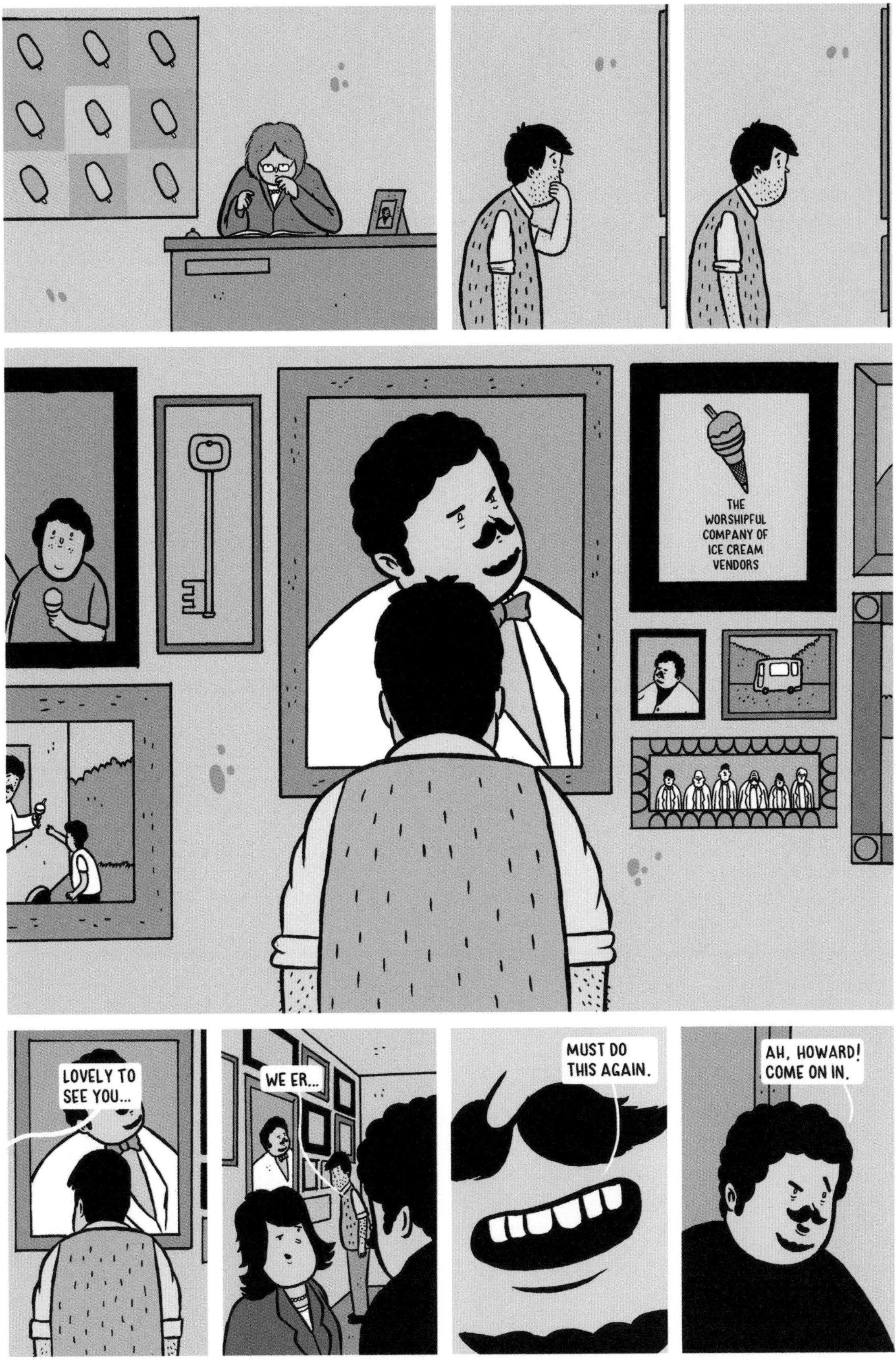
THE WORSHIPFUL COMPANY OF ICE CREAM VENDORS
LOVELY TO SEE YOU...
WE ER...
MUST DO THIS AGAIN.
AH, HOWARD! COME ON IN.

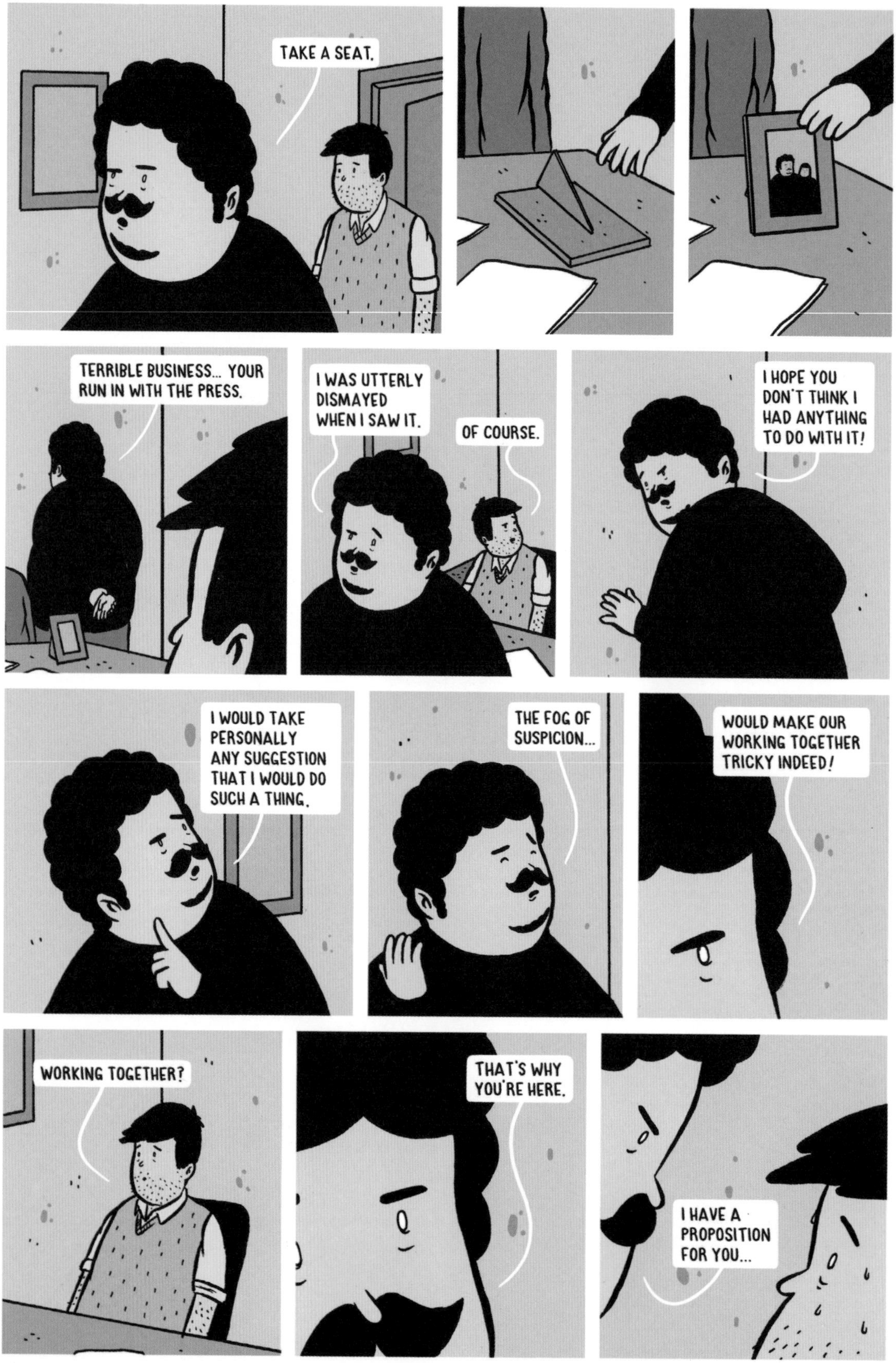
TAKE A SEAT.
TERRIBLE BUSINESS... YOUR RUN IN WITH THE PRESS.
I WAS UTTERLY DISMAYED WHEN I SAW IT.
OF COURSE.
I HOPE YOU DON'T THINK I HAD ANYTHING TO DO WITH IT!
I WOULD TAKE PERSONALLY ANY SUGGESTION THAT I WOULD DO SUCH A THING.
THE FOG OF SUSPICION...
WOULD MAKE OUR WORKING TOGETHER TRICKY INDEED!
WORKING TOGETHER?
THAT'S WHY YOU'RE HERE.
I HAVE A PROPOSITION FOR YOU...

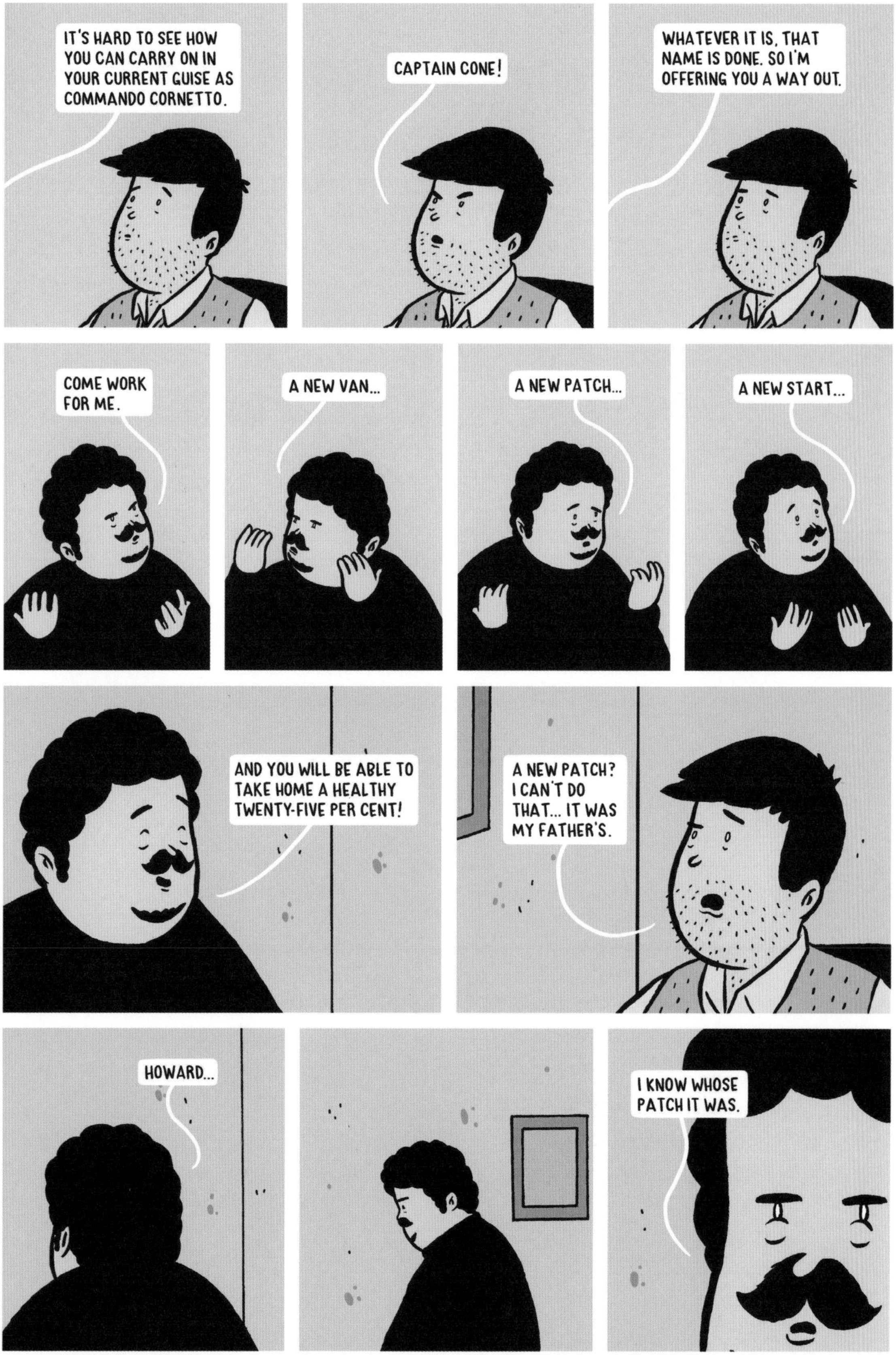
IT'S HARD TO SEE HOW YOU CAN CARRY ON IN YOUR CURRENT GUISE AS COMMANDO CORNETTO.
CAPTAIN CONE!
WHATEVER IT IS, THAT NAME IS DONE. SO I'M OFFERING YOU A WAY OUT.
COME WORK FOR ME.
A NEW VAN...
A NEW PATCH...
A NEW START...
AND YOU WILL BE ABLE TO TAKE HOME A HEALTHY TWENTY-FIVE PER CENT!
A NEW PATCH? I CAN'T DO THAT... IT WAS MY FATHER'S.
HOWARD...
I KNOW WHOSE PATCH IT WAS.

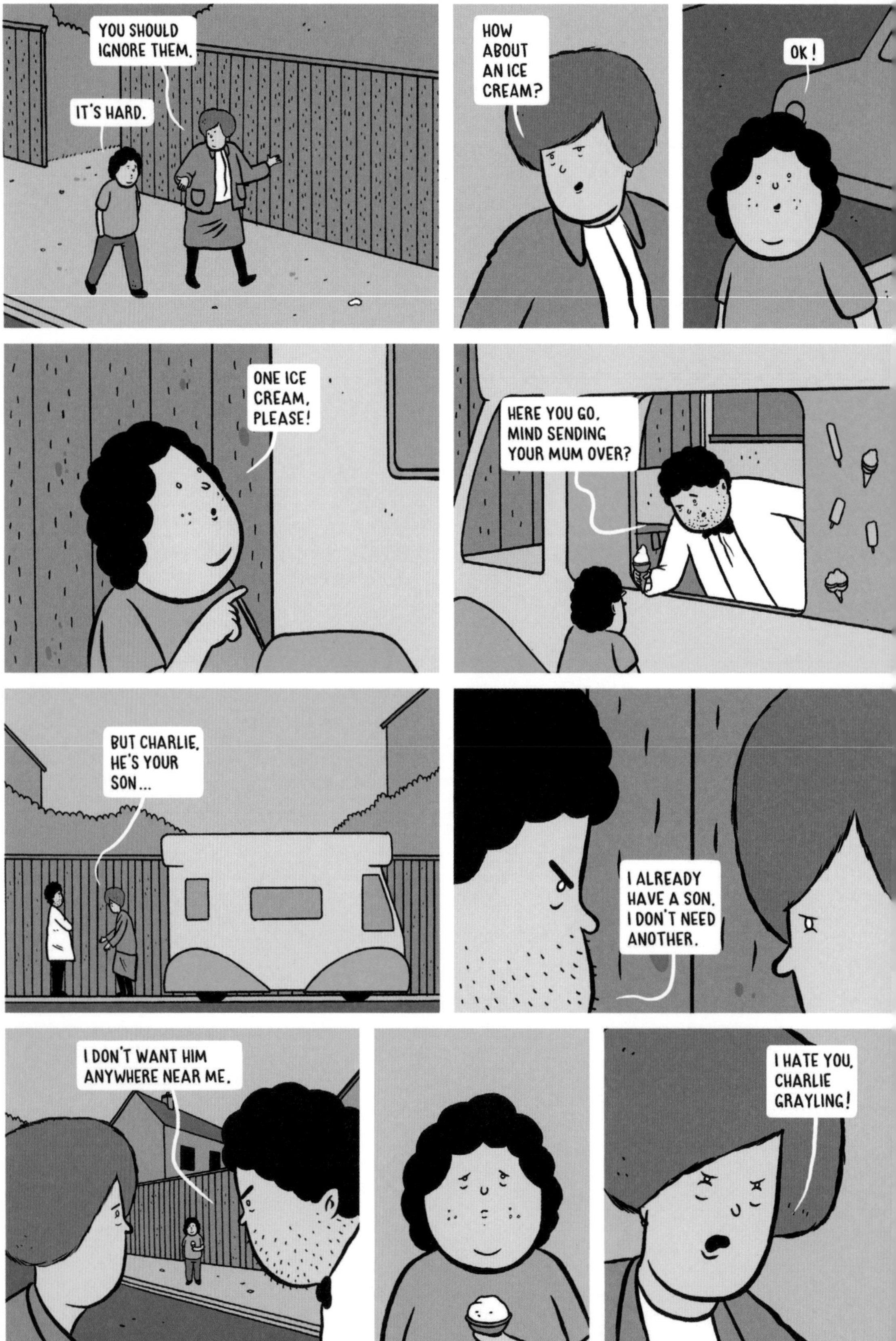
YOU SHOULD IGNORE THEM.
IT'S HARD.
HOW ABOUT AN ICE CREAM?
OK!
ONE ICE CREAM, PLEASE!
HERE YOU GO, MIND SENDING YOUR MUM OVER?
BUT CHARLIE, HE'S YOUR SON...
I ALREADY HAVE A SON. I DON'T NEED ANOTHER.
I DON'T WANT HIM ANYWHERE NEAR ME.
I HATE YOU, CHARLIE GRAYLING!

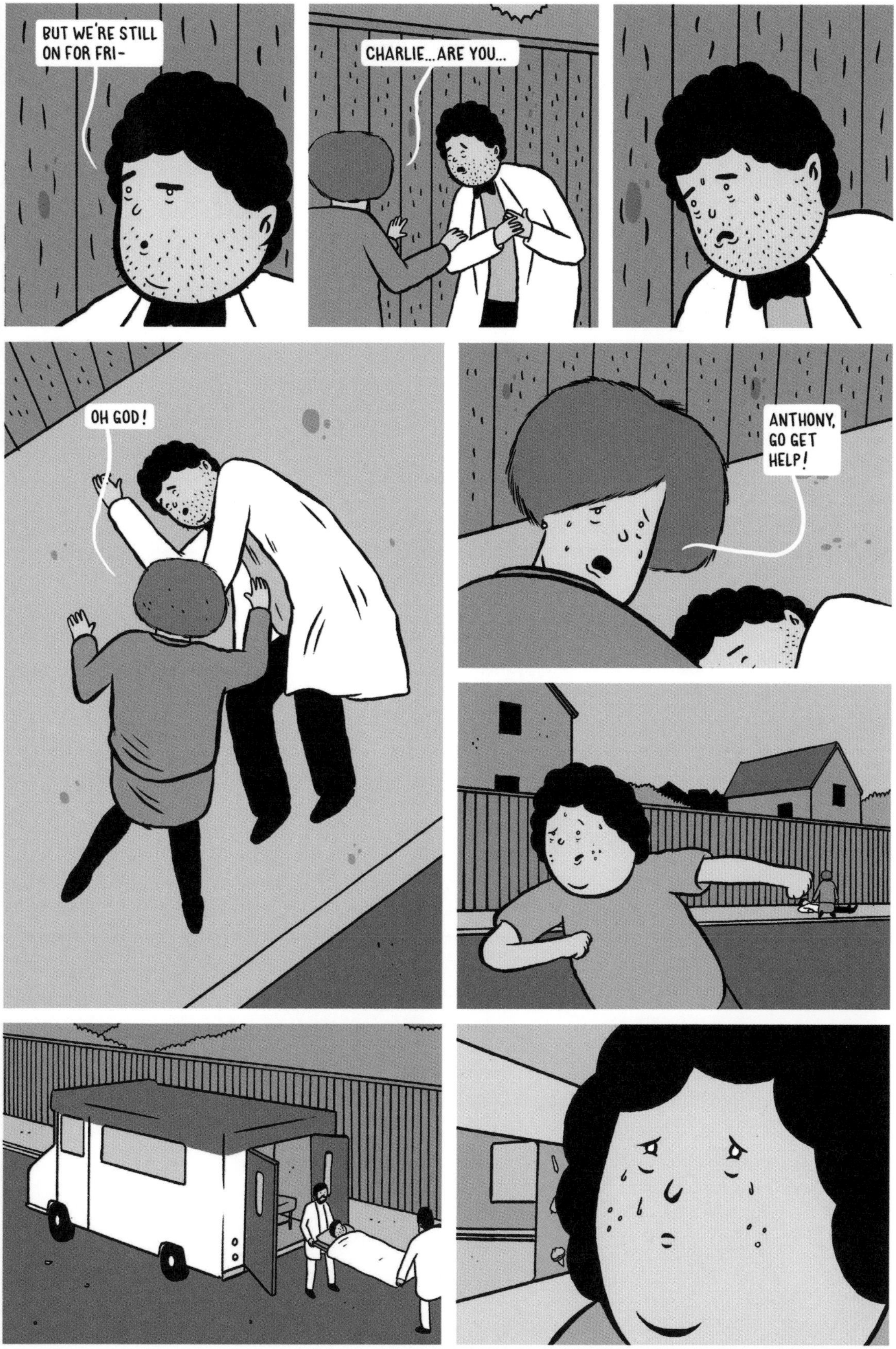
BUT WE'RE STILL ON FOR FRI-
CHARLIE...ARE YOU...
OH GOD!
ANTHONY, GO GET HELP!

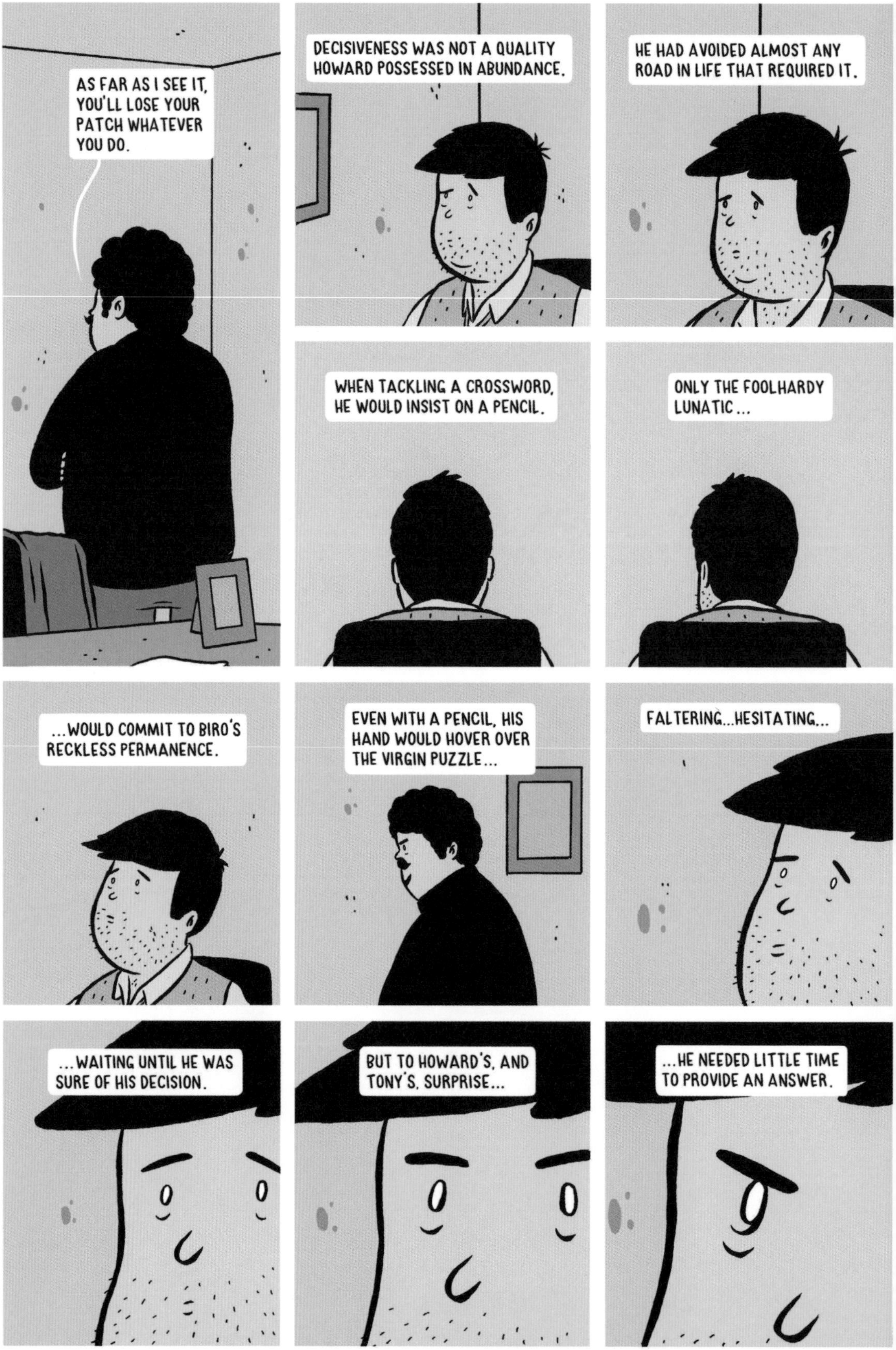
AS FAR AS I SEE IT, YOU'LL LOSE YOUR PATCH WHATEVER YOU DO.
DECISIVENESS WAS NOT A QUALITY HOWARD POSSESSED IN ABUNDANCE.
HE HAD AVOIDED ALMOST ANY ROAD IN LIFE THAT REQUIRED IT.
WHEN TACKLING A CROSSWORD, HE WOULD INSIST ON A PENCIL.
ONLY THE FOOLHARDY LUNATIC...
...WOULD COMMIT TO BIRO'S RECKLESS PERMANENCE.
EVEN WITH A PENCIL, HIS HAND WOULD HOVER OVER THE VIRGIN PUZZLE...
FALTERING...HESITATING...
...WAITING UNTIL HE WAS SURE OF HIS DECISION.
BUT TO HOWARD'S, AND TONY'S, SURPRISE...
...HE NEEDED LITTLE TIME TO PROVIDE AN ANSWER.

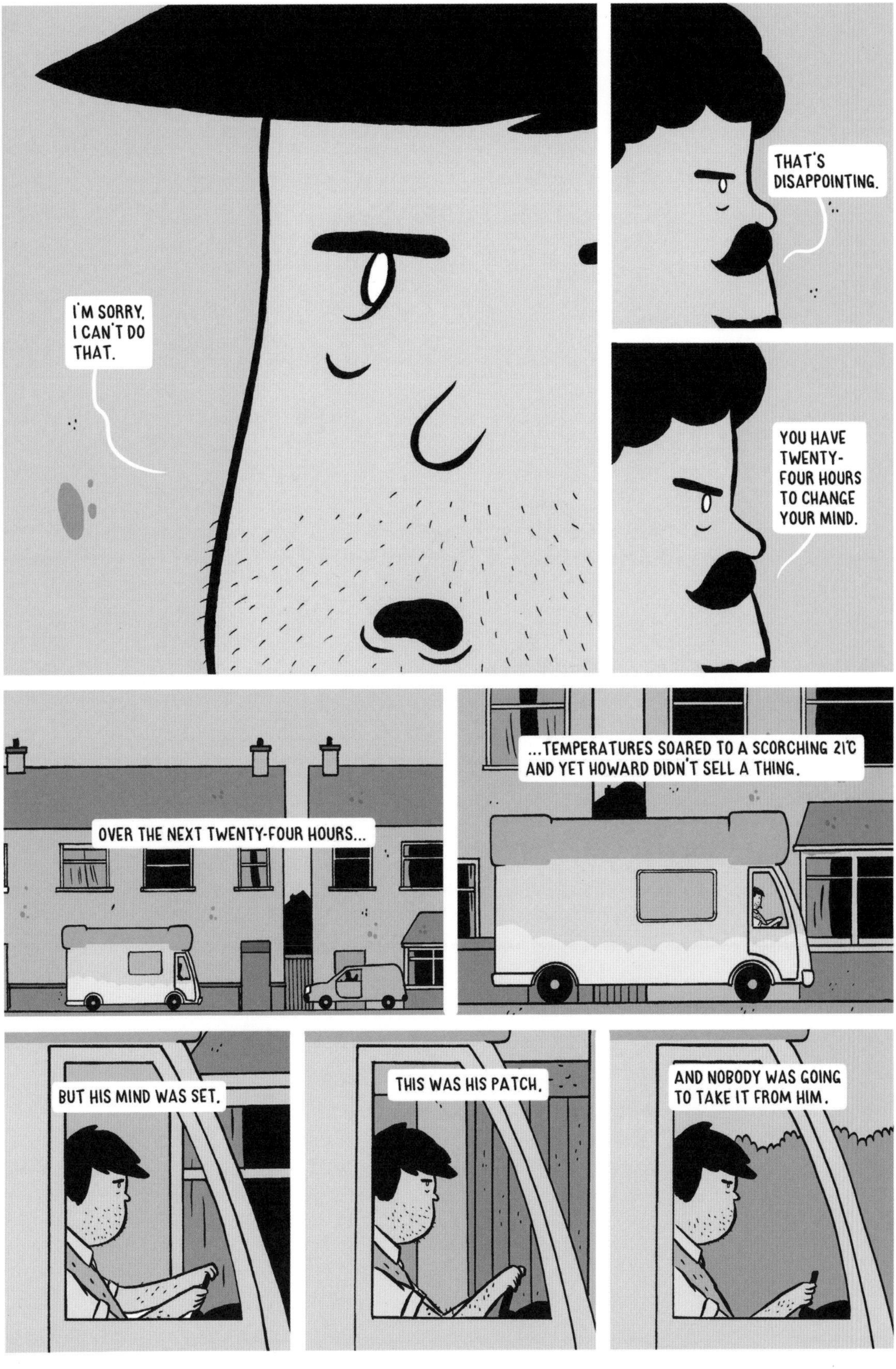
I'M SORRY, I CAN'T DO THAT.
THAT'S DISAPPOINTING.
YOU HAVE TWENTY-FOUR HOURS TO CHANGE YOUR MIND.
OVER THE NEXT TWENTY-FOUR HOURS...
...TEMPERATURES SOARED TO A SCORCHING 21°C AND YET HOWARD DIDN'T SELL A THING.
BUT HIS MIND WAS SET.
THIS WAS HIS PATCH,
AND NOBODY WAS GOING TO TAKE IT FROM HIM.

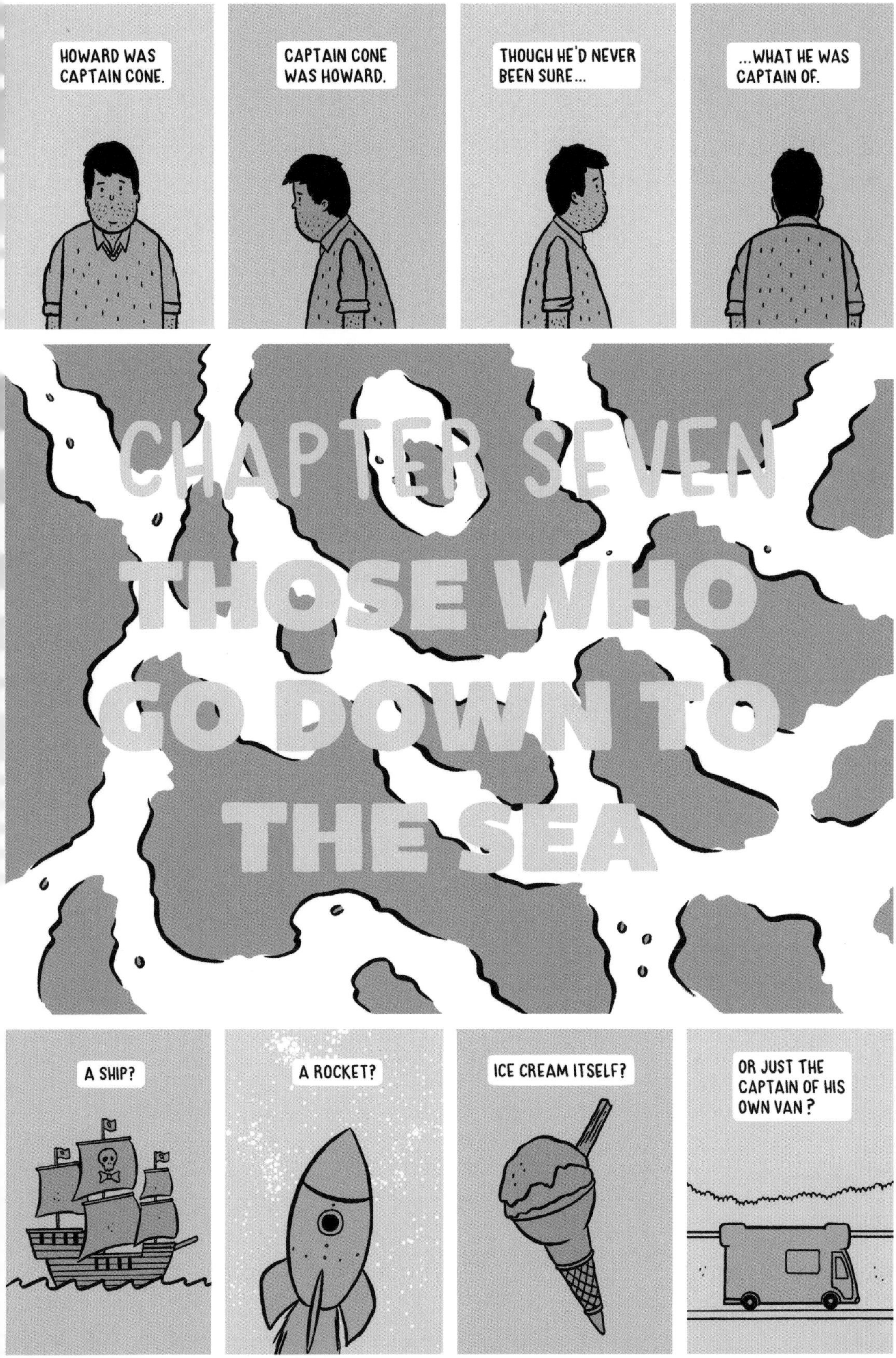
HOWARD WAS CAPTAIN CONE.
CAPTAIN CONE WAS HOWARD.
THOUGH HE'D NEVER BEEN SURE...
...WHAT HE WAS CAPTAIN OF.
CHAPTER SEVEN
THOSE WHO GO DOWN TO THE SEA
A SHIP?
A ROCKET?
ICE CREAM ITSELF?
OR JUST THE CAPTAIN OF HIS OWN VAN ?

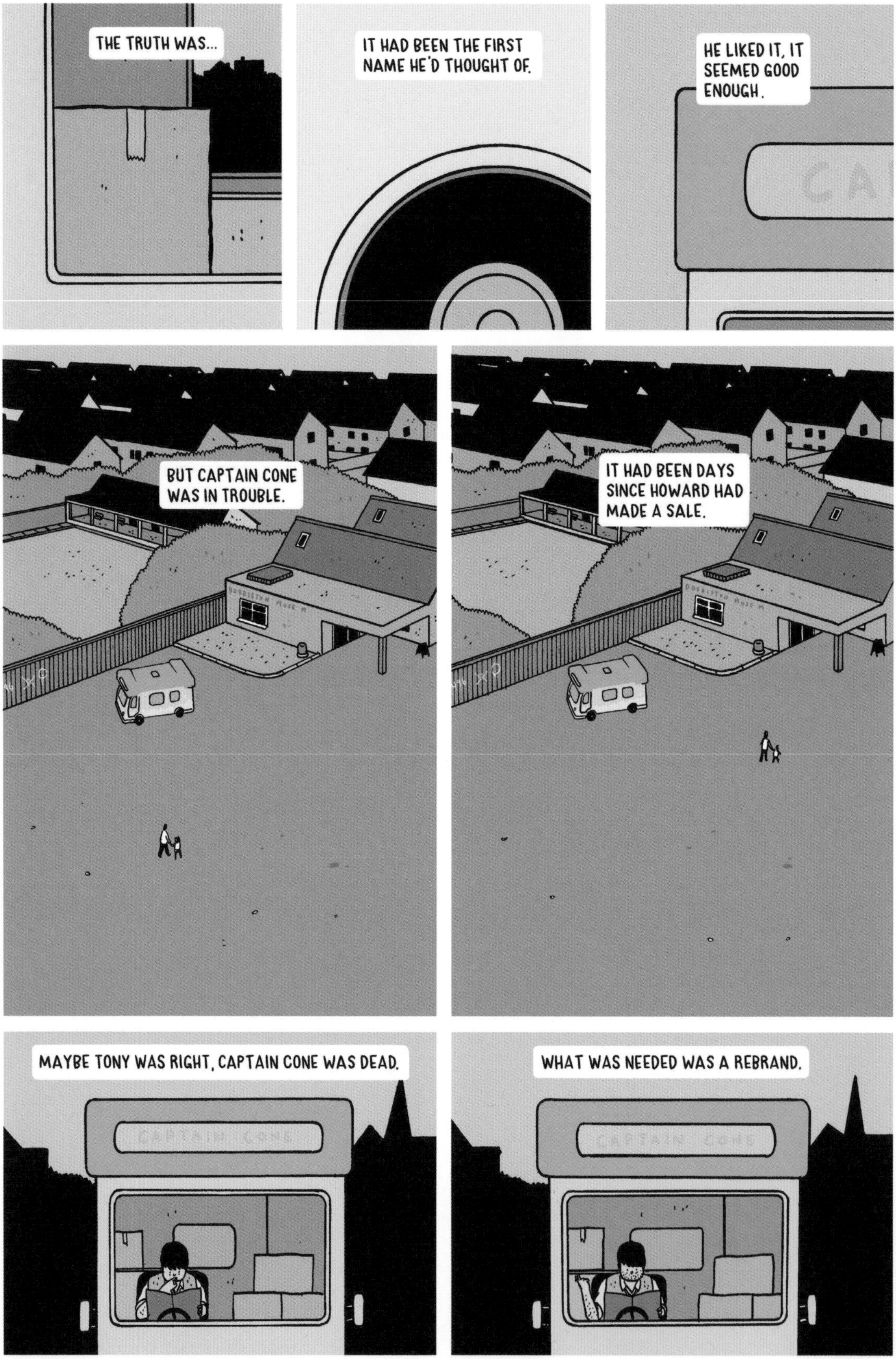
THE TRUTH WAS...
IT HAD BEEN THE FIRST NAME HE'D THOUGHT OF.
HE LIKED IT, IT SEEMED GOOD ENOUGH.
BUT CAPTAIN CONE WAS IN TROUBLE.
IT HAD BEEN DAYS SINCE HOWARD HAD MADE A SALE.
MAYBE TONY WAS RIGHT, CAPTAIN CONE WAS DEAD.
CAPTAIN CONE
WHAT WAS NEEDED WAS A REBRAND.
CAPTAIN CONE

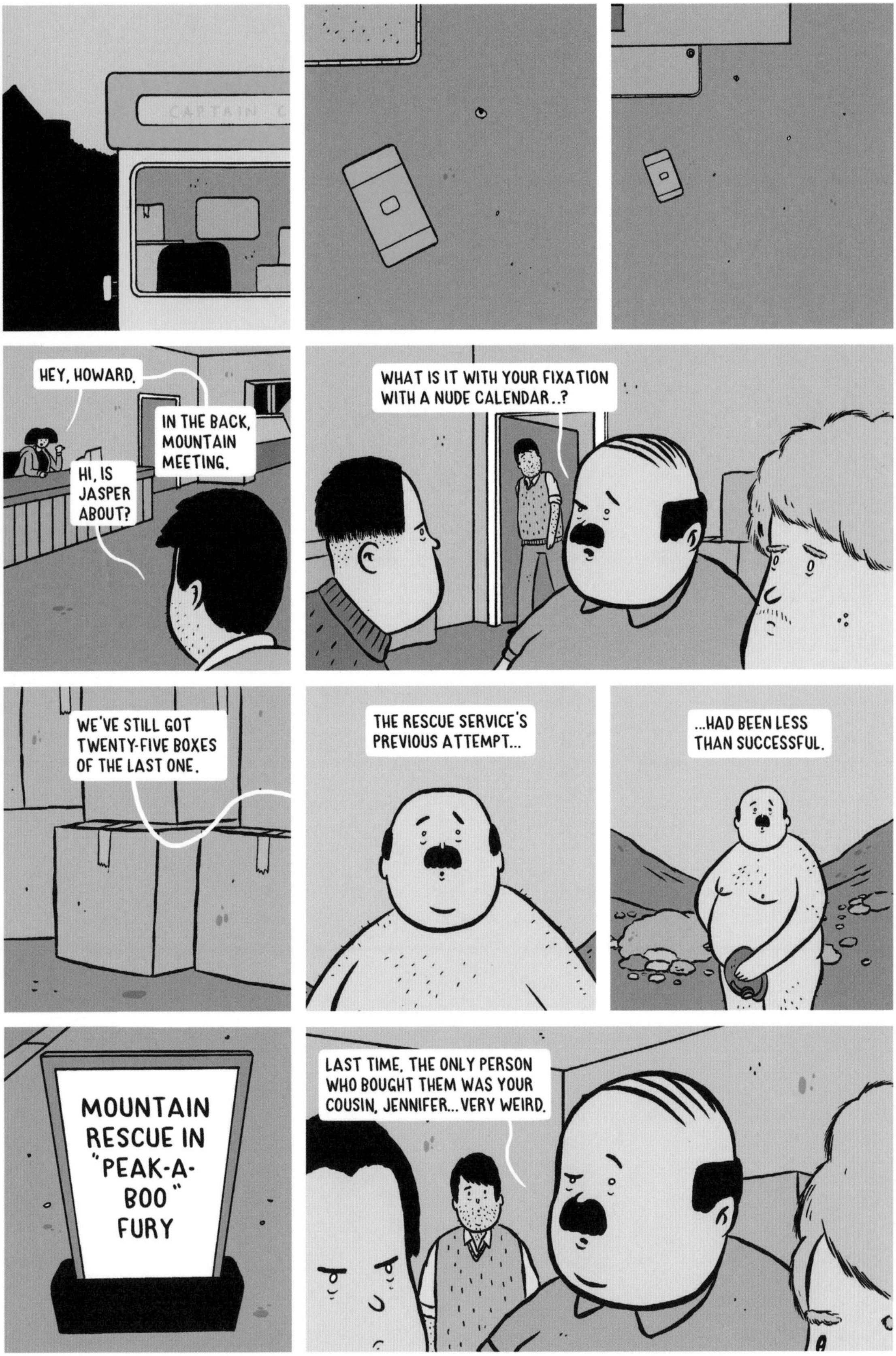
CAPTAIN C
HEY, HOWARD.
HI, IS JASPER ABOUT?
IN THE BACK, MOUNTAIN MEETING.
WHAT IS IT WITH YOUR FIXATION WITH A NUDE CALENDAR..?
WE'VE STILL GOT TWENTY-FIVE BOXES OF THE LAST ONE.
THE RESCUE SERVICE'S PREVIOUS ATTEMPT...
...HAD BEEN LESS THAN SUCCESSFUL.
MOUNTAIN RESCUE IN "PEAK-A-BOO" FURY
LAST TIME, THE ONLY PERSON WHO BOUGHT THEM WAS YOUR COUSIN, JENNIFER... VERY WEIRD.

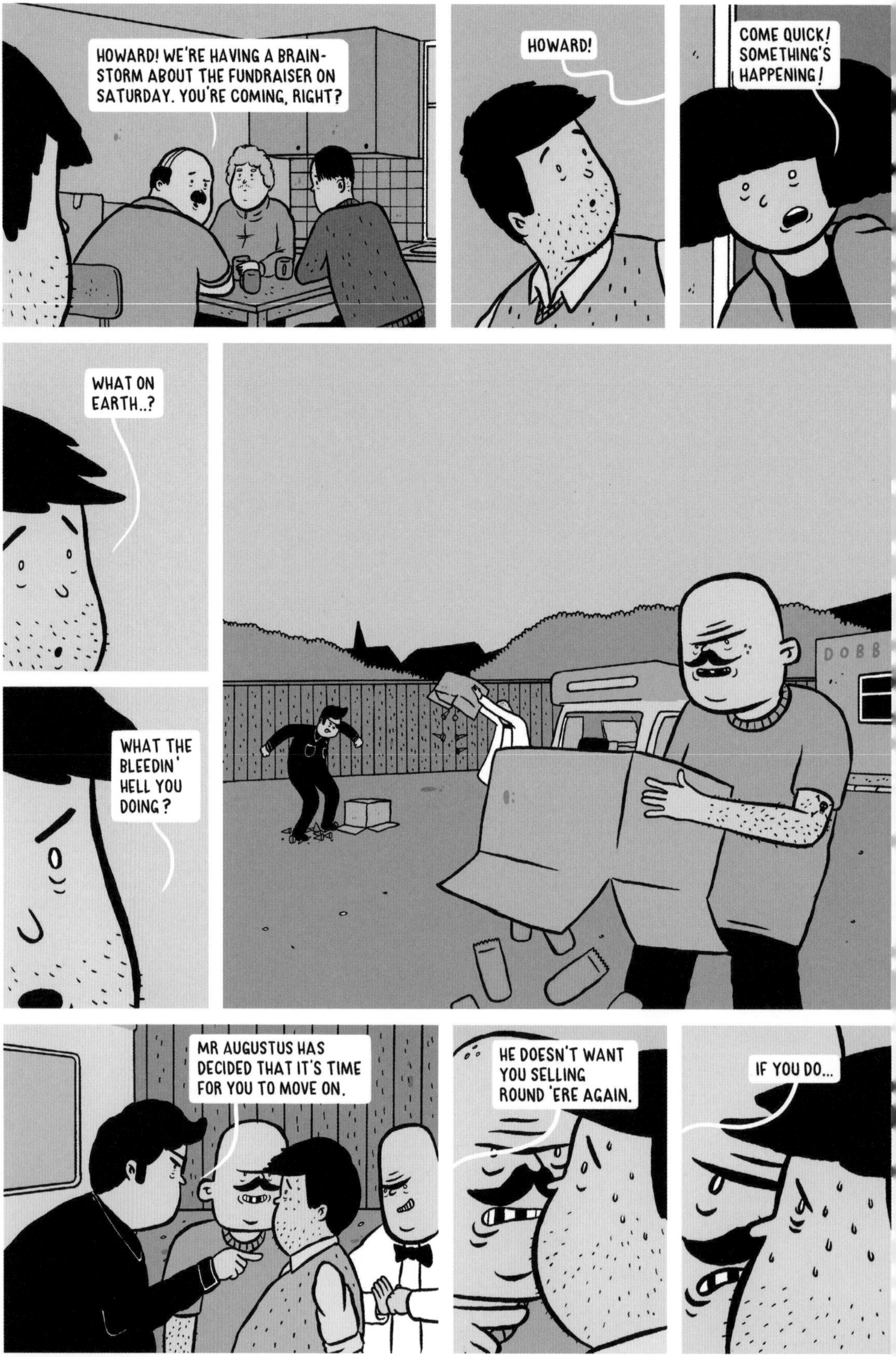
HOWARD! WE'RE HAVING A BRAIN-STORM ABOUT THE FUNDRAISER ON SATURDAY. YOU'RE COMING, RIGHT?
HOWARD!
COME QUICK! SOMETHING'S HAPPENING!
WHAT ON EARTH..?
DOBB
WHAT THE BLEEDIN' HELL YOU DOING?
MR AUGUSTUS HAS DECIDED THAT IT'S TIME FOR YOU TO MOVE ON.
HE DOESN'T WANT YOU SELLING ROUND 'ERE AGAIN.
IF YOU DO...

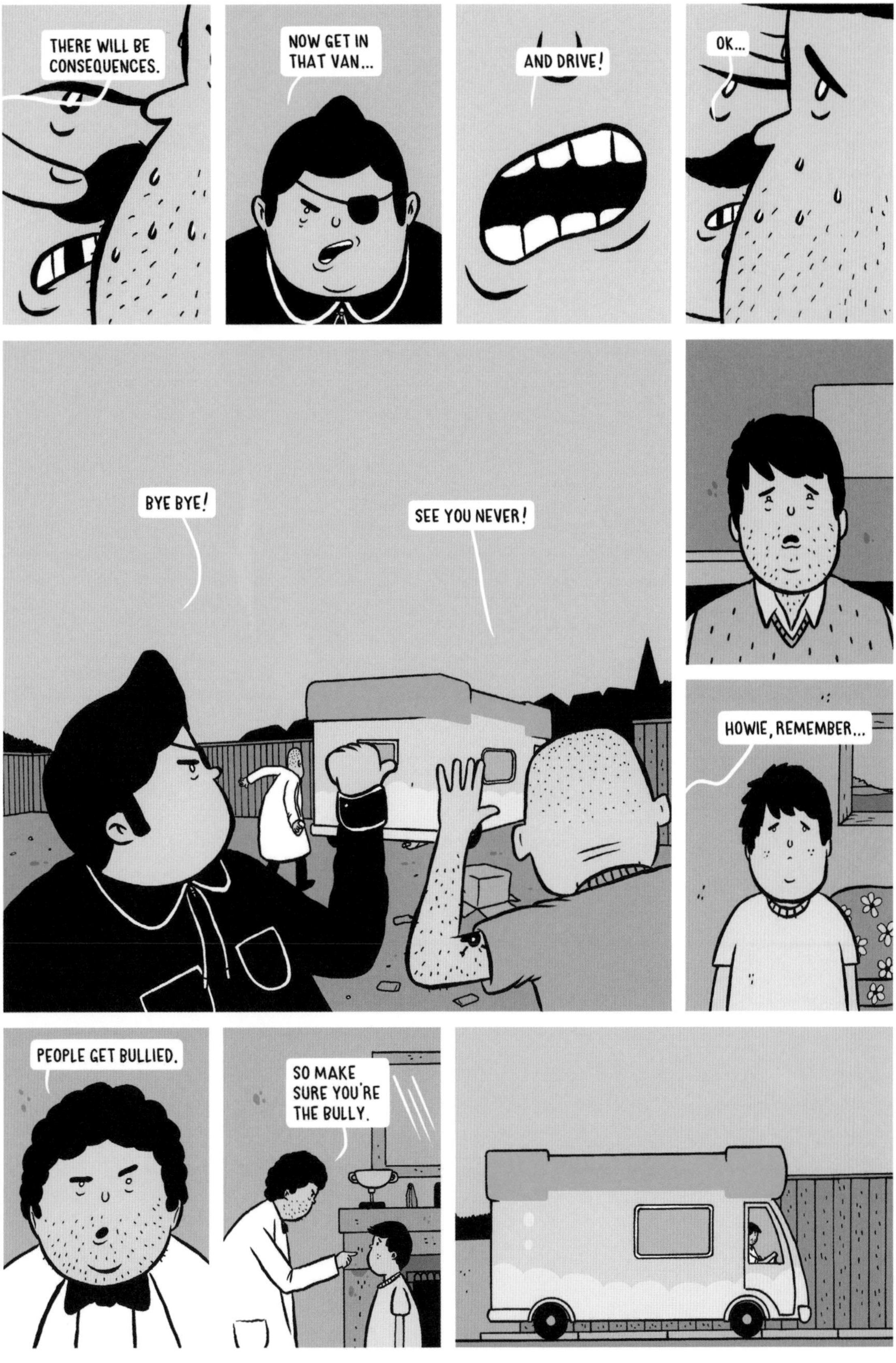
THERE WILL BE CONSEQUENCES.
NOW GET IN THAT VAN...
AND DRIVE!
OK...
BYE BYE!
SEE YOU NEVER!
HOWIE, REMEMBER...
PEOPLE GET BULLIED.
SO MAKE SURE YOU'RE THE BULLY.

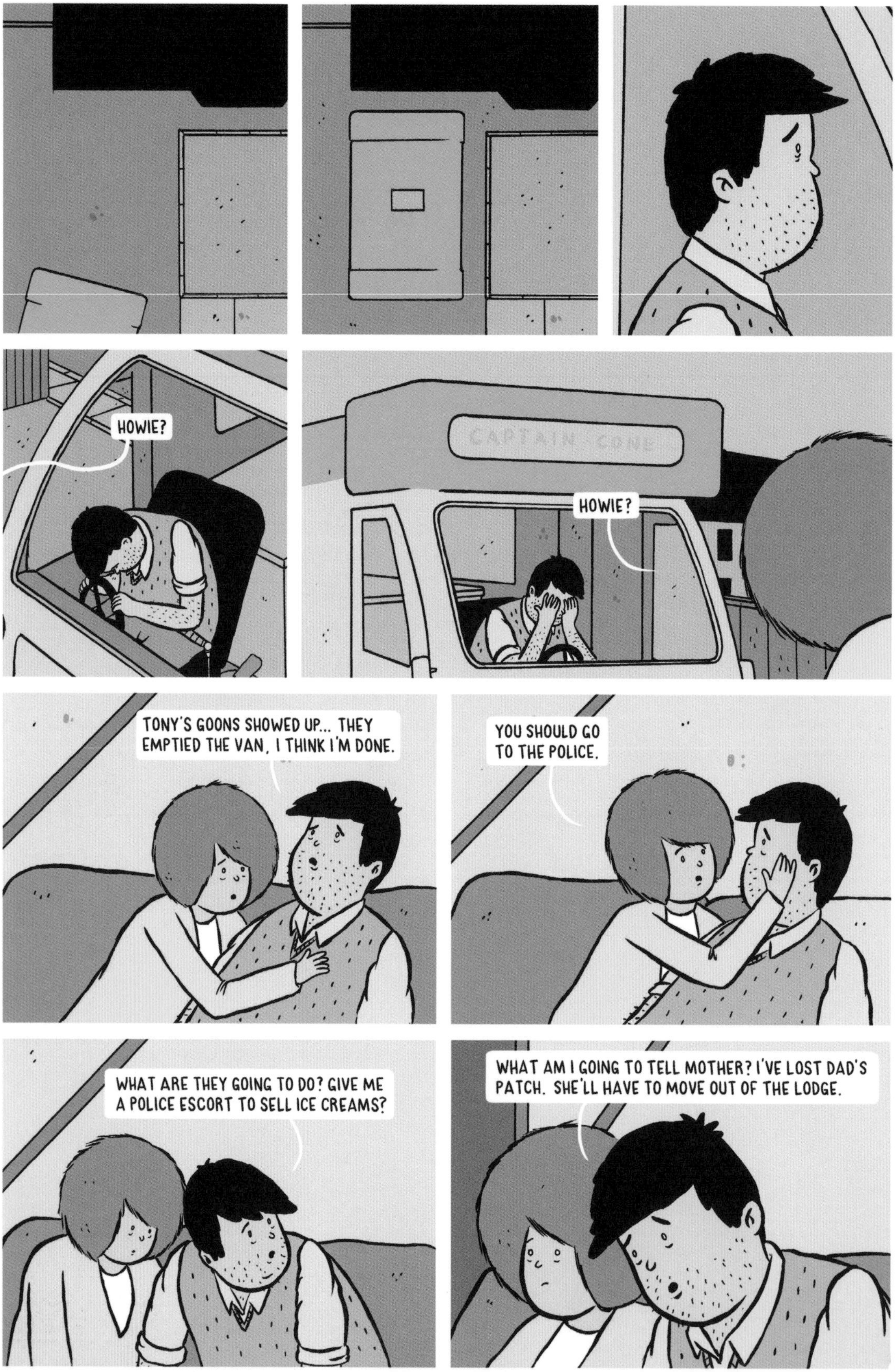
HOWIE?
CAPTAIN CONE
HOWIE?
TONY'S GOONS SHOWED UP... THEY EMPTIED THE VAN, I THINK I'M DONE.
YOU SHOULD GO TO THE POLICE.
WHAT ARE THEY GOING TO DO? GIVE ME A POLICE ESCORT TO SELL ICE CREAMS?
WHAT AM I GOING TO TELL MOTHER? I'VE LOST DAD'S PATCH. SHE'LL HAVE TO MOVE OUT OF THE LODGE.

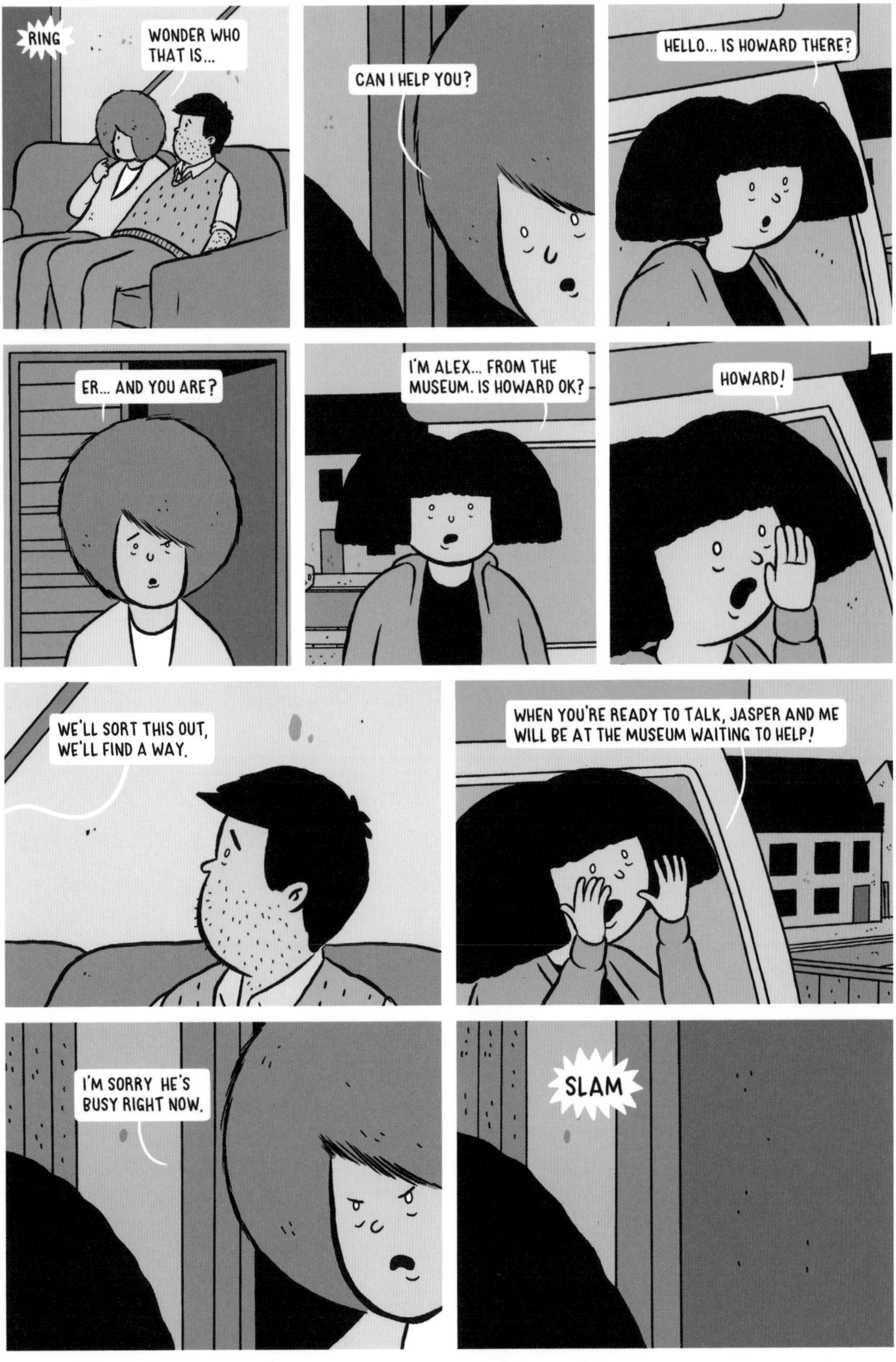
RING
WONDER WHO THAT IS...
CAN I HELP YOU?
HELLO... IS HOWARD THERE?
ER... AND YOU ARE?
I'M ALEX... FROM THE MUSEUM. IS HOWARD OK?
HOWARD!
WE'LL SORT THIS OUT, WE'LL FIND A WAY.
WHEN YOU'RE READY TO TALK, JASPER AND ME WILL BE AT THE MUSEUM WAITING TO HELP!
I'M SORRY HE'S BUSY RIGHT NOW.
SLAM

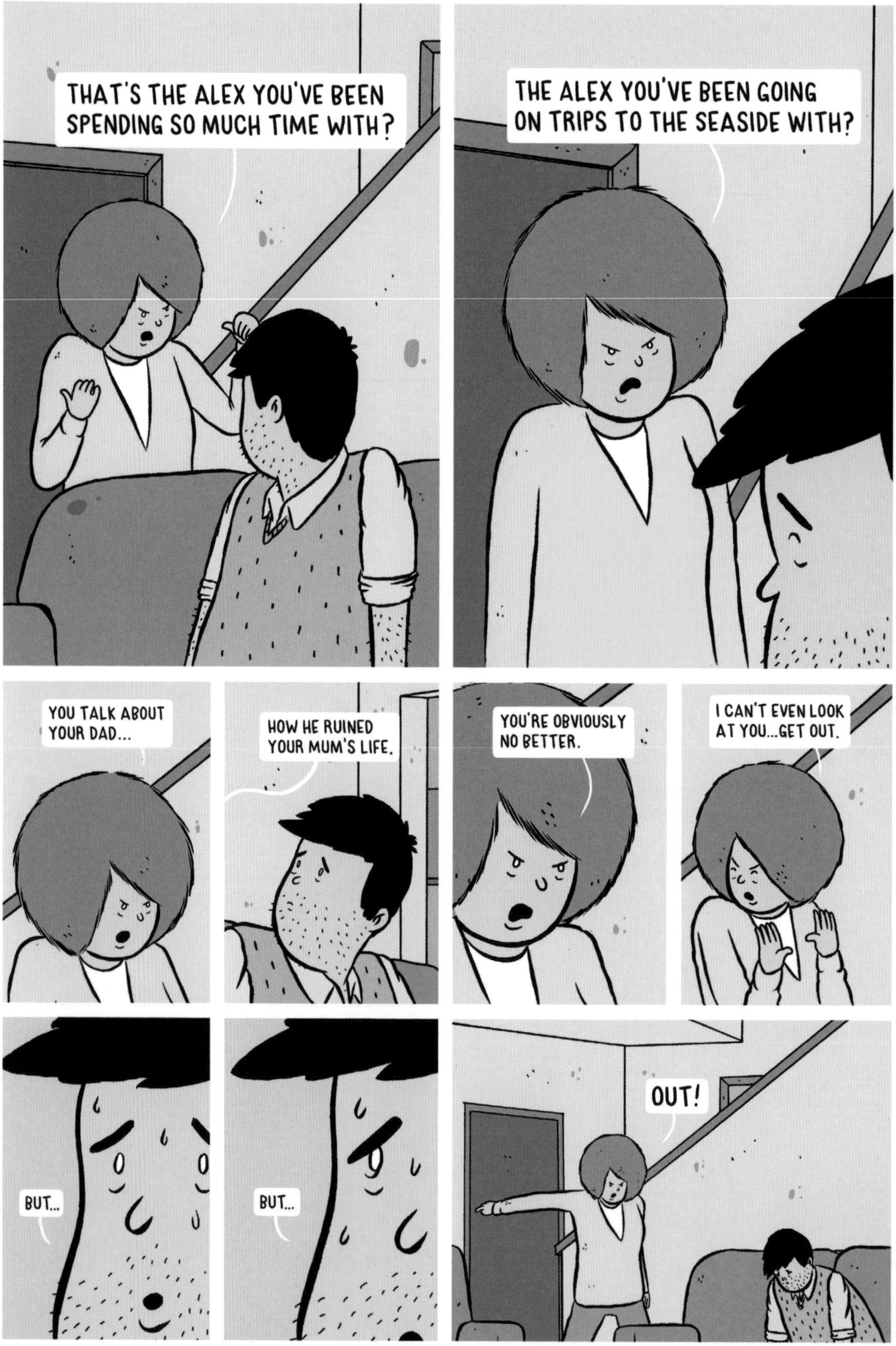
THAT'S THE ALEX YOU'VE BEEN SPENDING SO MUCH TIME WITH?
THE ALEX YOU'VE BEEN GOING ON TRIPS TO THE SEASIDE WITH?
YOU TALK ABOUT YOUR DAD...
HOW HE RUINED YOUR MUM'S LIFE.
YOU'RE OBVIOUSLY NO BETTER.
I CAN'T EVEN LOOK AT YOU...GET OUT.
BUT...
BUT...
OUT!

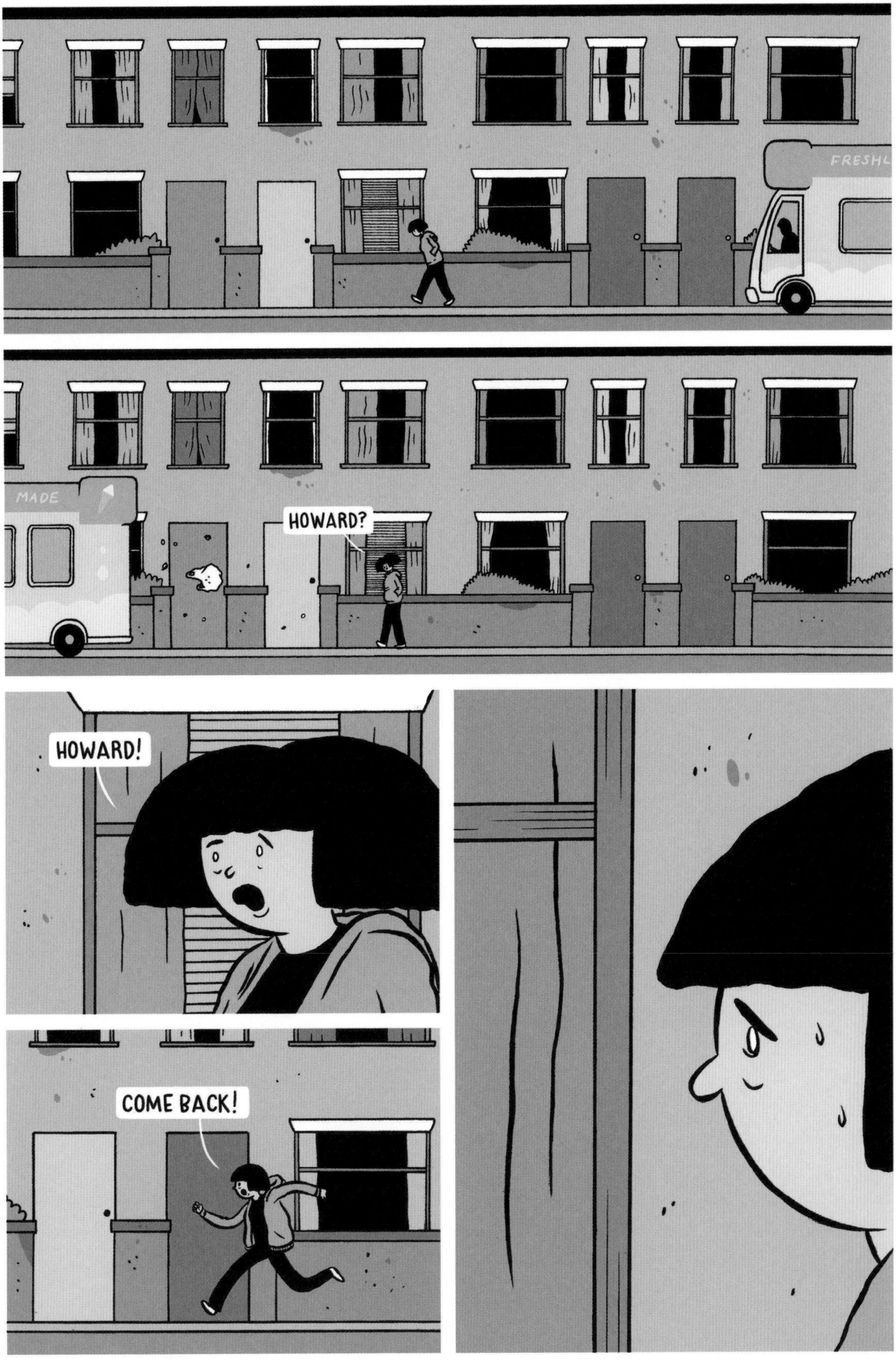
FRESHL
MADE
HOWARD?
HOWARD!
COME BACK!

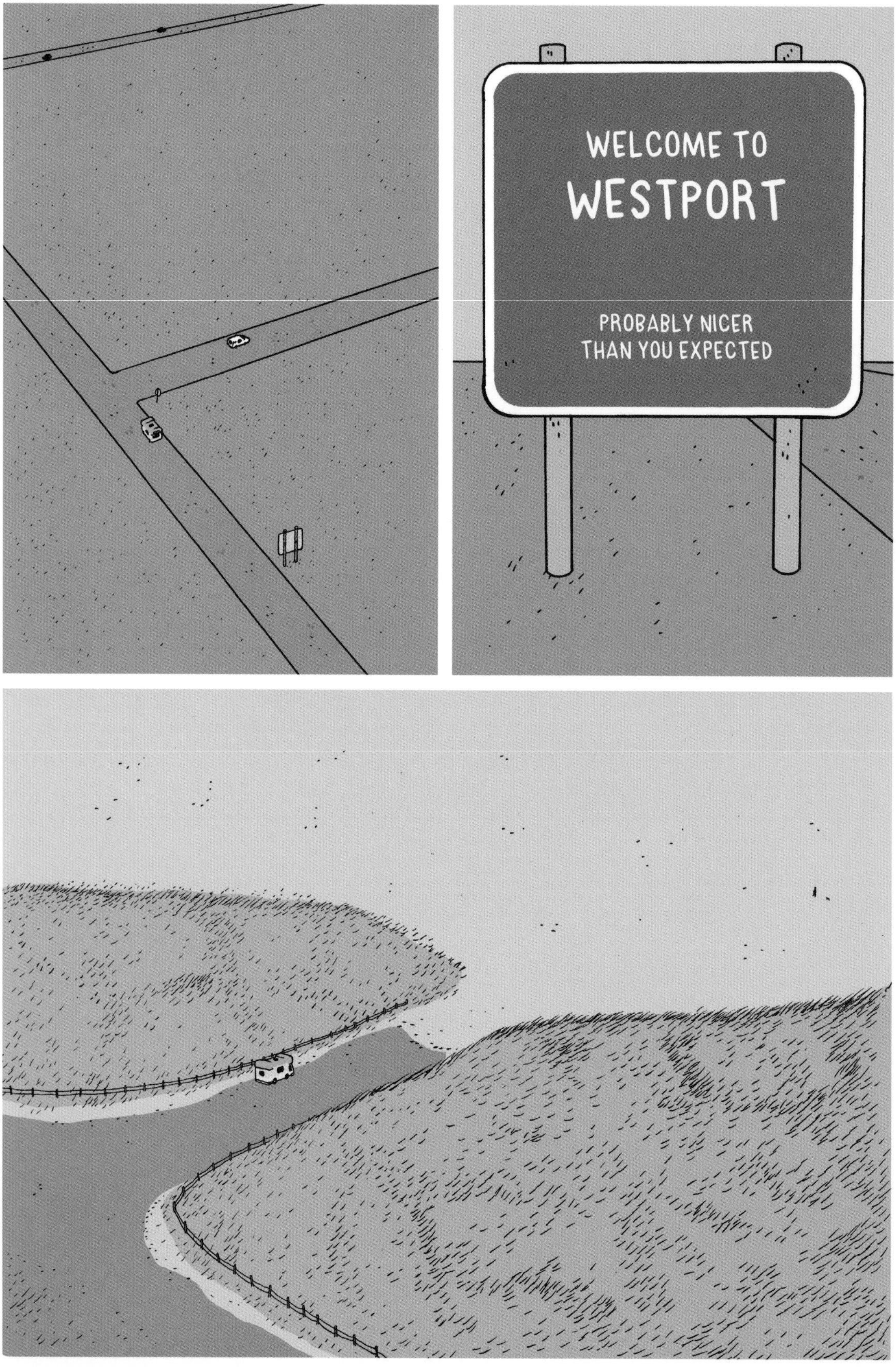
WELCOME TO
WESTPORT
PROBABLY NICER
THAN YOU EXPECTED

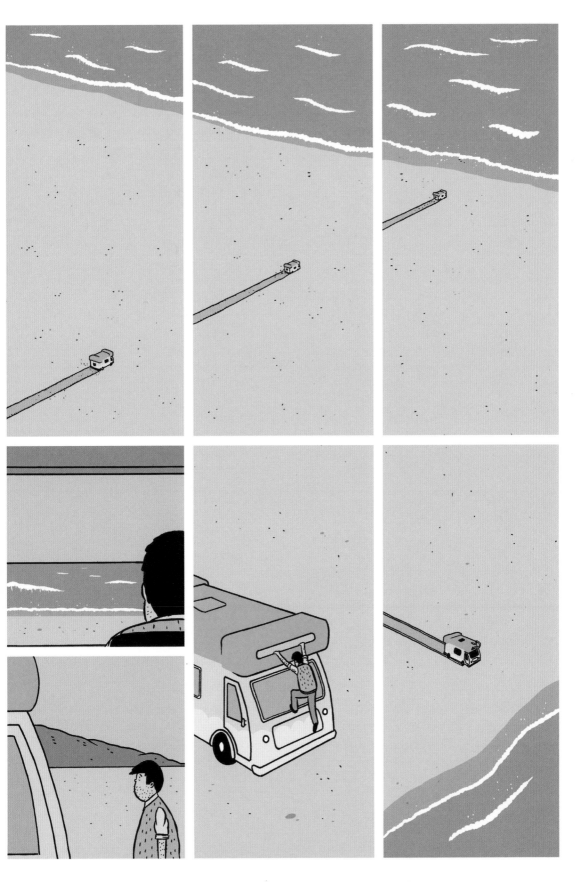

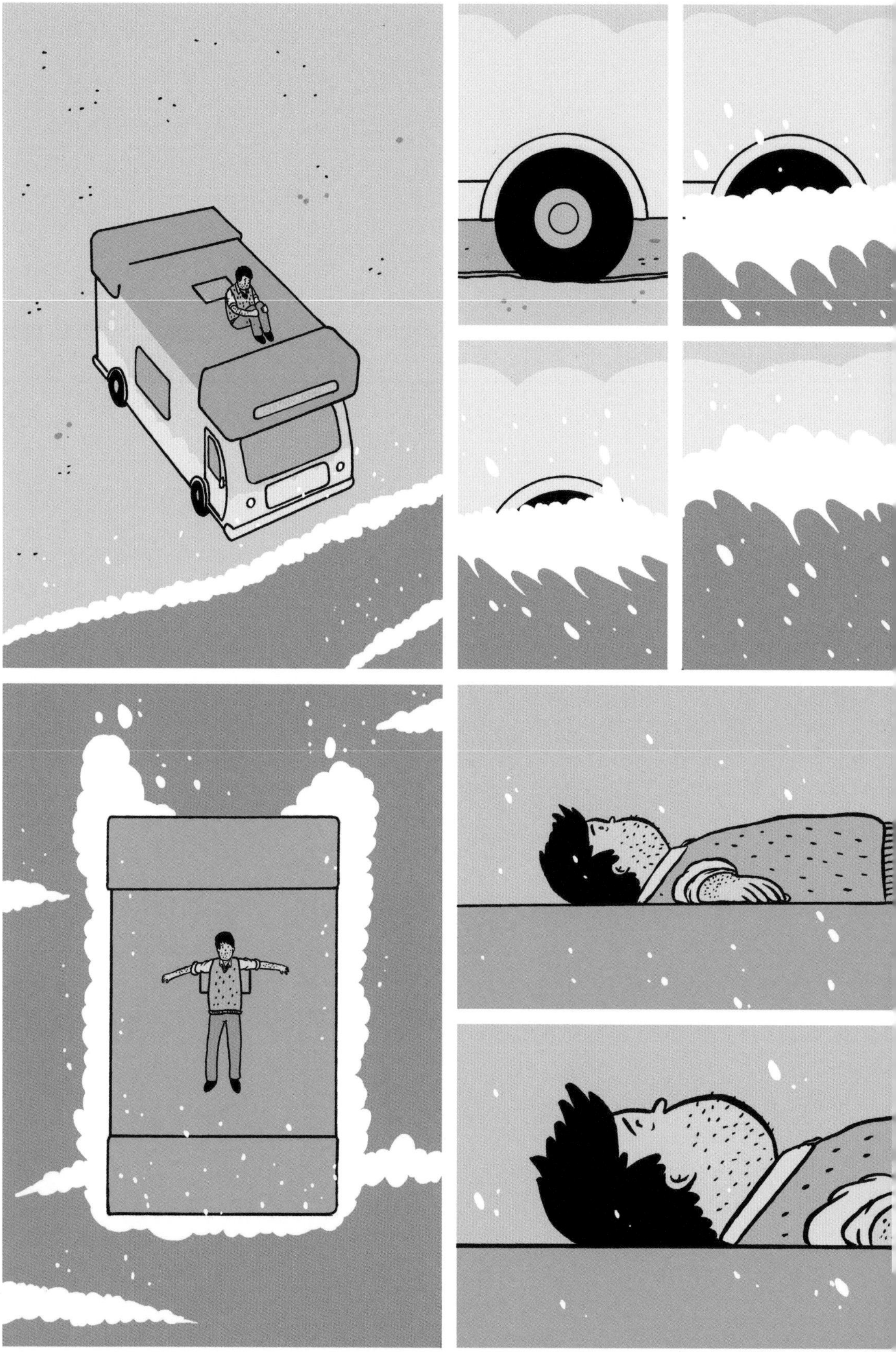

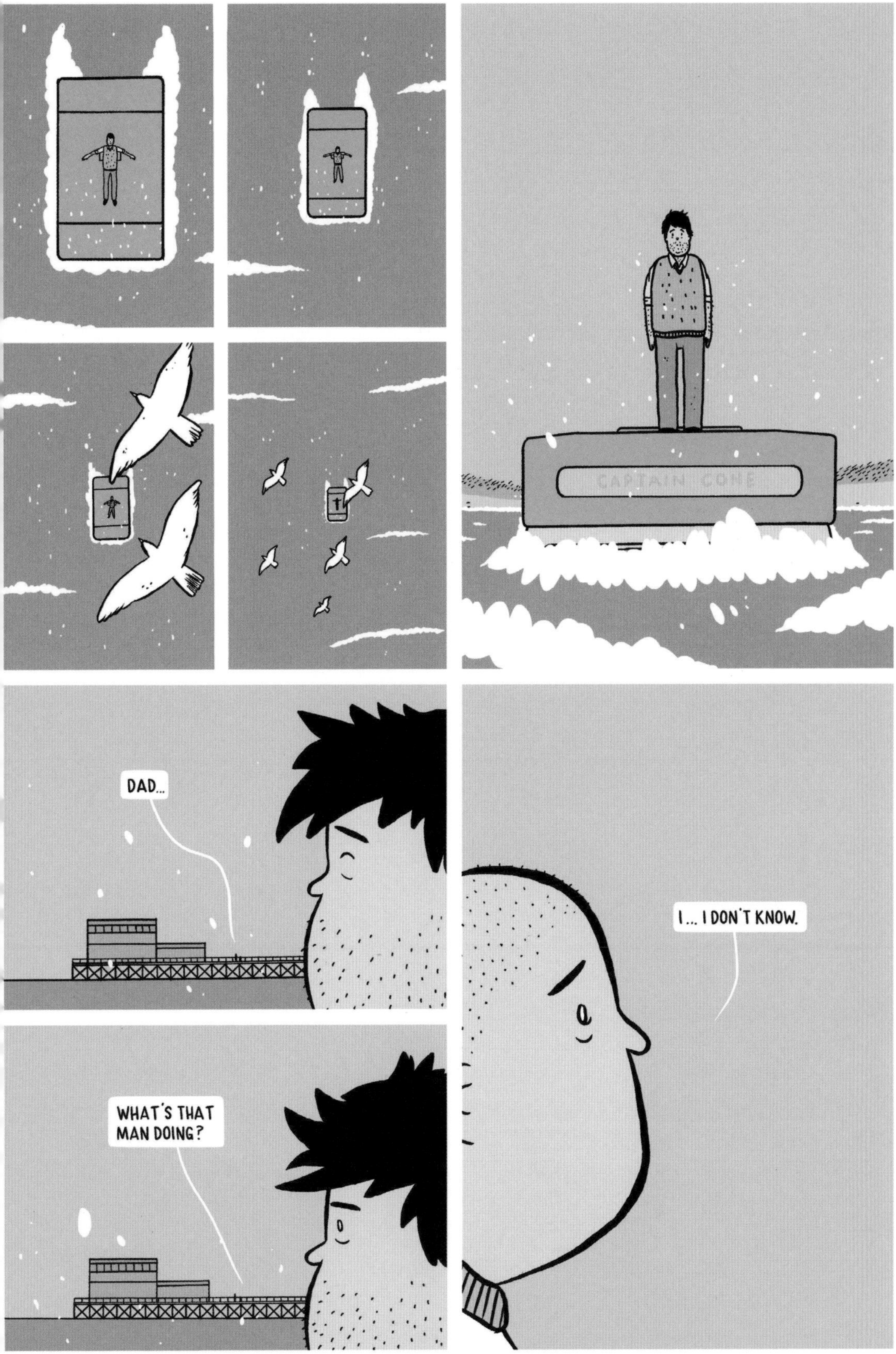
CAPTAIN CONE
DAD...
WHAT'S THAT MAN DOING?
I... I DON'T KNOW.

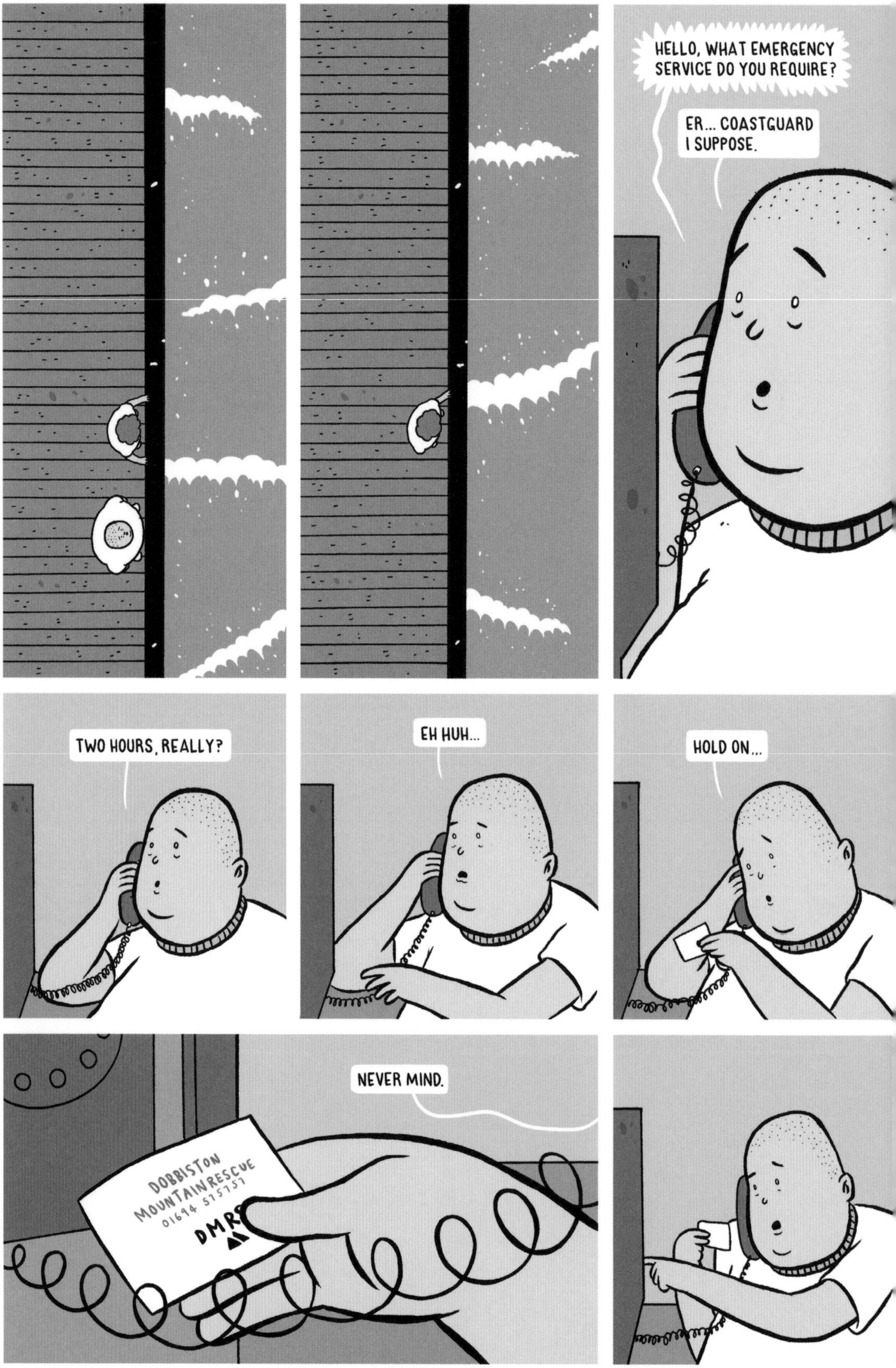
HELLO, WHAT EMERGENCY SERVICE DO YOU REQUIRE?
ER... COASTGUARD I SUPPOSE.
TWO HOURS, REALLY?
EH HUH...
HOLD ON...
NEVER MIND.
DOBBISTON MOUNTAIN RESCUE
01694 575757
DMR

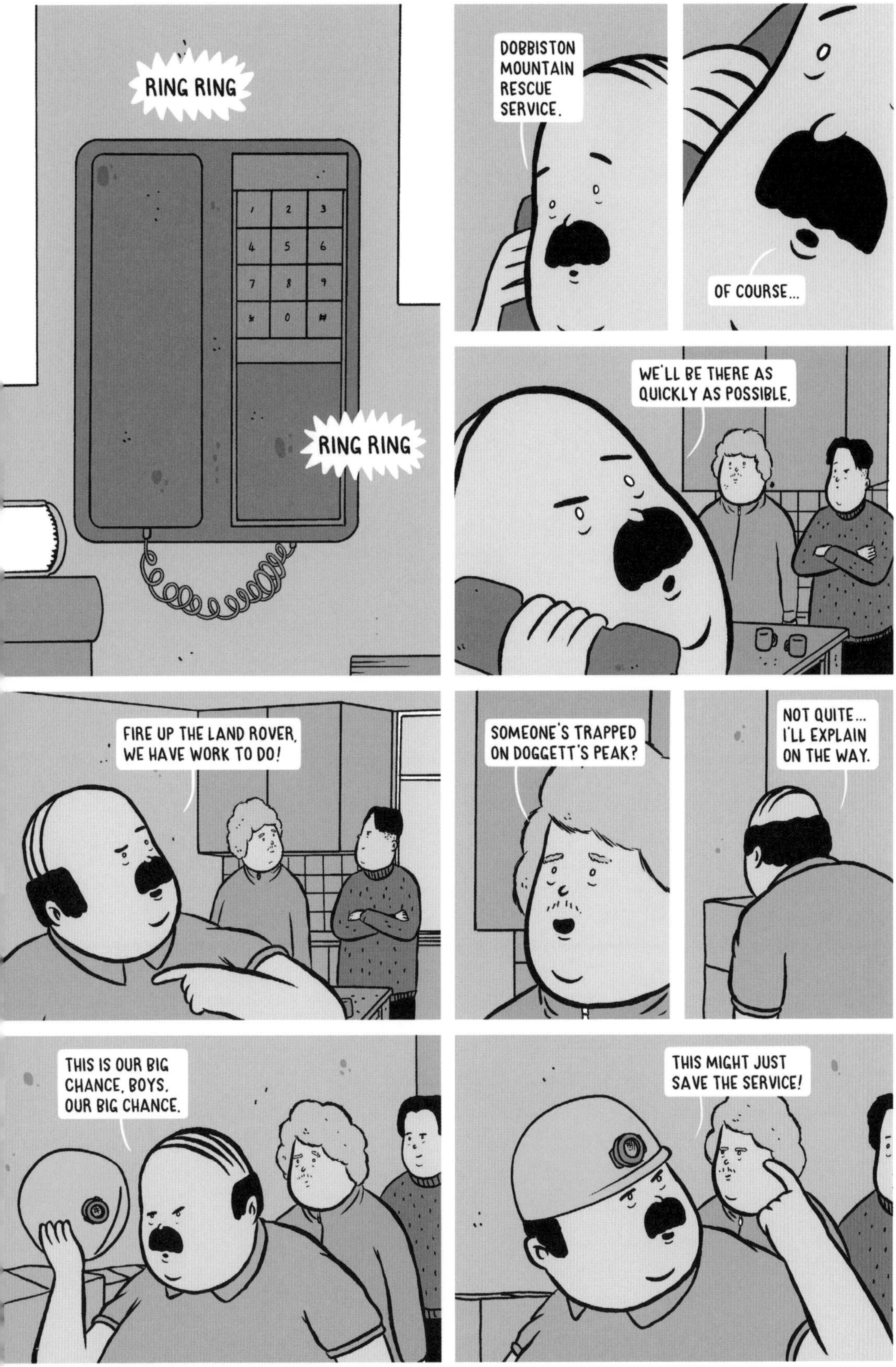
RING RING
RING RING
DOBBISTON MOUNTAIN RESCUE SERVICE.
OF COURSE...
WE'LL BE THERE AS QUICKLY AS POSSIBLE.
FIRE UP THE LAND ROVER, WE HAVE WORK TO DO!
SOMEONE'S TRAPPED ON DOGGETT'S PEAK?
NOT QUITE... I'LL EXPLAIN ON THE WAY.
THIS IS OUR BIG CHANCE, BOYS, OUR BIG CHANCE.
THIS MIGHT JUST SAVE THE SERVICE!

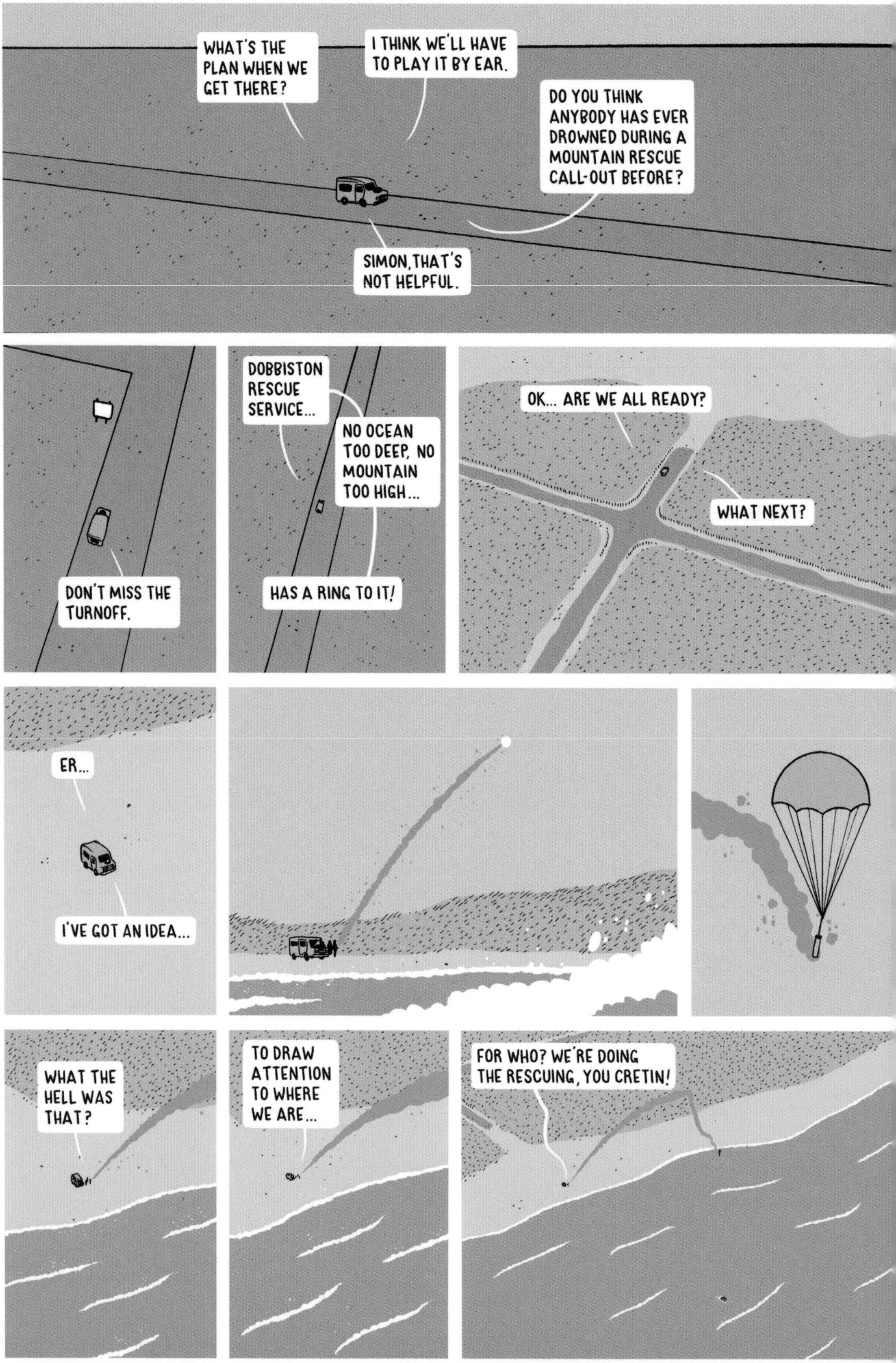
WHAT'S THE PLAN WHEN WE GET THERE?
I THINK WE'LL HAVE TO PLAY IT BY EAR.
DO YOU THINK ANYBODY HAS EVER DROWNED DURING A MOUNTAIN RESCUE CALL-OUT BEFORE?
SIMON, THAT'S NOT HELPFUL.
DON'T MISS THE TURNOFF.
DOBBISTON RESCUE SERVICE...
NO OCEAN TOO DEEP, NO MOUNTAIN TOO HIGH...
HAS A RING TO IT!
OK... ARE WE ALL READY?
WHAT NEXT?
ER...
I'VE GOT AN IDEA...
WHAT THE HELL WAS THAT?
TO DRAW ATTENTION TO WHERE WE ARE...
FOR WHO? WE'RE DOING THE RESCUING, YOU CRETIN!

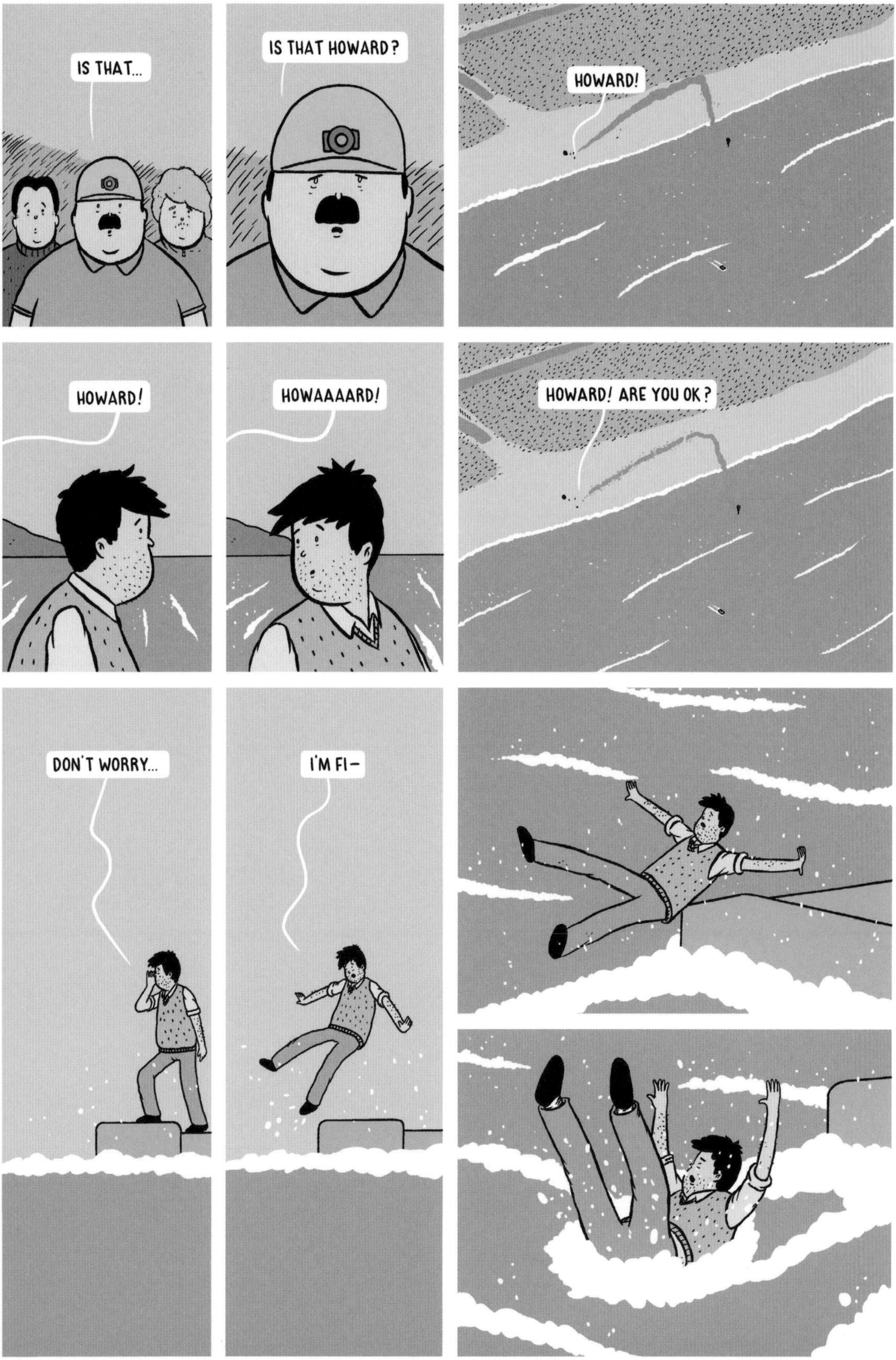
IS THAT...
IS THAT HOWARD?
HOWARD!
HOWARD!
HOWAAAARD!
HOWARD! ARE YOU OK?
DON'T WORRY...
I'M FI–

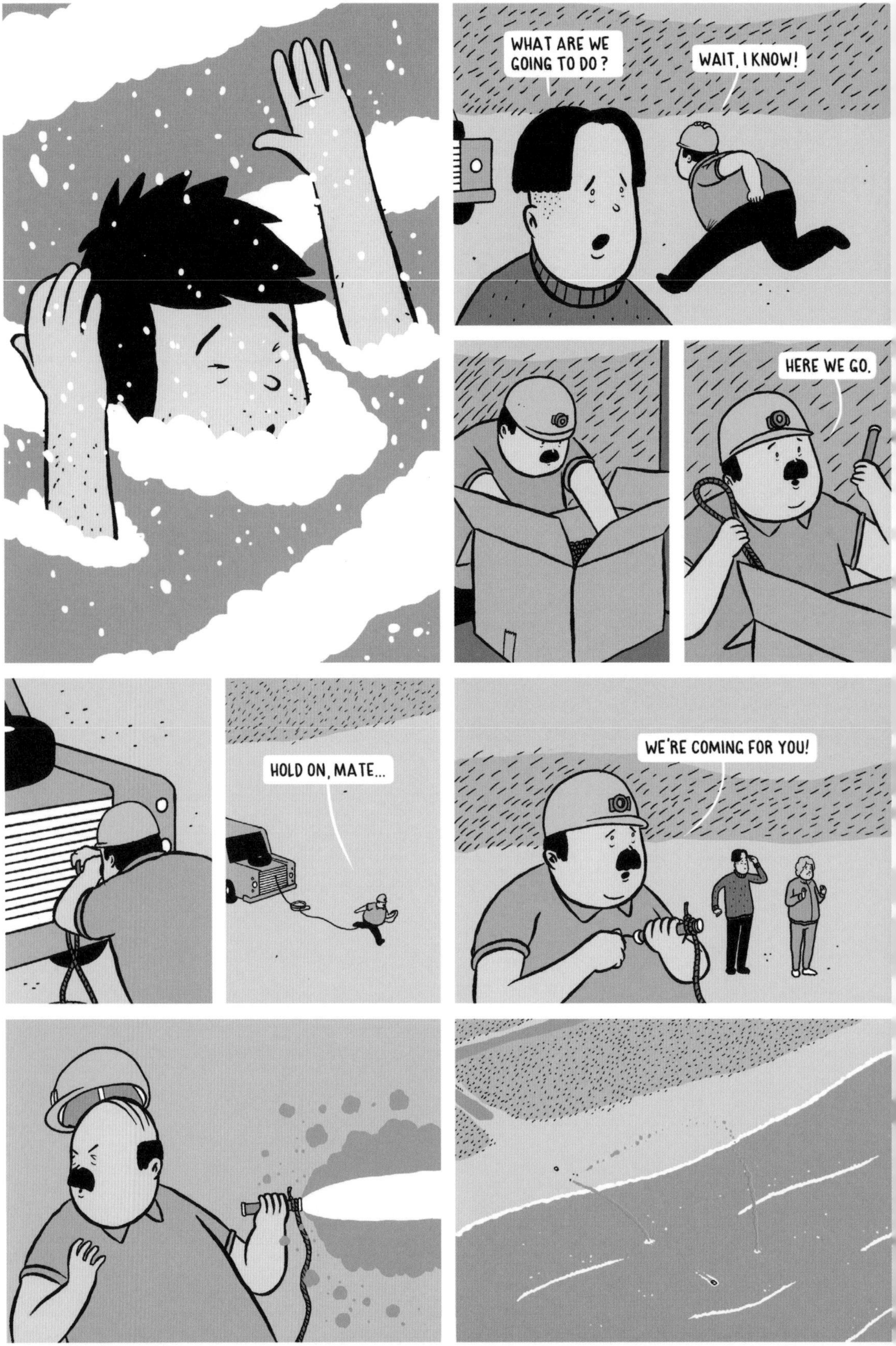
WHAT ARE WE GOING TO DO?
WAIT, I KNOW!
HERE WE GO.
HOLD ON, MATE...
WE'RE COMING FOR YOU!

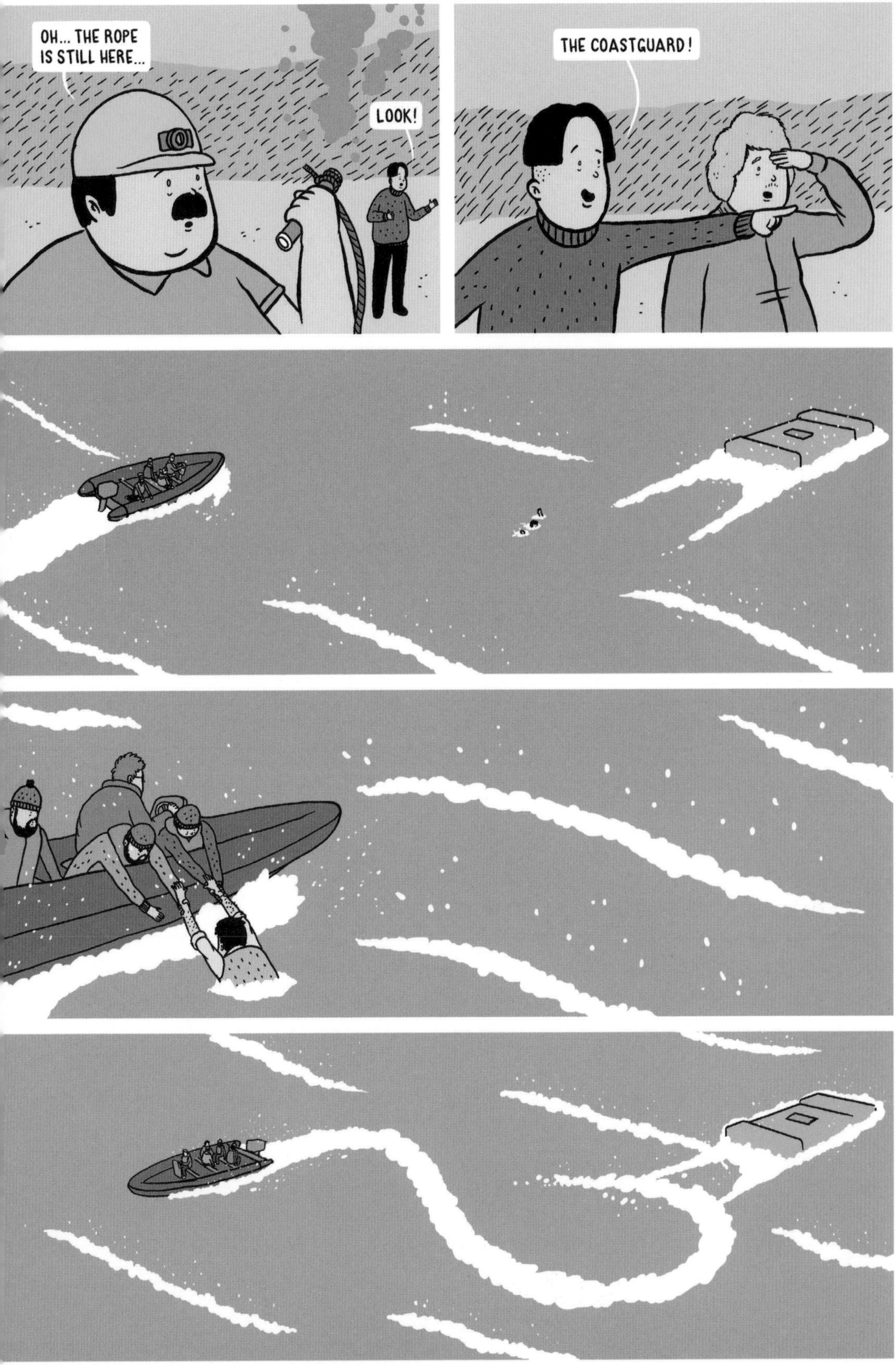
OH... THE ROPE IS STILL HERE...
LOOK!
THE COASTGUARD!

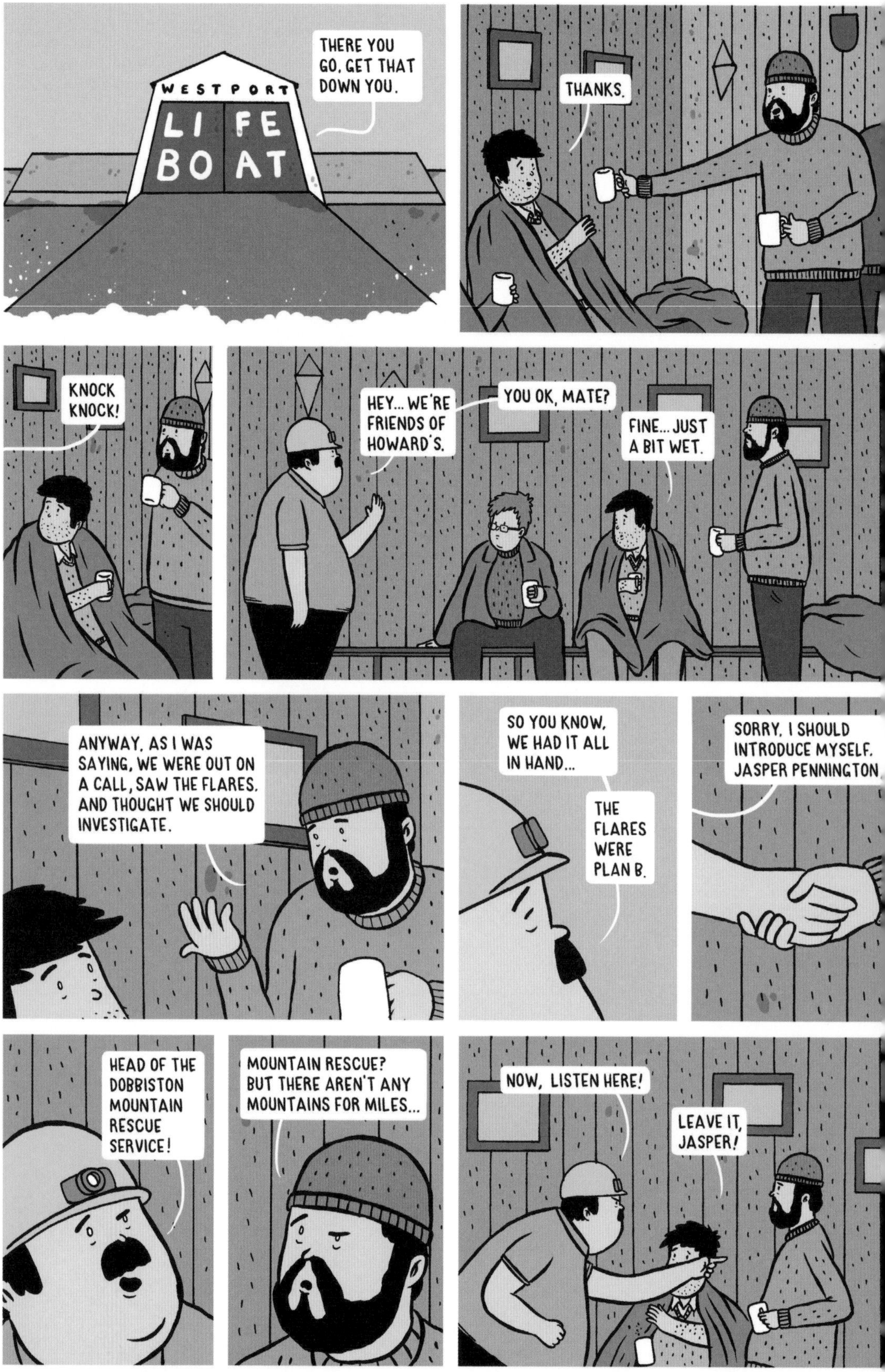
WESTPORT
LIFE BOAT
THERE YOU GO, GET THAT DOWN YOU.
THANKS.
KNOCK KNOCK!
HEY... WE'RE FRIENDS OF HOWARD'S.
YOU OK, MATE?
FINE... JUST A BIT WET.
ANYWAY, AS I WAS SAYING, WE WERE OUT ON A CALL, SAW THE FLARES, AND THOUGHT WE SHOULD INVESTIGATE.
SO YOU KNOW, WE HAD IT ALL IN HAND...
THE FLARES WERE PLAN B.
SORRY, I SHOULD INTRODUCE MYSELF. JASPER PENNINGTON,
HEAD OF THE DOBBISTON MOUNTAIN RESCUE SERVICE!
MOUNTAIN RESCUE? BUT THERE AREN'T ANY MOUNTAINS FOR MILES...
NOW, LISTEN HERE!
LEAVE IT, JASPER!

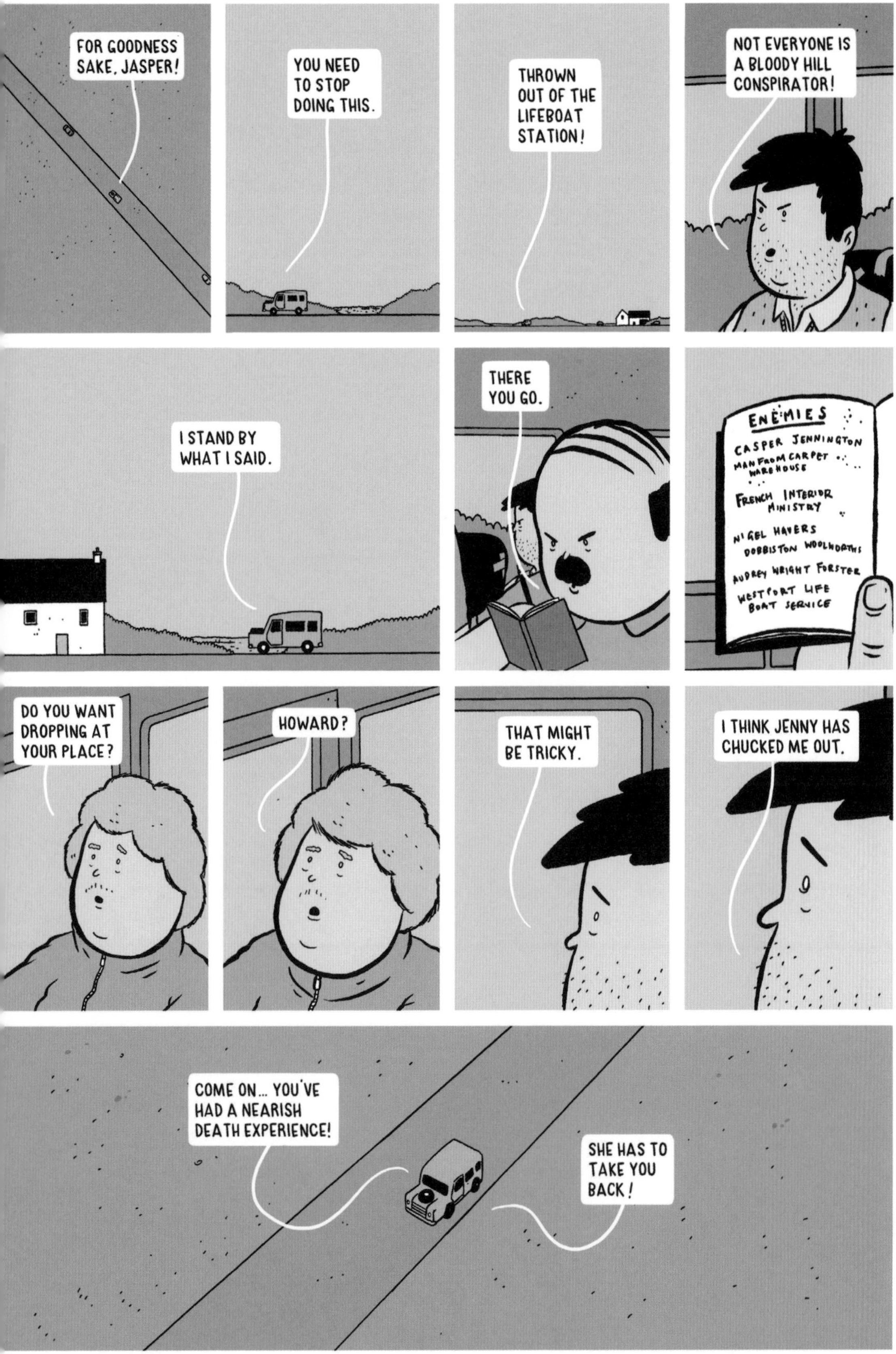
FOR GOODNESS SAKE, JASPER!
YOU NEED TO STOP DOING THIS.
THROWN OUT OF THE LIFEBOAT STATION!
NOT EVERYONE IS A BLOODY HILL CONSPIRATOR!
I STAND BY WHAT I SAID.
THERE YOU GO.
ENEMIES
CASPER JENNINGTON
MAN FROM CARPET WAREHOUSE
FRENCH INTERIOR MINISTRY
NIGEL HAVERS
DOBBISTON WOOLWORTHS
AUDREY WRIGHT FORSTER
WESTPORT LIFE BOAT SERVICE
DO YOU WANT DROPPING AT YOUR PLACE?
HOWARD?
THAT MIGHT BE TRICKY.
I THINK JENNY HAS CHUCKED ME OUT.
COME ON... YOU'VE HAD A NEARISH DEATH EXPERIENCE!
SHE HAS TO TAKE YOU BACK!

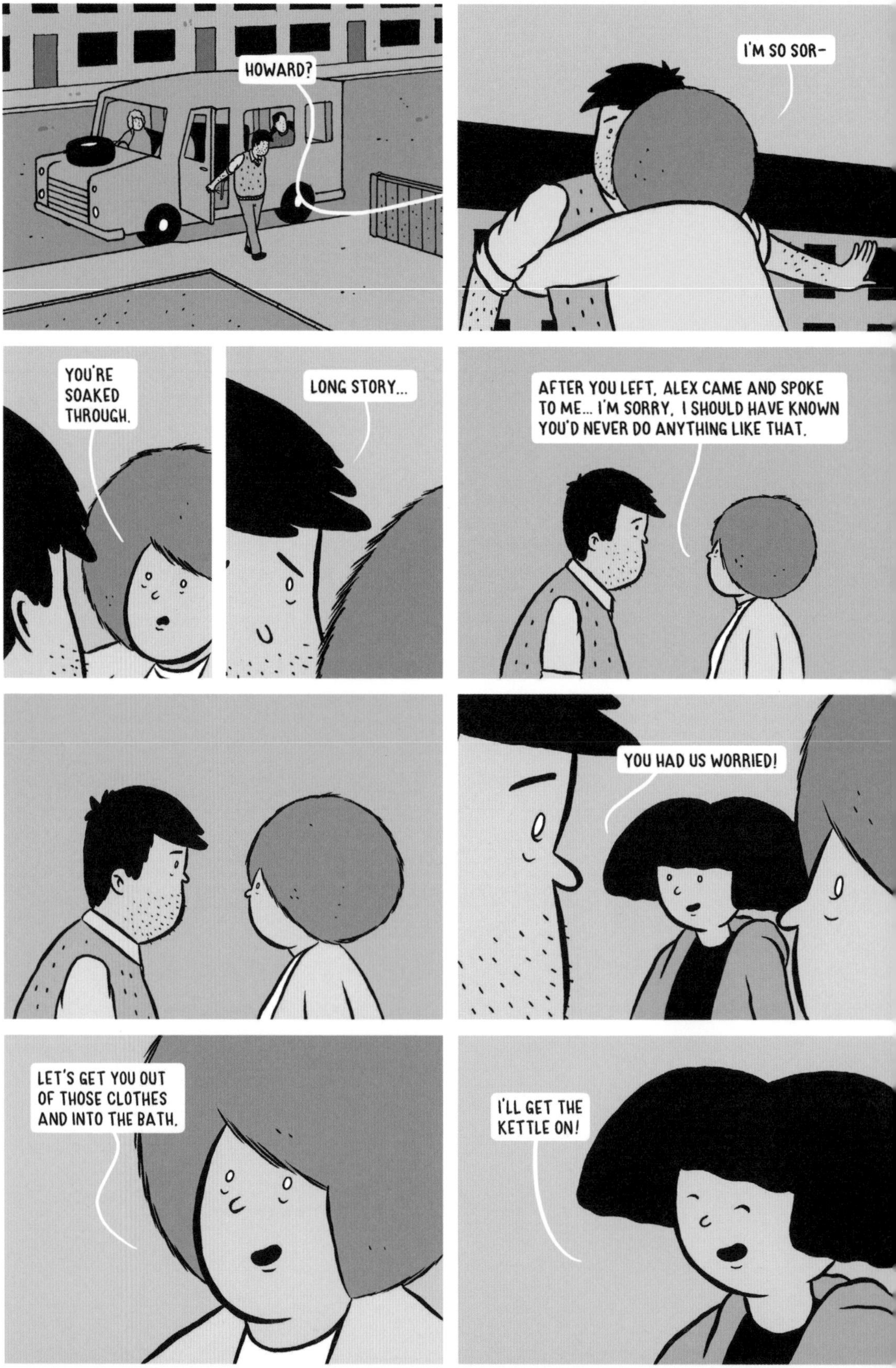
HOWARD?
I'M SO SOR-
YOU'RE SOAKED THROUGH.
LONG STORY...
AFTER YOU LEFT, ALEX CAME AND SPOKE TO ME... I'M SORRY, I SHOULD HAVE KNOWN YOU'D NEVER DO ANYTHING LIKE THAT.
YOU HAD US WORRIED!
LET'S GET YOU OUT OF THOSE CLOTHES AND INTO THE BATH.
I'LL GET THE KETTLE ON!

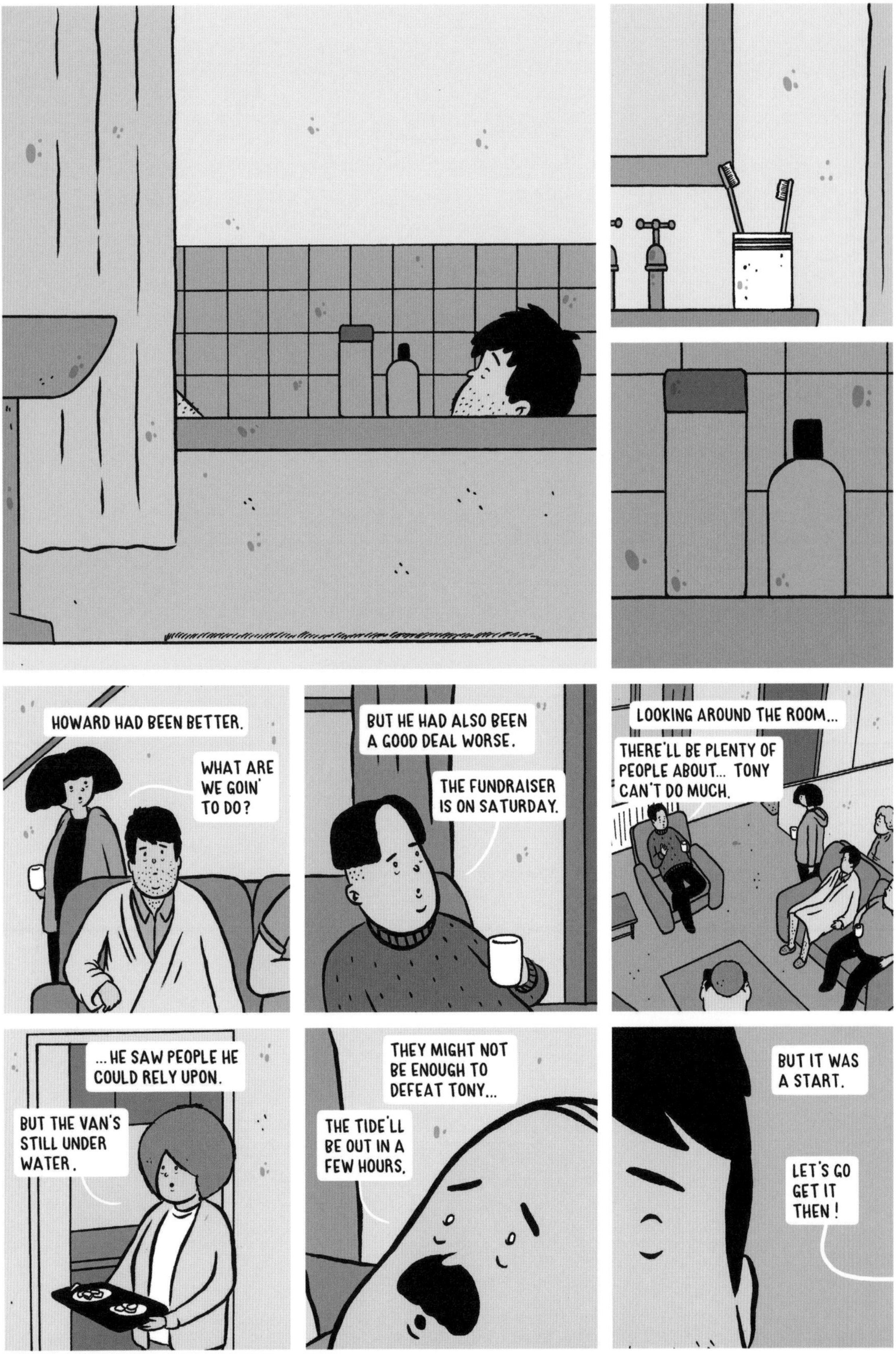
HOWARD HAD BEEN BETTER.
WHAT ARE WE GOIN' TO DO?
BUT HE HAD ALSO BEEN A GOOD DEAL WORSE.
THE FUNDRAISER IS ON SATURDAY.
LOOKING AROUND THE ROOM...
THERE'LL BE PLENTY OF PEOPLE ABOUT... TONY CAN'T DO MUCH.
... HE SAW PEOPLE HE COULD RELY UPON.
BUT THE VAN'S STILL UNDER WATER.
THEY MIGHT NOT BE ENOUGH TO DEFEAT TONY...
THE TIDE'LL BE OUT IN A FEW HOURS.
BUT IT WAS A START.
LET'S GO GET IT THEN!

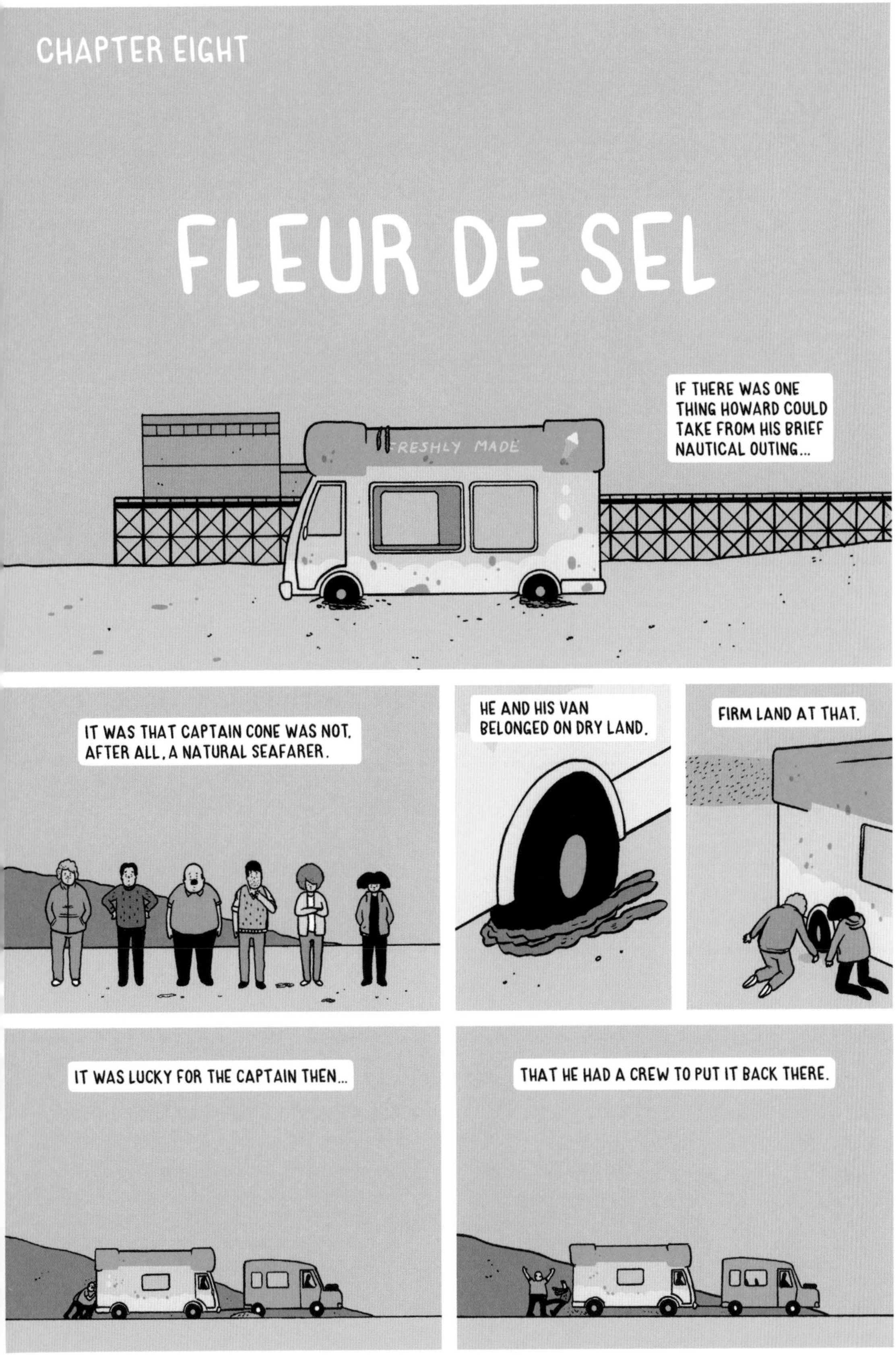
CHAPTER EIGHT
FLEUR DE SEL
IF THERE WAS ONE THING HOWARD COULD TAKE FROM HIS BRIEF NAUTICAL OUTING...
FRESHLY MADE
IT WAS THAT CAPTAIN CONE WAS NOT, AFTER ALL, A NATURAL SEAFARER.
HE AND HIS VAN BELONGED ON DRY LAND.
FIRM LAND AT THAT.
IT WAS LUCKY FOR THE CAPTAIN THEN...
THAT HE HAD A CREW TO PUT IT BACK THERE.

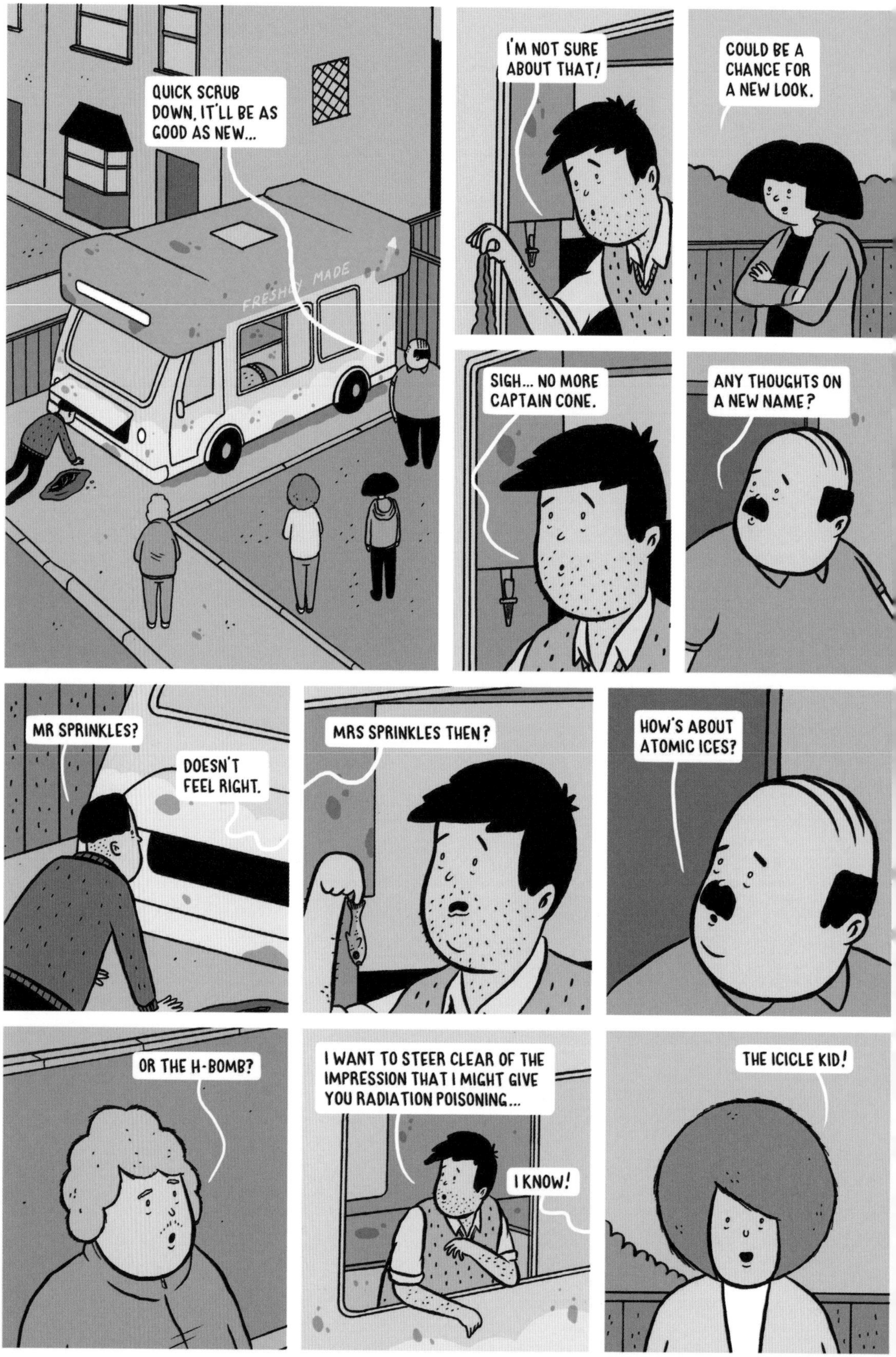
QUICK SCRUB DOWN, IT'LL BE AS GOOD AS NEW...
FRESHLY MADE
I'M NOT SURE ABOUT THAT!
COULD BE A CHANCE FOR A NEW LOOK.
SIGH... NO MORE CAPTAIN CONE.
ANY THOUGHTS ON A NEW NAME?
MR SPRINKLES?
DOESN'T FEEL RIGHT.
MRS SPRINKLES THEN?
HOW'S ABOUT ATOMIC ICES?
OR THE H-BOMB?
I WANT TO STEER CLEAR OF THE IMPRESSION THAT I MIGHT GIVE YOU RADIATION POISONING...
I KNOW!
THE ICICLE KID!

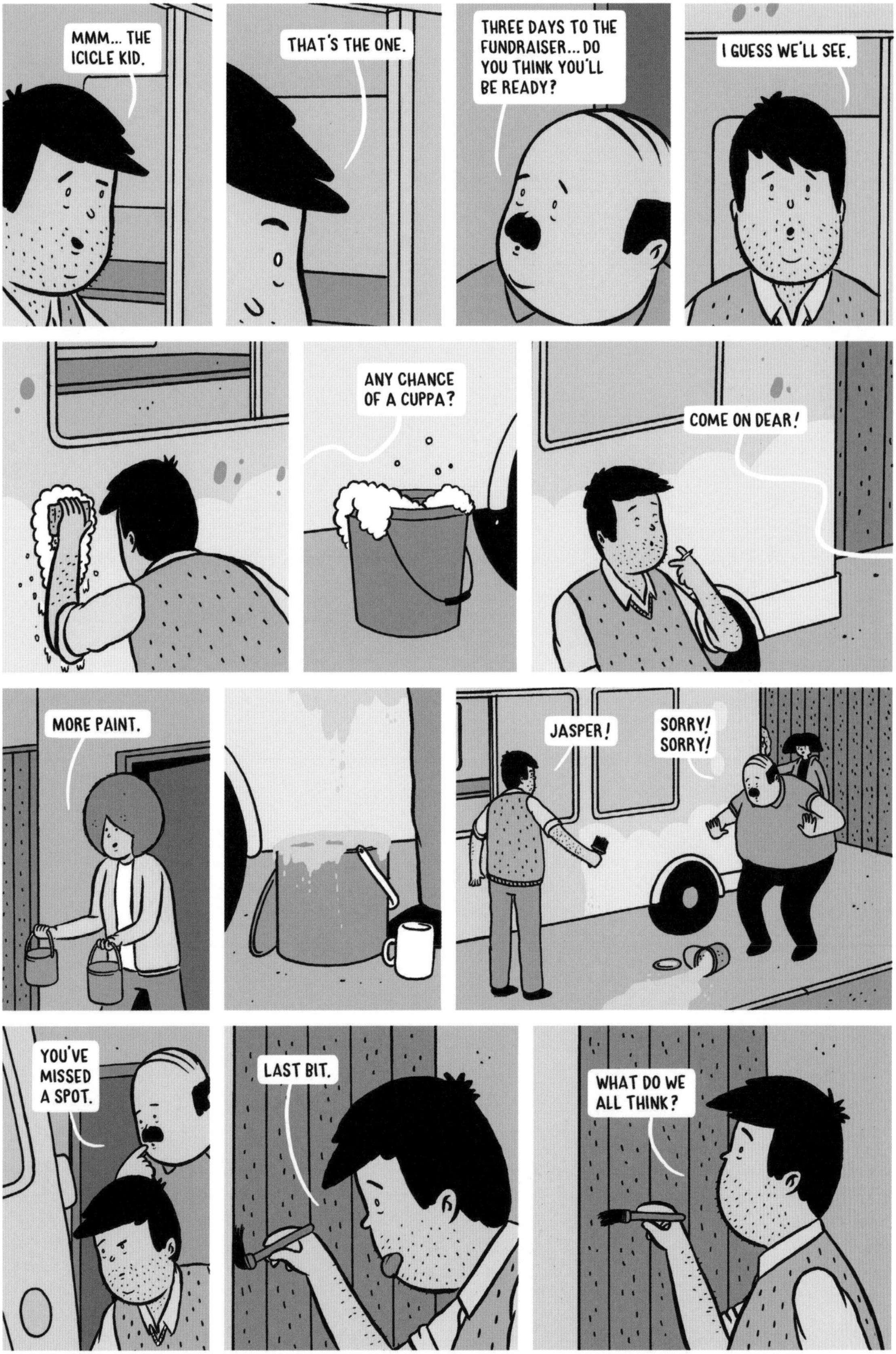
MMM... THE ICICLE KID.
THAT'S THE ONE.
THREE DAYS TO THE FUNDRAISER... DO YOU THINK YOU'LL BE READY?
I GUESS WE'LL SEE.
ANY CHANCE OF A CUPPA?
COME ON DEAR!
MORE PAINT.
JASPER!
SORRY! SORRY!
YOU'VE MISSED A SPOT.
LAST BIT.
WHAT DO WE ALL THINK?

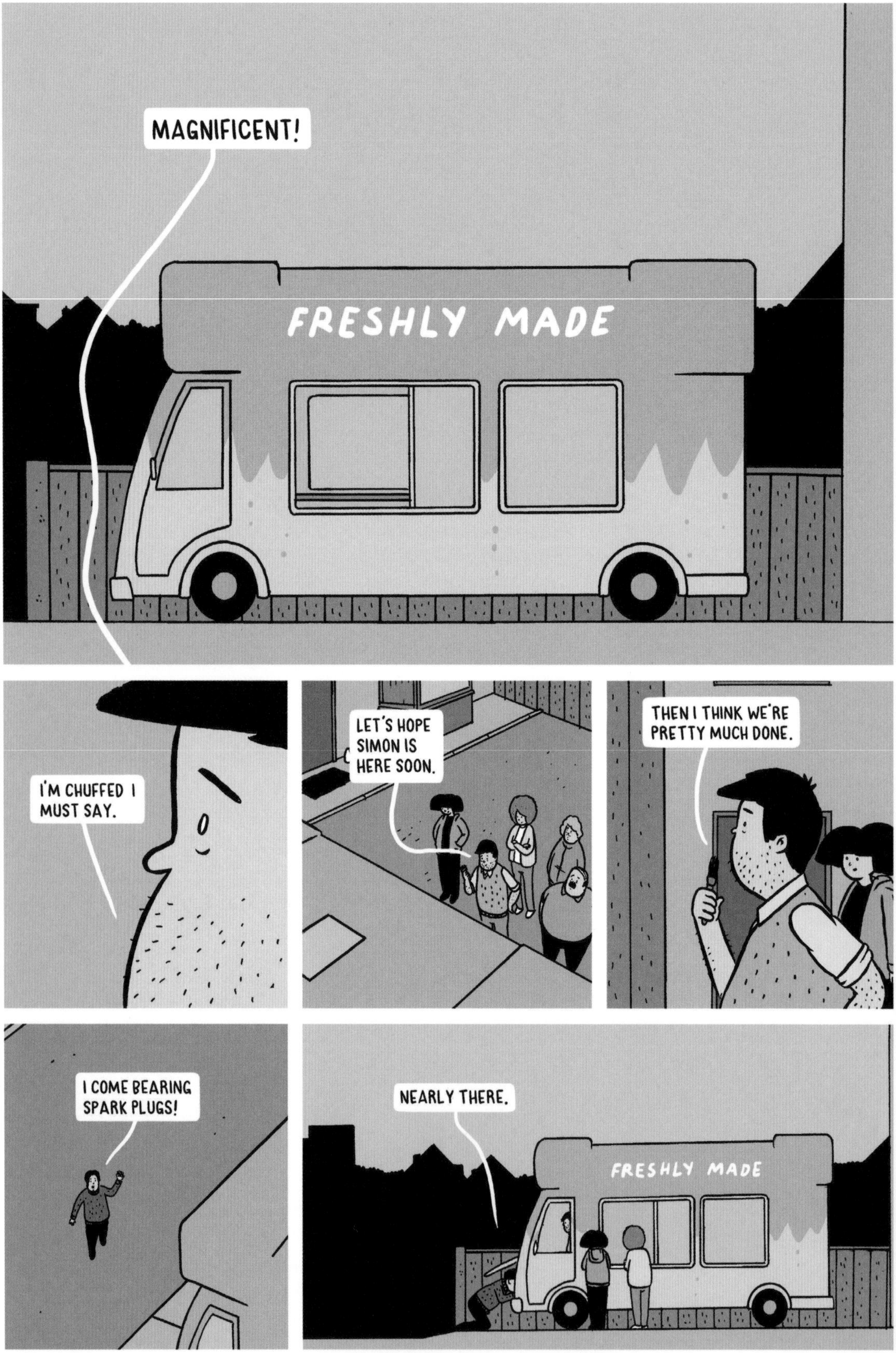
MAGNIFICENT!
FRESHLY MADE
I'M CHUFFED I MUST SAY.
LET'S HOPE SIMON IS HERE SOON.
THEN I THINK WE'RE PRETTY MUCH DONE.
I COME BEARING SPARK PLUGS!
NEARLY THERE.
FRESHLY MADE

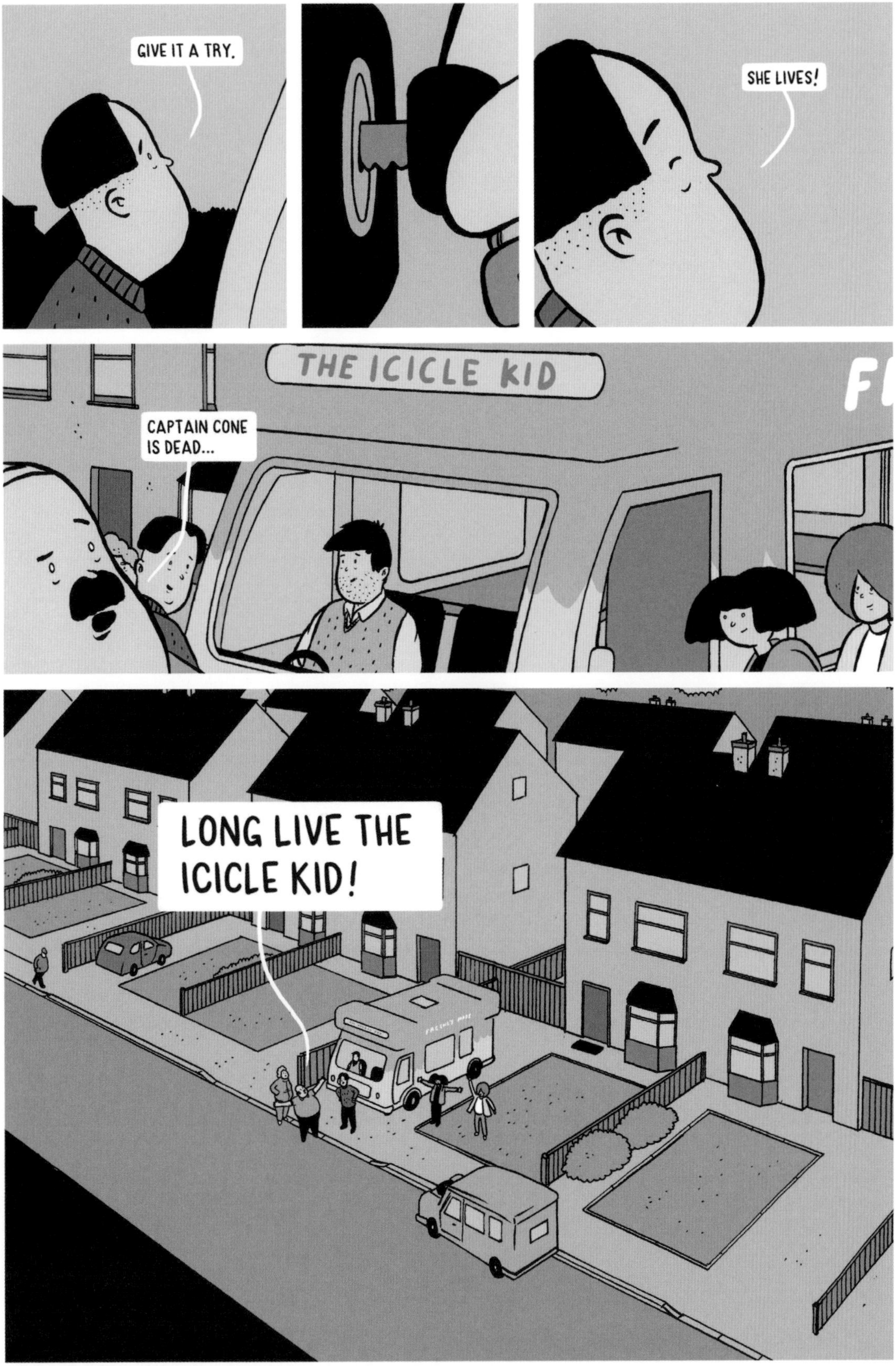
GIVE IT A TRY.
SHE LIVES!
THE ICICLE KID
CAPTAIN CONE IS DEAD...
LONG LIVE THE ICICLE KID!

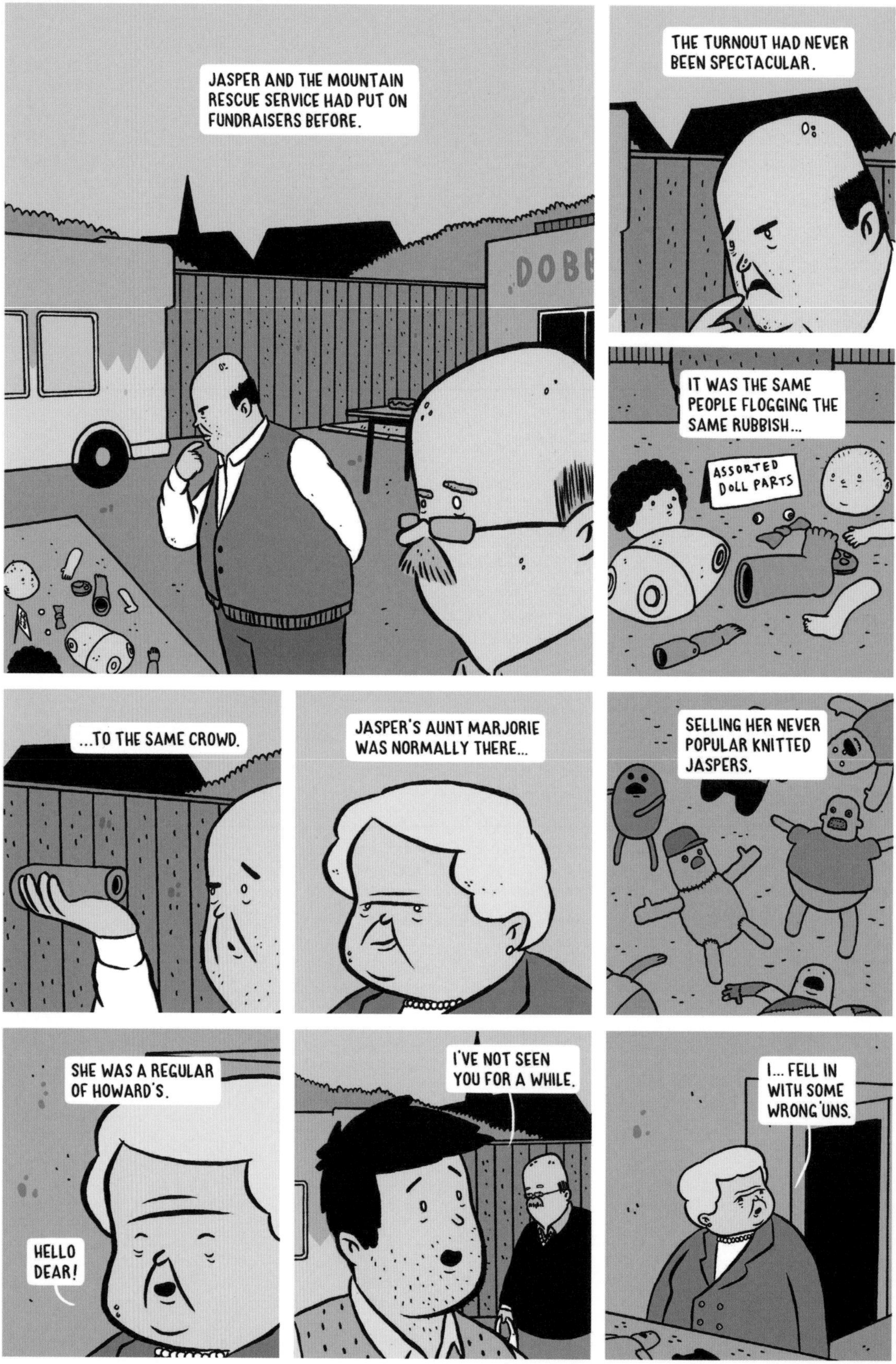
JASPER AND THE MOUNTAIN RESCUE SERVICE HAD PUT ON FUNDRAISERS BEFORE.
DOBB
THE TURNOUT HAD NEVER BEEN SPECTACULAR.
IT WAS THE SAME PEOPLE FLOGGING THE SAME RUBBISH...
ASSORTED DOLL PARTS
...TO THE SAME CROWD.
JASPER'S AUNT MARJORIE WAS NORMALLY THERE...
SELLING HER NEVER POPULAR KNITTED JASPERS.
SHE WAS A REGULAR OF HOWARD'S.
HELLO DEAR!
I'VE NOT SEEN YOU FOR A WHILE.
I... FELL IN WITH SOME WRONG 'UNS.

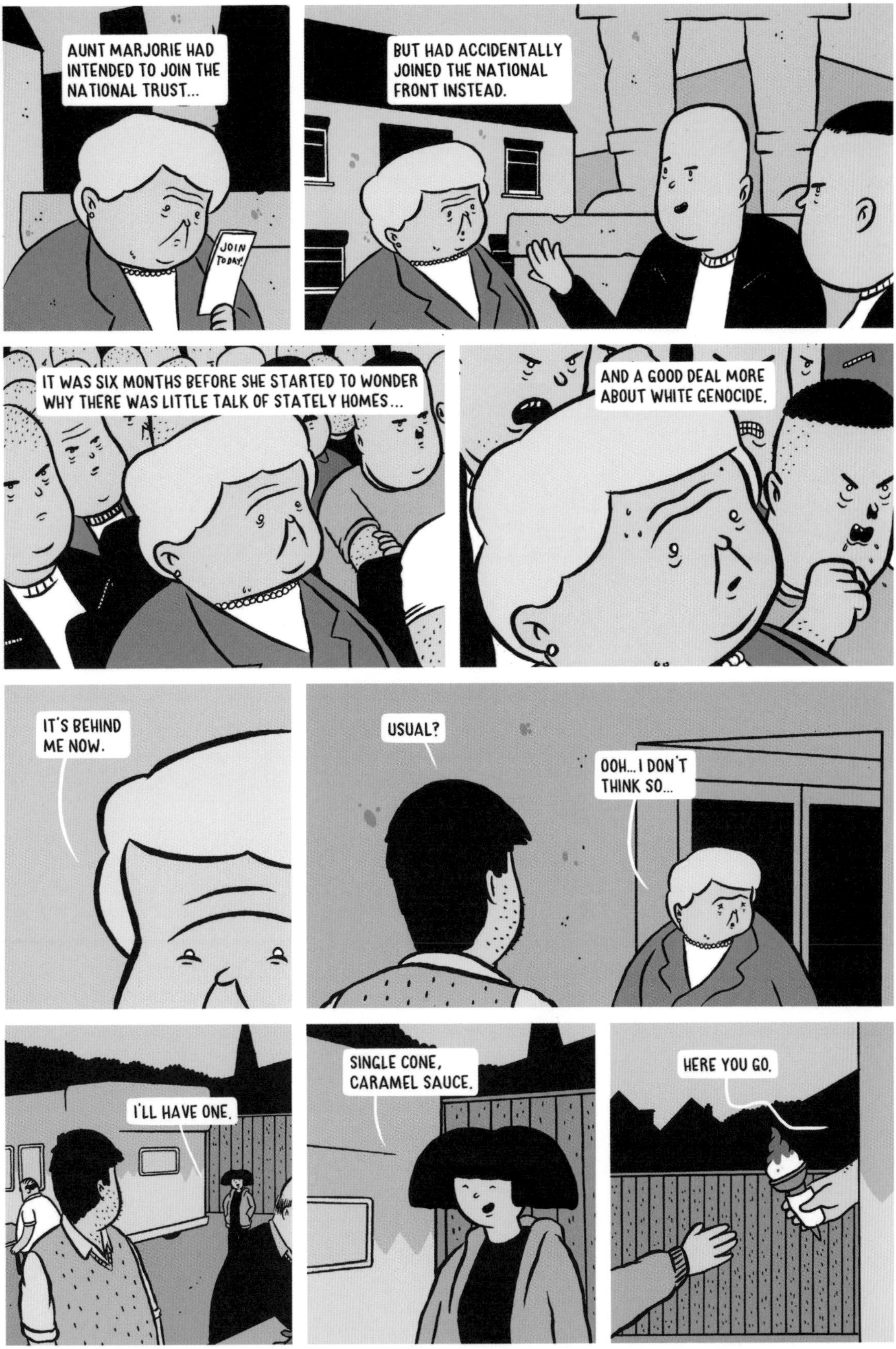
AUNT MARJORIE HAD INTENDED TO JOIN THE NATIONAL TRUST...
JOIN TODAY!
BUT HAD ACCIDENTALLY JOINED THE NATIONAL FRONT INSTEAD.
IT WAS SIX MONTHS BEFORE SHE STARTED TO WONDER WHY THERE WAS LITTLE TALK OF STATELY HOMES...
AND A GOOD DEAL MORE ABOUT WHITE GENOCIDE.
IT'S BEHIND ME NOW.
USUAL?
OOH... I DON'T THINK SO...
I'LL HAVE ONE.
SINGLE CONE, CARAMEL SAUCE.
HERE YOU GO.

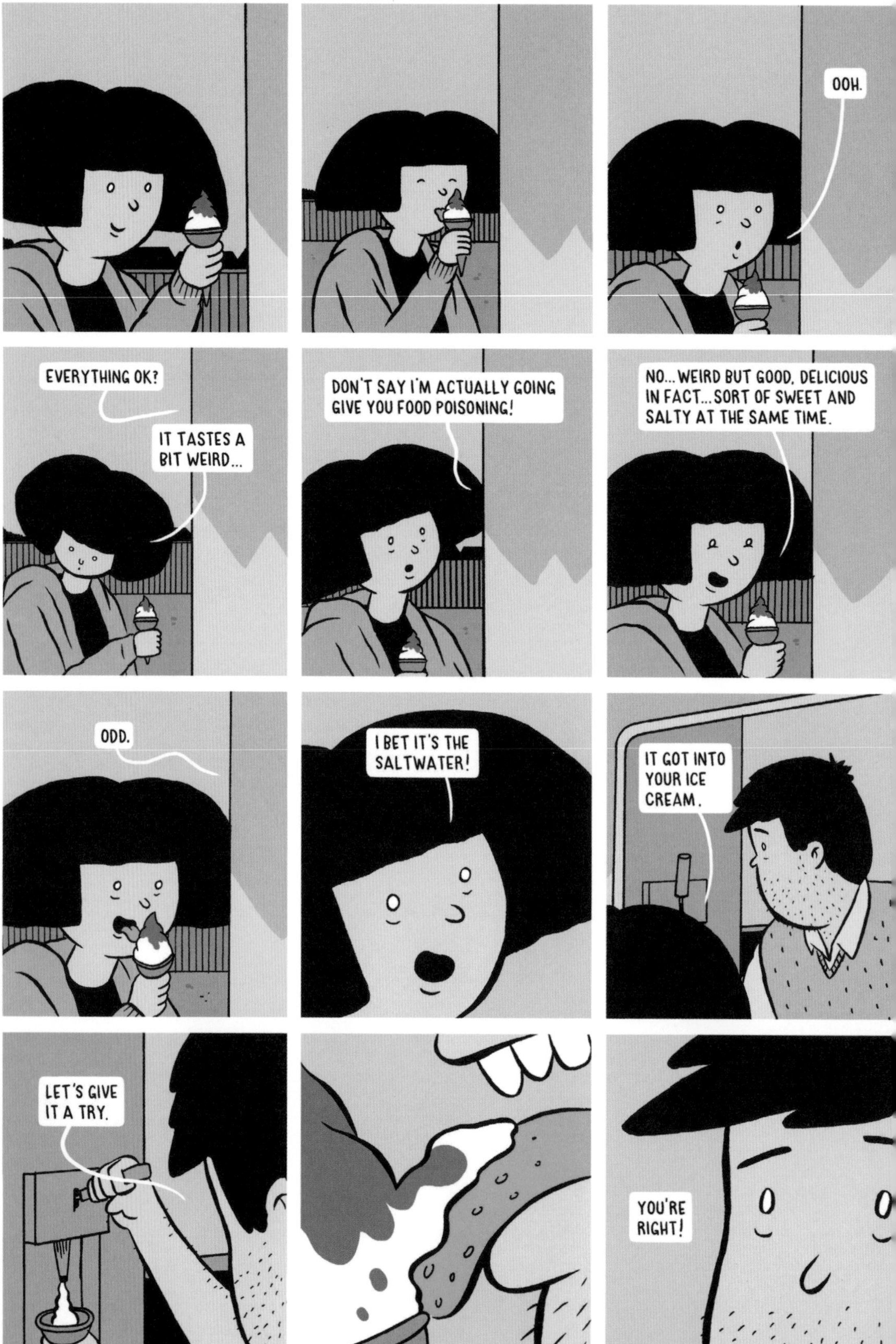
OOH.
EVERYTHING OK?
IT TASTES A BIT WEIRD...
DON'T SAY I'M ACTUALLY GOING GIVE YOU FOOD POISONING!
NO... WEIRD BUT GOOD, DELICIOUS IN FACT... SORT OF SWEET AND SALTY AT THE SAME TIME.
ODD.
I BET IT'S THE SALTWATER!
IT GOT INTO YOUR ICE CREAM.
LET'S GIVE IT A TRY.
YOU'RE RIGHT!

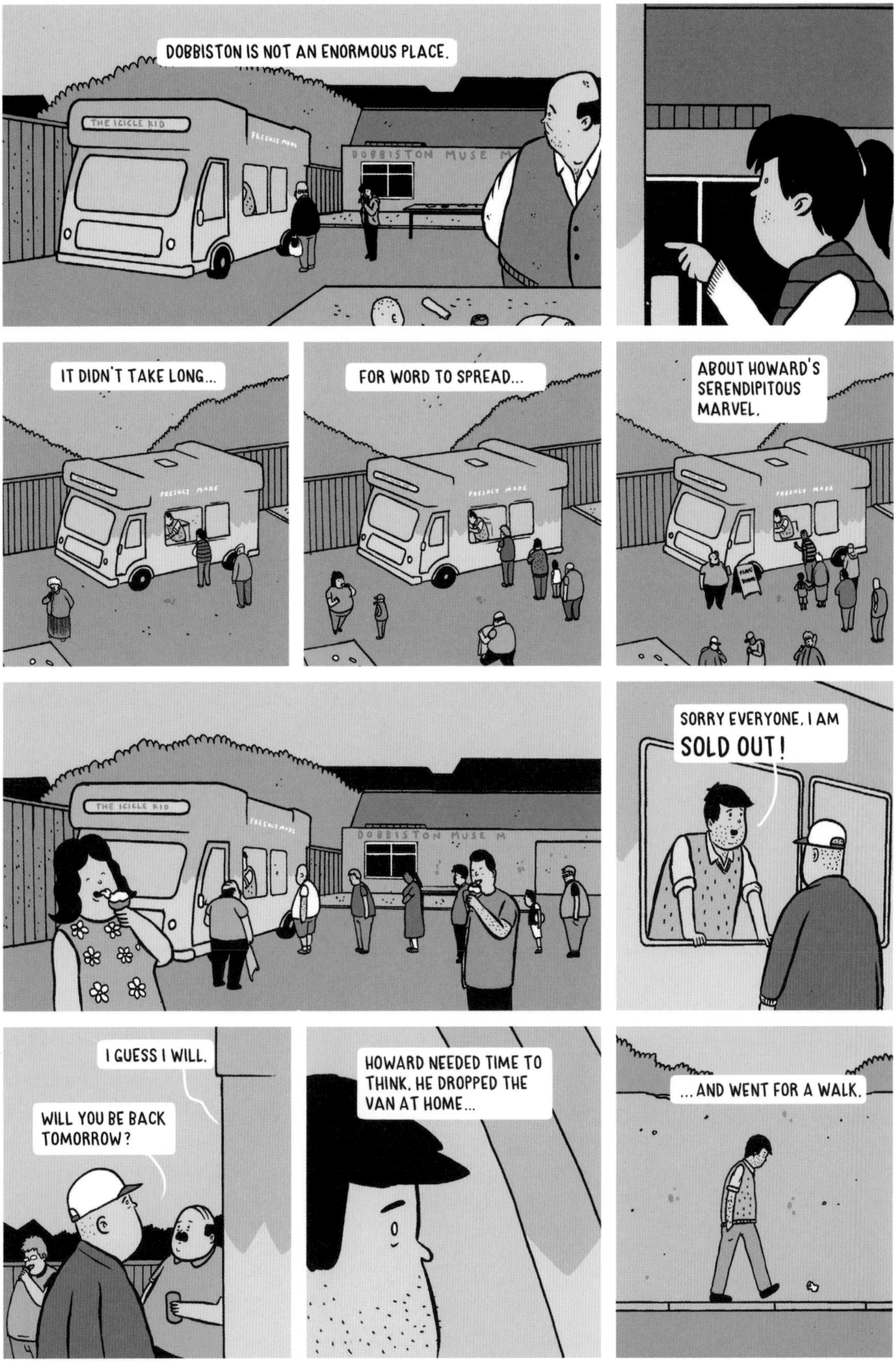
DOBBISTON IS NOT AN ENORMOUS PLACE.
THE ICICLE KID
DOBBISTON MUSE M
IT DIDN'T TAKE LONG...
FOR WORD TO SPREAD...
ABOUT HOWARD'S SERENDIPITOUS MARVEL.
THE ICICLE KID
DOBBISTON MUSE M
SORRY EVERYONE, I AM SOLD OUT!
WILL YOU BE BACK TOMORROW?
I GUESS I WILL.
HOWARD NEEDED TIME TO THINK. HE DROPPED THE VAN AT HOME...
... AND WENT FOR A WALK.

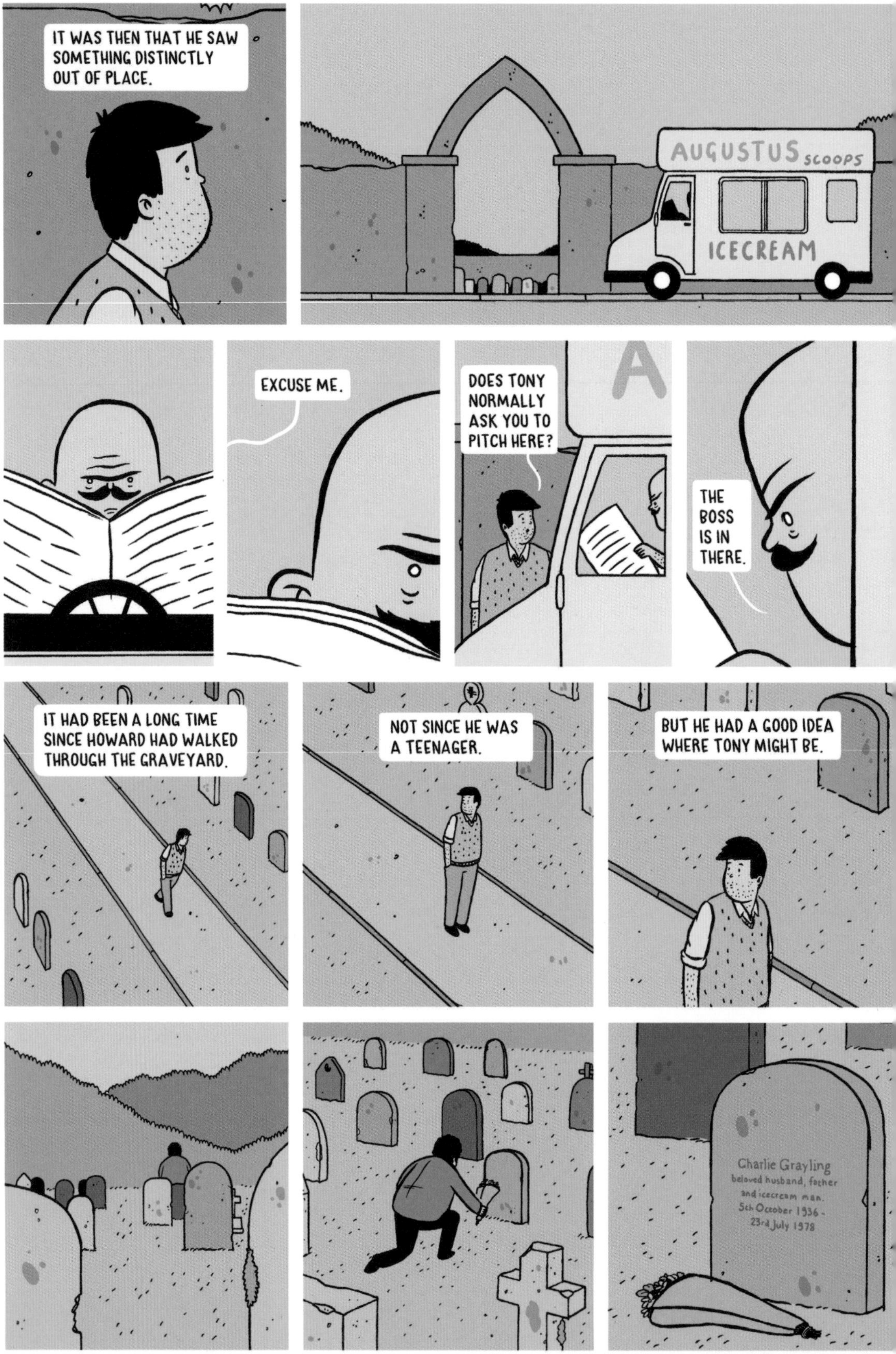
IT WAS THEN THAT HE SAW SOMETHING DISTINCTLY OUT OF PLACE.
AUGUSTUS SCOOPS
ICECREAM
EXCUSE ME.
DOES TONY NORMALLY ASK YOU TO PITCH HERE?
THE BOSS IS IN THERE.
IT HAD BEEN A LONG TIME SINCE HOWARD HAD WALKED THROUGH THE GRAVEYARD.
NOT SINCE HE WAS A TEENAGER.
BUT HE HAD A GOOD IDEA WHERE TONY MIGHT BE.
Charlie Grayling
beloved husband, father
and icecream man.
5th October 1936 -
23rd July 1978

THE FLOWERS ARE NICE.

MOTHER LIKES ME TO DO IT EVERY COUPLE OF WEEKS. SHE'S TOO FRAIL TO DO IT HERSELF.

YOU KNOW...

YOU REMIND ME OF HIM.

YEAH?

I DON'T MEAN THAT AS A COMPLIMENT.

Charlie Grayling
beloved husband, father
and ice-cream man
5th October 1926.
Died July 1972.

I HATED HIM.

I STILL HATE HIM.

WHAT HE DID TO MY MUM.

TONY, FOR WHAT HE DID TO YOUR MUM.

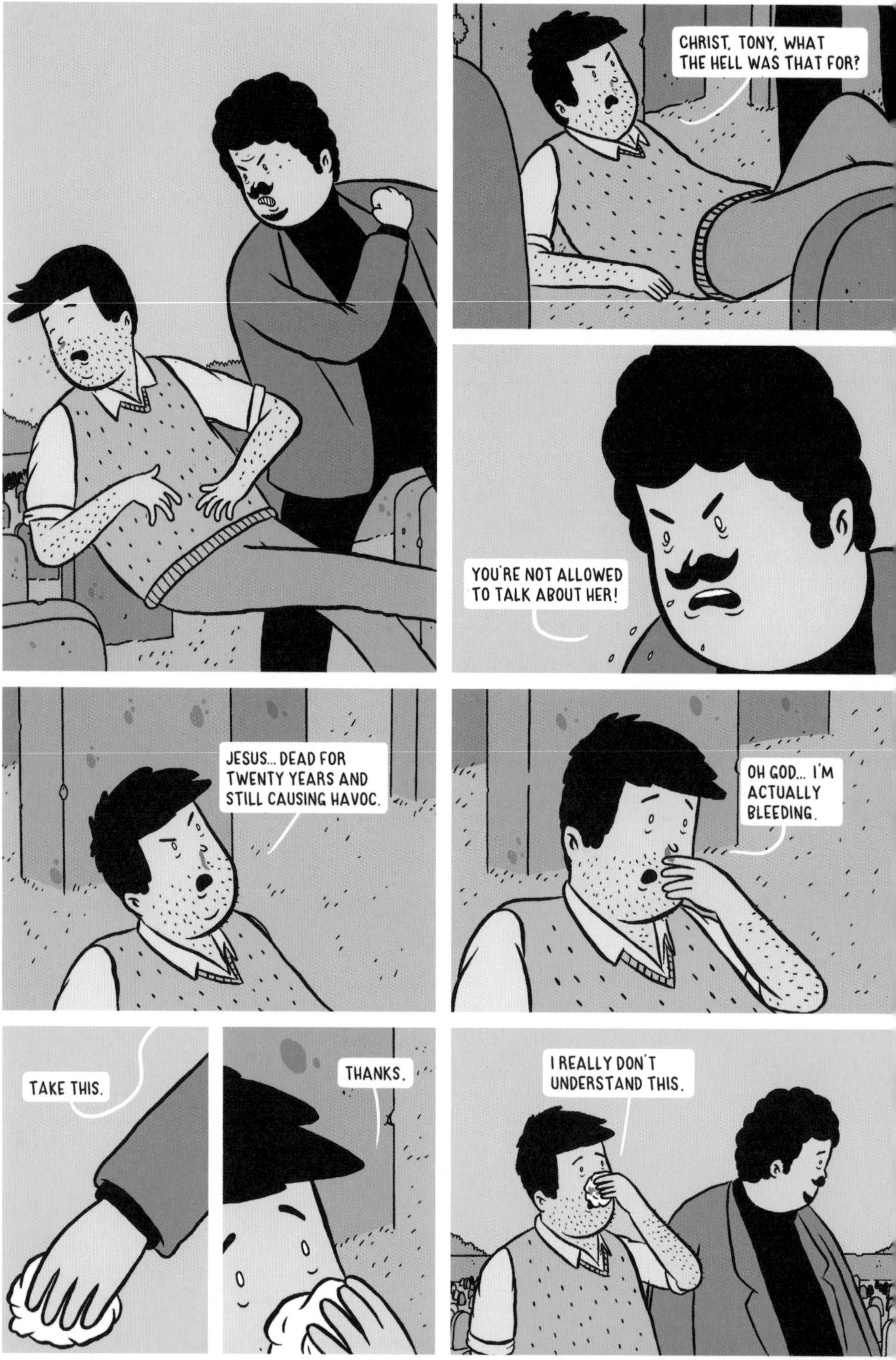
CHRIST, TONY, WHAT THE HELL WAS THAT FOR?
YOU'RE NOT ALLOWED TO TALK ABOUT HER!
JESUS... DEAD FOR TWENTY YEARS AND STILL CAUSING HAVOC.
OH GOD... I'M ACTUALLY BLEEDING.
TAKE THIS.
THANKS.
I REALLY DON'T UNDERSTAND THIS.

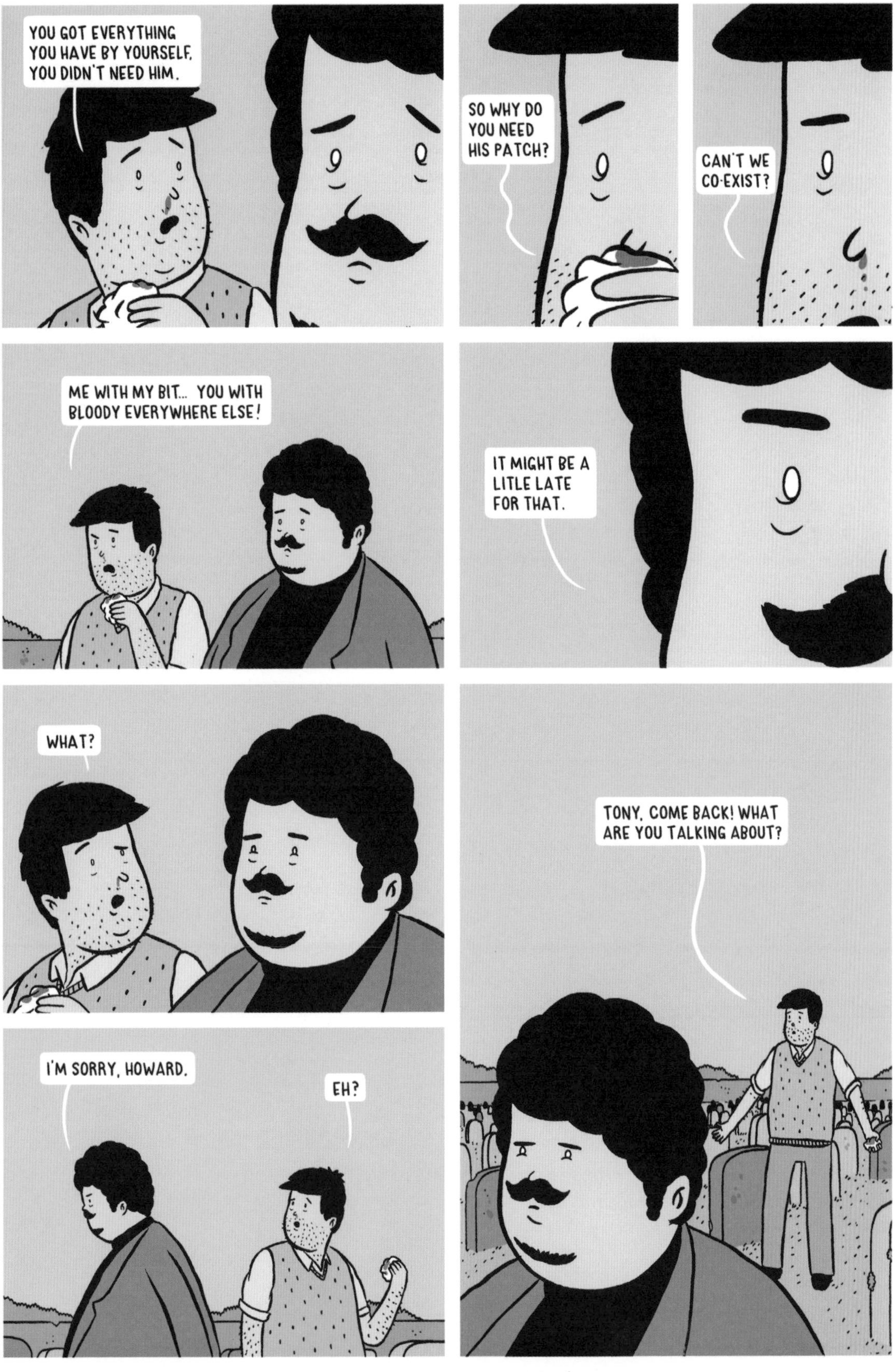
YOU GOT EVERYTHING YOU HAVE BY YOURSELF. YOU DIDN'T NEED HIM.
SO WHY DO YOU NEED HIS PATCH?
CAN'T WE CO-EXIST?
ME WITH MY BIT... YOU WITH BLOODY EVERYWHERE ELSE!
IT MIGHT BE A LITLE LATE FOR THAT.
WHAT?
I'M SORRY, HOWARD.
EH?
TONY, COME BACK! WHAT ARE YOU TALKING ABOUT?

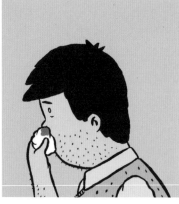
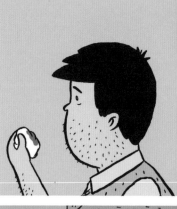

LOOK AT THE STATE OF YOU.

I'M SORRY...

I HOPE WHOEVER DID THIS TO YOU IS IN A BAD WAY.

MUM SAID...

I DON'T CARE WHAT YOUR MOTHER SAID!

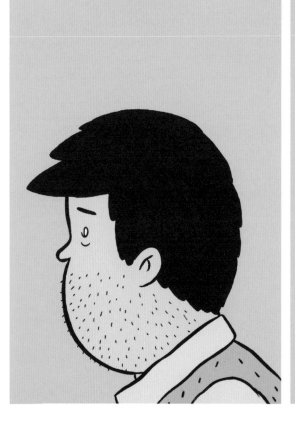

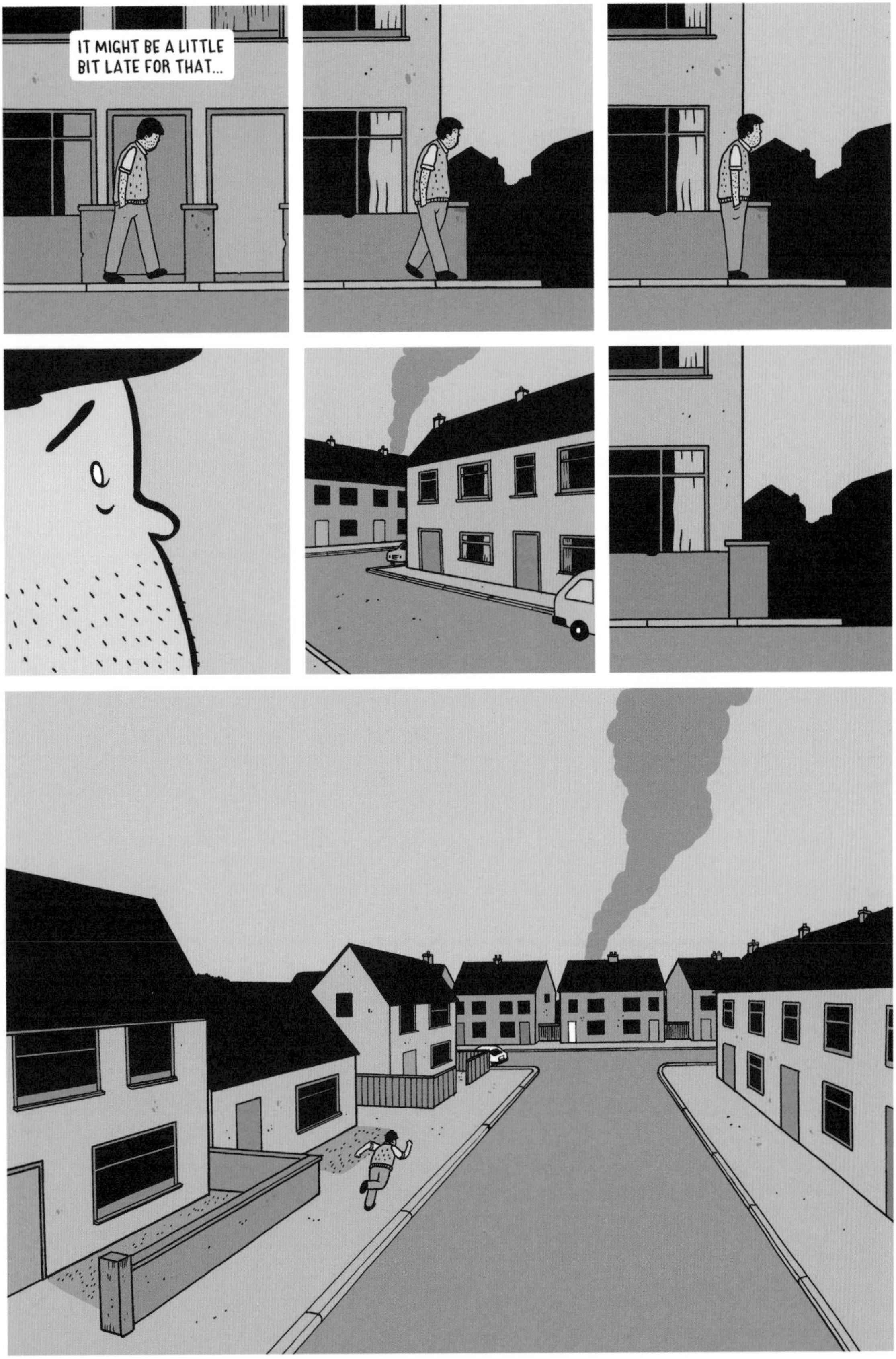
IT MIGHT BE A LITTLE BIT LATE FOR THAT...

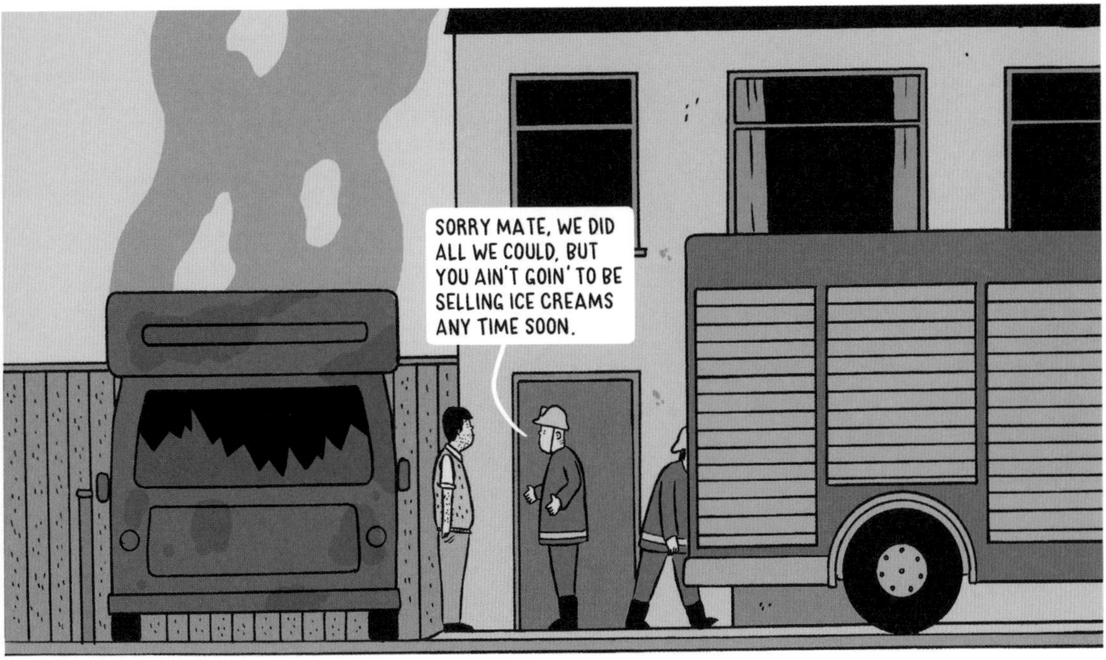
SORRY MATE, WE DID ALL WE COULD, BUT YOU AIN'T GOIN' TO BE SELLING ICE CREAMS ANY TIME SOON.

HOWARD, THE ICE CREAM MAGNATE

CHAPTER NINE

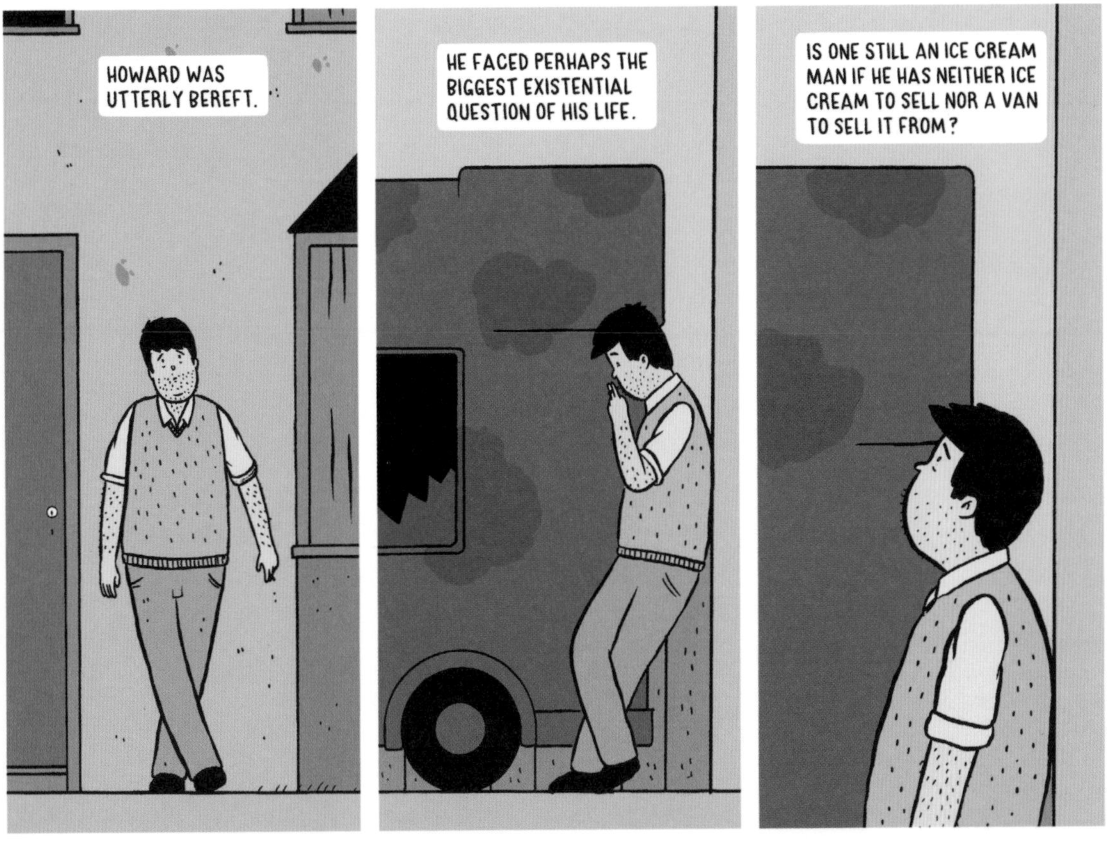
HOWARD WAS UTTERLY BEREFT.
HE FACED PERHAPS THE BIGGEST EXISTENTIAL QUESTION OF HIS LIFE.
IS ONE STILL AN ICE CREAM MAN IF HE HAS NEITHER ICE CREAM TO SELL NOR A VAN TO SELL IT FROM?

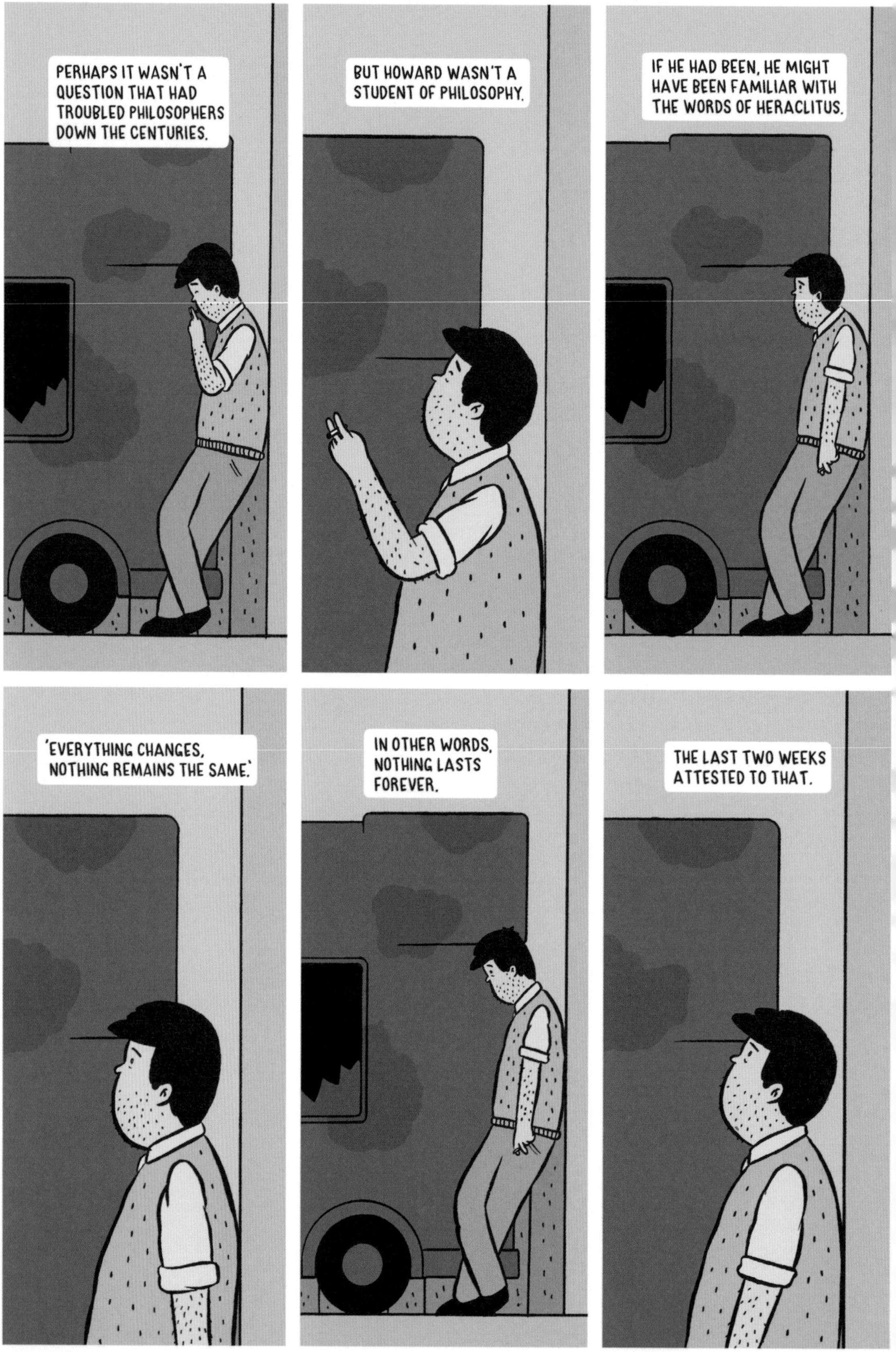
PERHAPS IT WASN'T A QUESTION THAT HAD TROUBLED PHILOSOPHERS DOWN THE CENTURIES.
BUT HOWARD WASN'T A STUDENT OF PHILOSOPHY.
IF HE HAD BEEN, HE MIGHT HAVE BEEN FAMILIAR WITH THE WORDS OF HERACLITUS.
'EVERYTHING CHANGES, NOTHING REMAINS THE SAME.'
IN OTHER WORDS, NOTHING LASTS FOREVER.
THE LAST TWO WEEKS ATTESTED TO THAT.

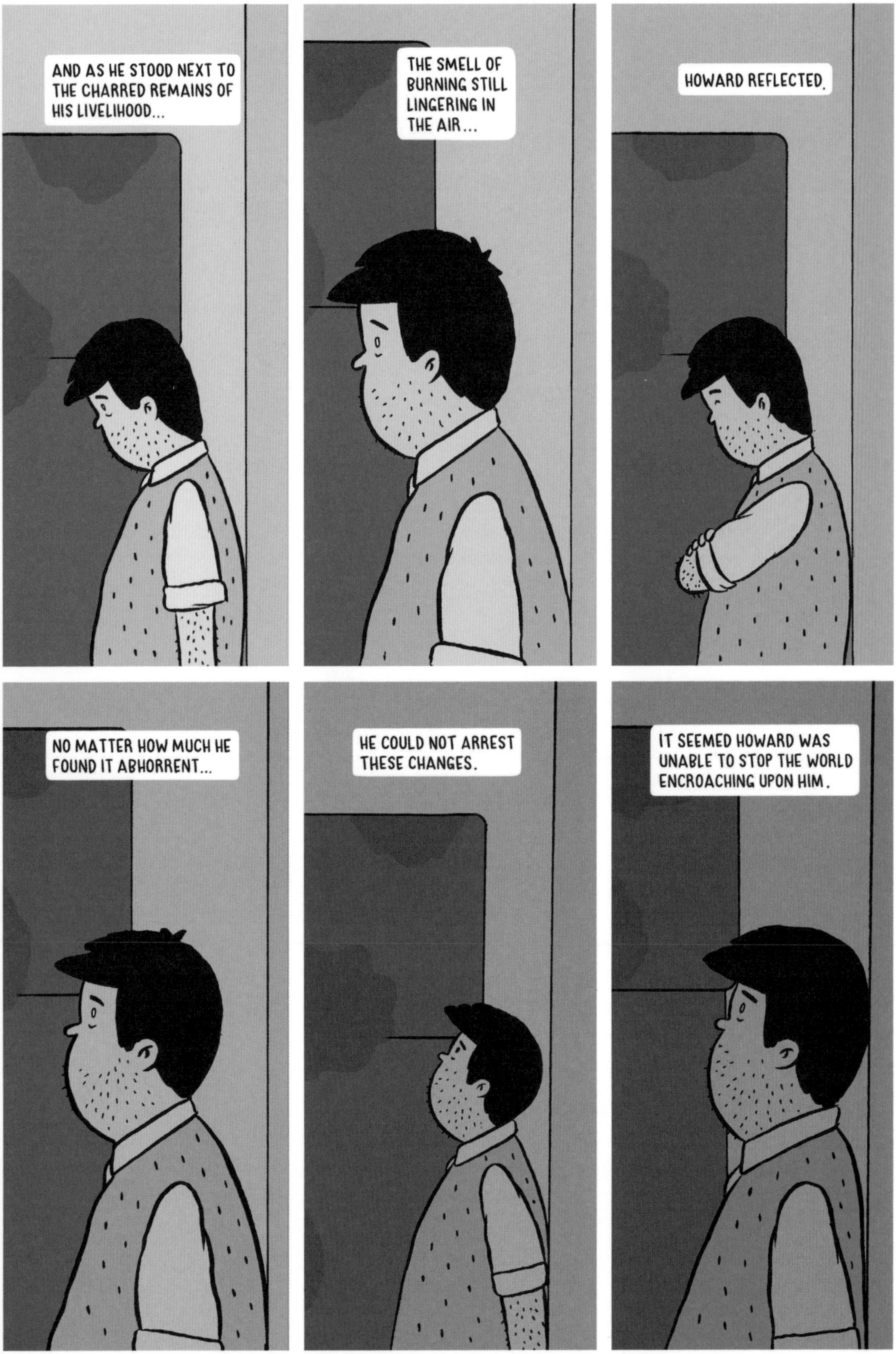
AND AS HE STOOD NEXT TO THE CHARRED REMAINS OF HIS LIVELIHOOD...
THE SMELL OF BURNING STILL LINGERING IN THE AIR...
HOWARD REFLECTED.
NO MATTER HOW MUCH HE FOUND IT ABHORRENT...
HE COULD NOT ARREST THESE CHANGES.
IT SEEMED HOWARD WAS UNABLE TO STOP THE WORLD ENCROACHING UPON HIM.

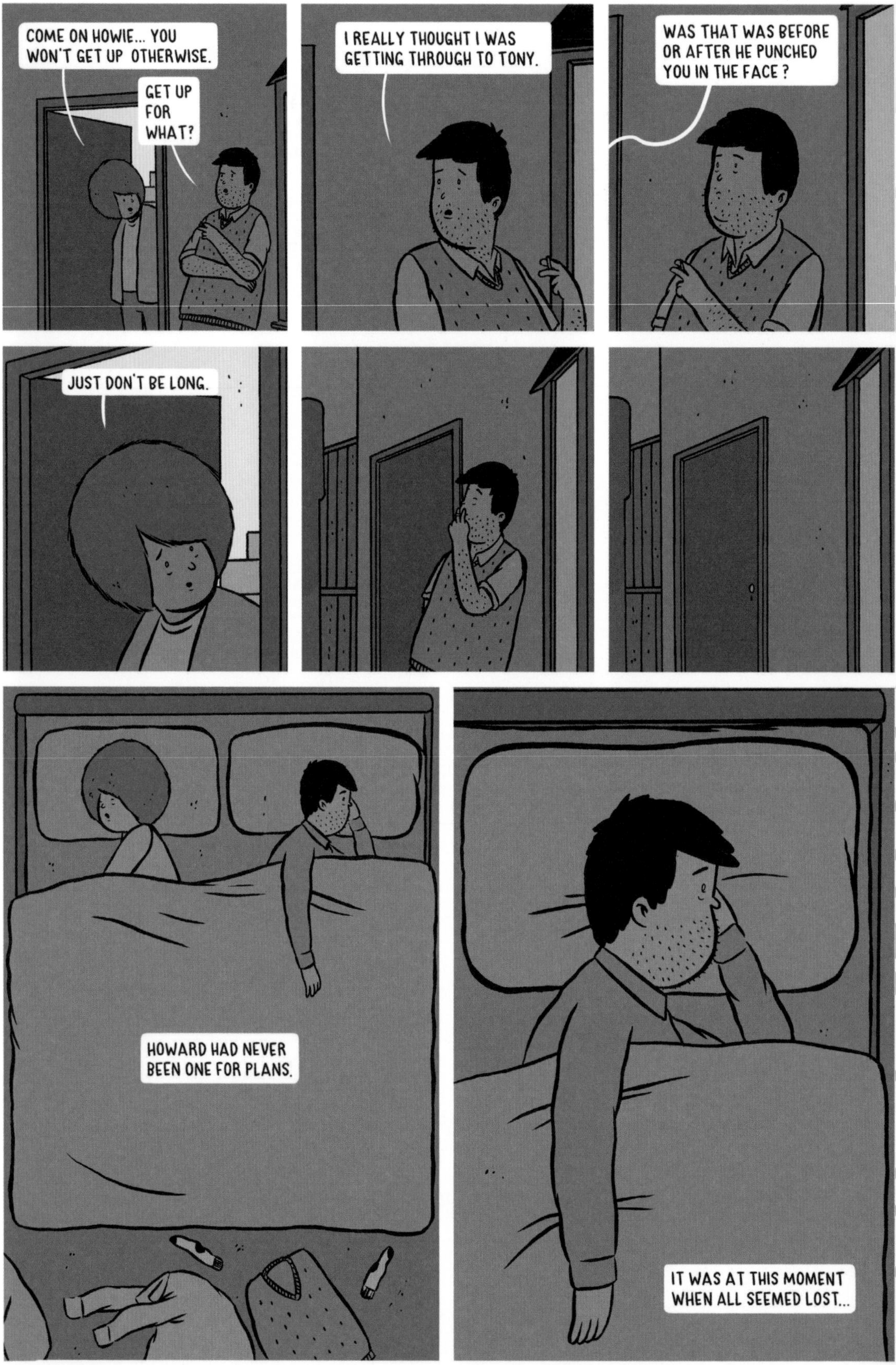
COME ON HOWIE... YOU WON'T GET UP OTHERWISE.
GET UP FOR WHAT?
I REALLY THOUGHT I WAS GETTING THROUGH TO TONY.
WAS THAT WAS BEFORE OR AFTER HE PUNCHED YOU IN THE FACE ?
JUST DON'T BE LONG.
HOWARD HAD NEVER BEEN ONE FOR PLANS.
IT WAS AT THIS MOMENT WHEN ALL SEEMED LOST...

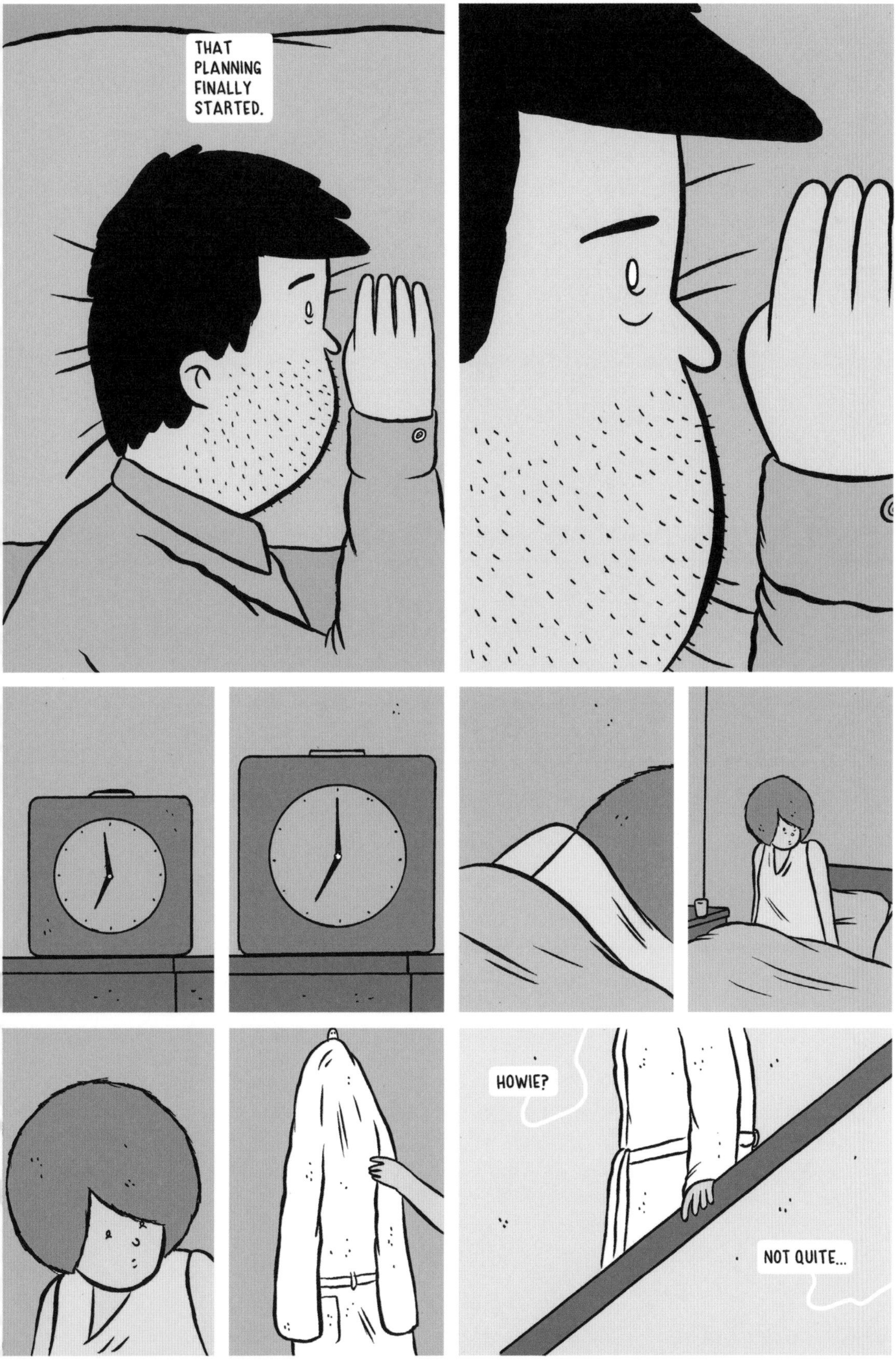
THAT PLANNING FINALLY STARTED.
HOWIE?
NOT QUITE...

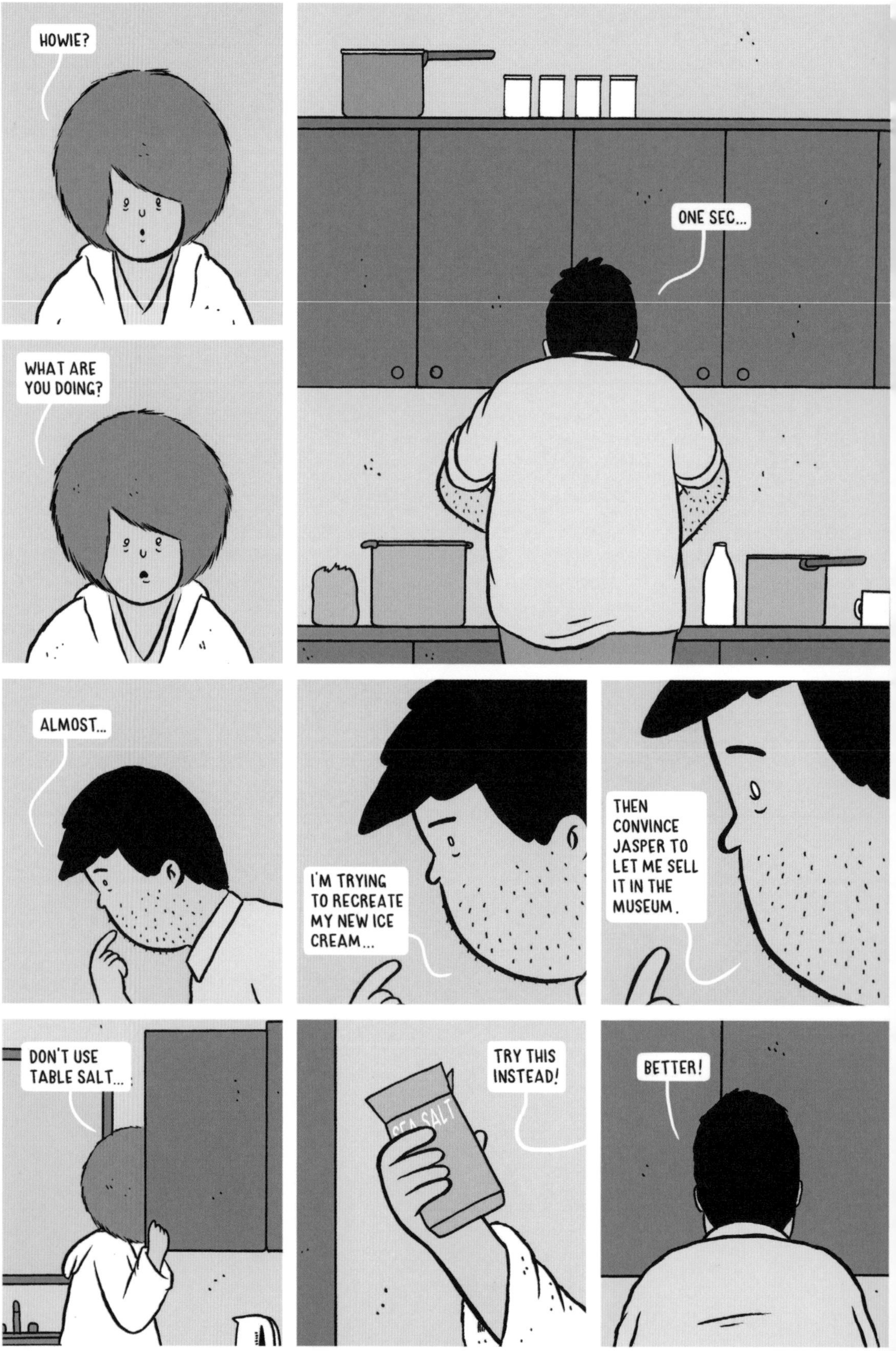
HOWIE?
ONE SEC...
WHAT ARE YOU DOING?
ALMOST...
I'M TRYING TO RECREATE MY NEW ICE CREAM...
THEN CONVINCE JASPER TO LET ME SELL IT IN THE MUSEUM.
DON'T USE TABLE SALT...
TRY THIS INSTEAD!
SEA SALT
BETTER!

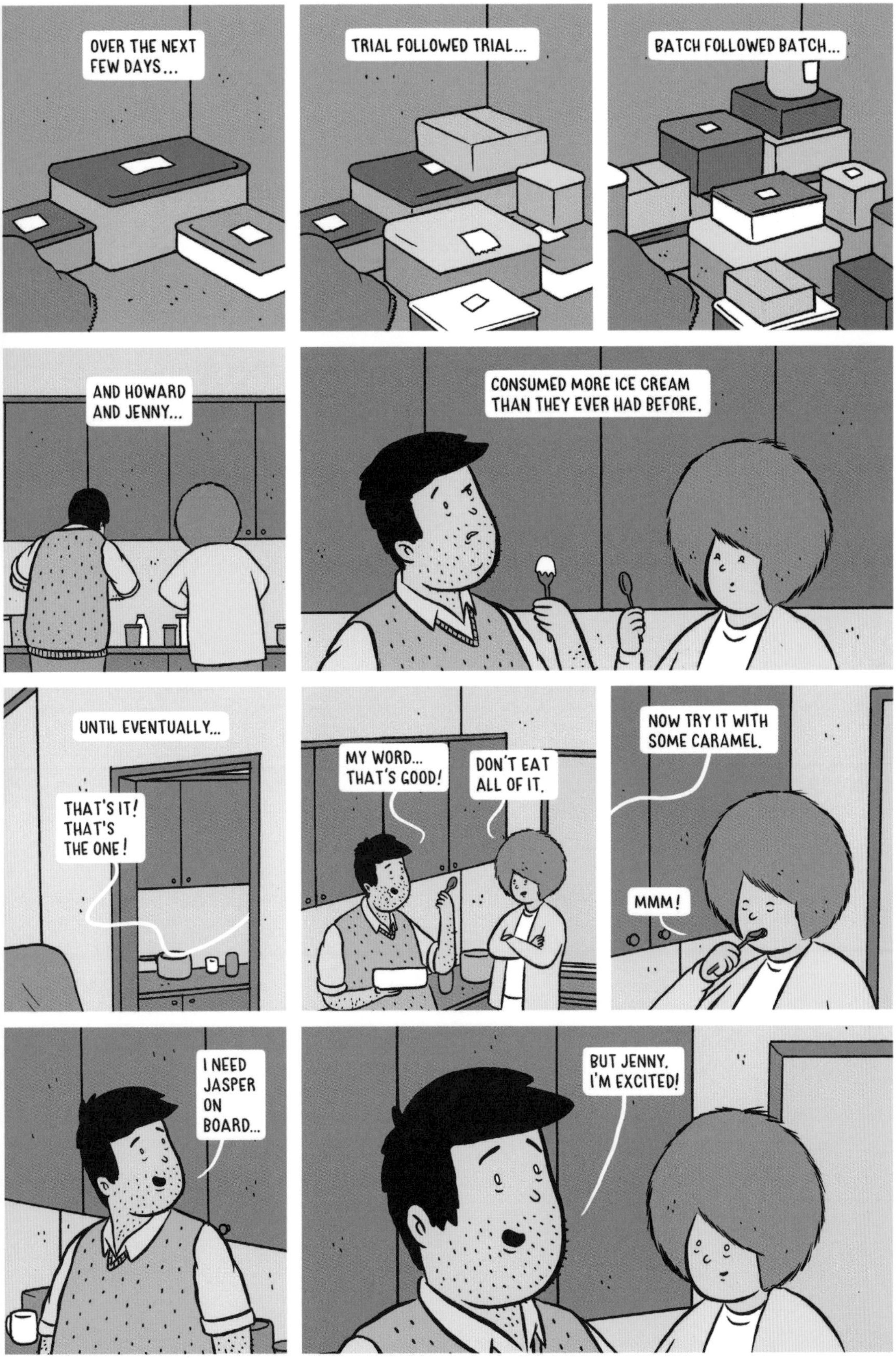
OVER THE NEXT FEW DAYS...
TRIAL FOLLOWED TRIAL...
BATCH FOLLOWED BATCH...
AND HOWARD AND JENNY...
CONSUMED MORE ICE CREAM THAN THEY EVER HAD BEFORE.
UNTIL EVENTUALLY...
THAT'S IT! THAT'S THE ONE!
MY WORD... THAT'S GOOD!
DON'T EAT ALL OF IT.
NOW TRY IT WITH SOME CARAMEL.
MMM!
I NEED JASPER ON BOARD...
BUT JENNY, I'M EXCITED!

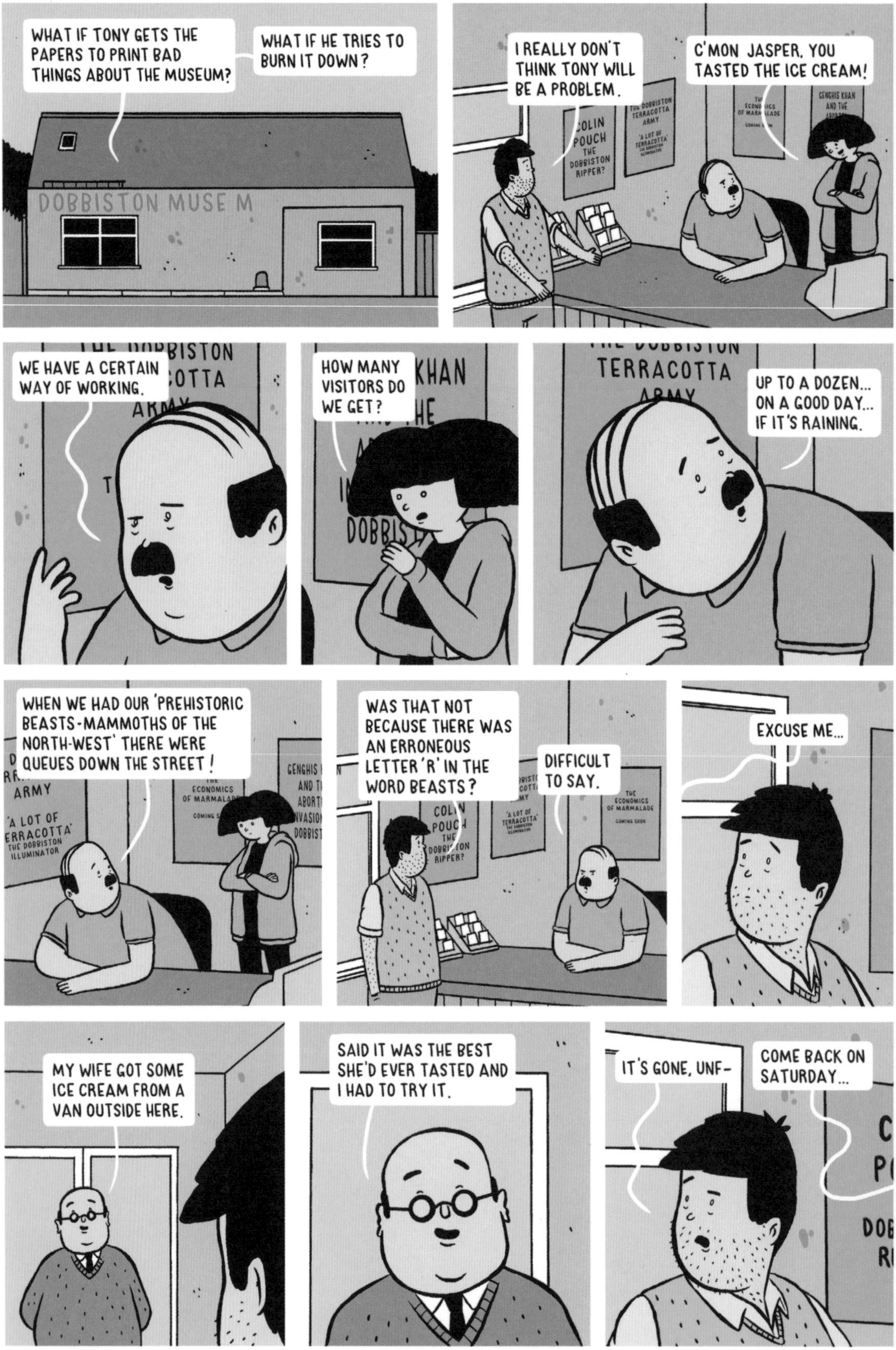
WHAT IF TONY GETS THE PAPERS TO PRINT BAD THINGS ABOUT THE MUSEUM?
WHAT IF HE TRIES TO BURN IT DOWN?
DOBBISTON MUSE M
I REALLY DON'T THINK TONY WILL BE A PROBLEM.
C'MON JASPER, YOU TASTED THE ICE CREAM!
WE HAVE A CERTAIN WAY OF WORKING.
HOW MANY VISITORS DO WE GET?
UP TO A DOZEN... ON A GOOD DAY... IF IT'S RAINING.
WHEN WE HAD OUR 'PREHISTORIC BEASTS-MAMMOTHS OF THE NORTH-WEST' THERE WERE QUEUES DOWN THE STREET!
WAS THAT NOT BECAUSE THERE WAS AN ERRONEOUS LETTER 'R' IN THE WORD BEASTS?
DIFFICULT TO SAY.
EXCUSE ME...
MY WIFE GOT SOME ICE CREAM FROM A VAN OUTSIDE HERE.
SAID IT WAS THE BEST SHE'D EVER TASTED AND I HAD TO TRY IT.
IT'S GONE, UNF-
COME BACK ON SATURDAY...

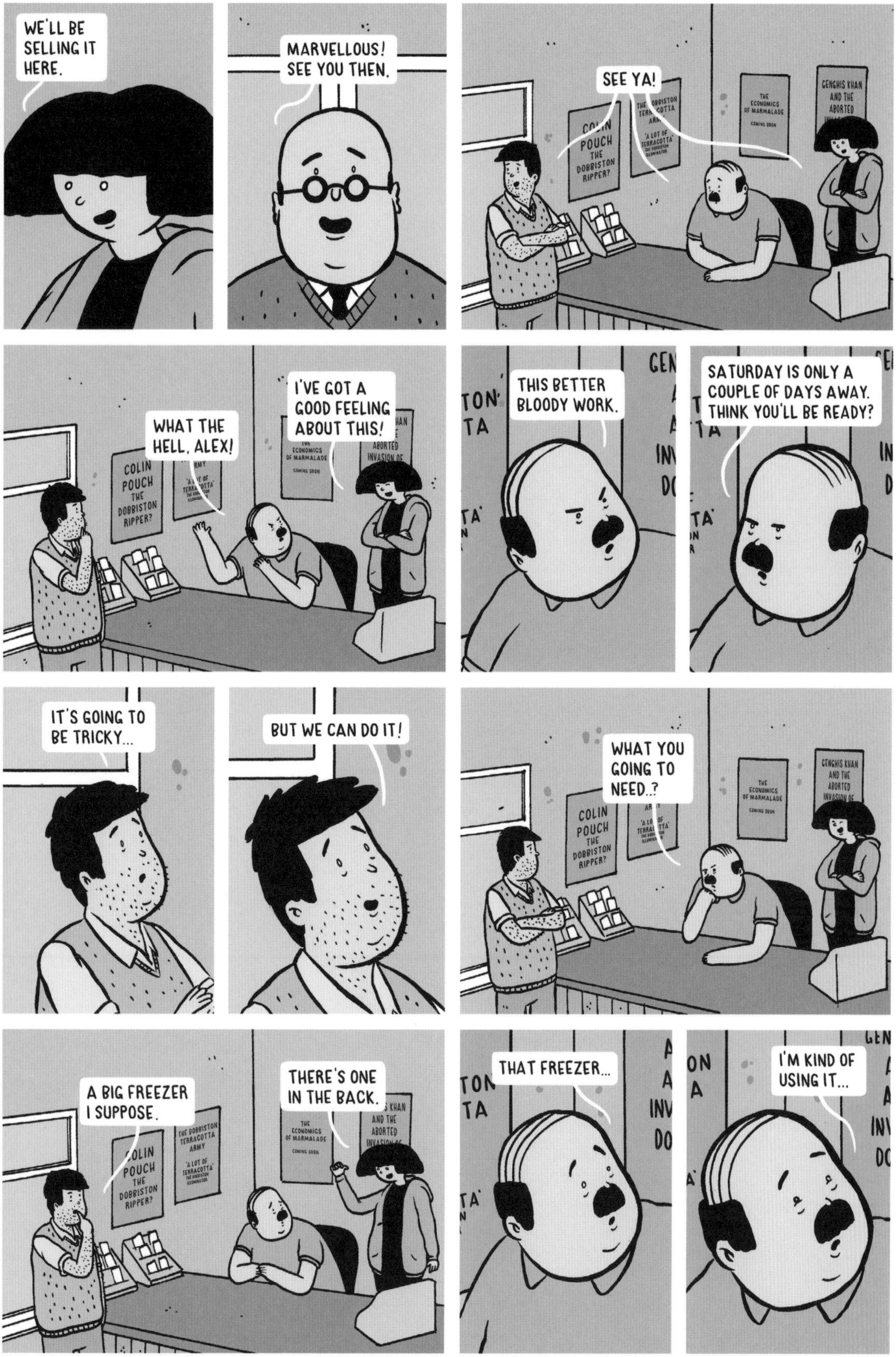
WE'LL BE SELLING IT HERE.
MARVELLOUS! SEE YOU THEN.
SEE YA!
WHAT THE HELL, ALEX!
I'VE GOT A GOOD FEELING ABOUT THIS!
THIS BETTER BLOODY WORK.
SATURDAY IS ONLY A COUPLE OF DAYS AWAY. THINK YOU'LL BE READY?
IT'S GOING TO BE TRICKY...
BUT WE CAN DO IT!
WHAT YOU GOING TO NEED..?
A BIG FREEZER I SUPPOSE.
THERE'S ONE IN THE BACK.
THAT FREEZER...
I'M KIND OF USING IT...

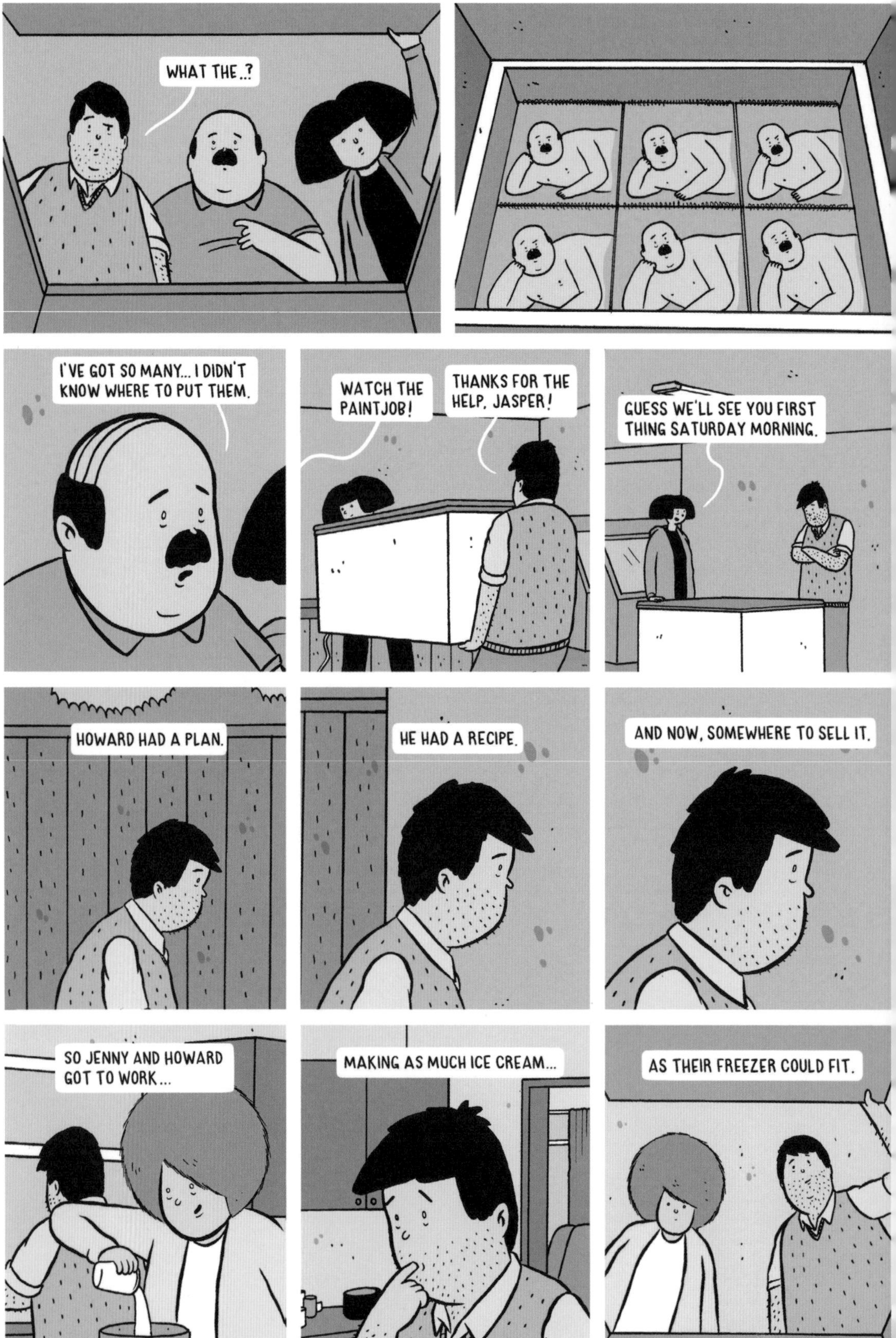
WHAT THE..?
I'VE GOT SO MANY... I DIDN'T KNOW WHERE TO PUT THEM.
WATCH THE PAINTJOB!
THANKS FOR THE HELP, JASPER!
GUESS WE'LL SEE YOU FIRST THING SATURDAY MORNING.
HOWARD HAD A PLAN.
HE HAD A RECIPE.
AND NOW, SOMEWHERE TO SELL IT.
SO JENNY AND HOWARD GOT TO WORK...
MAKING AS MUCH ICE CREAM...
AS THEIR FREEZER COULD FIT.

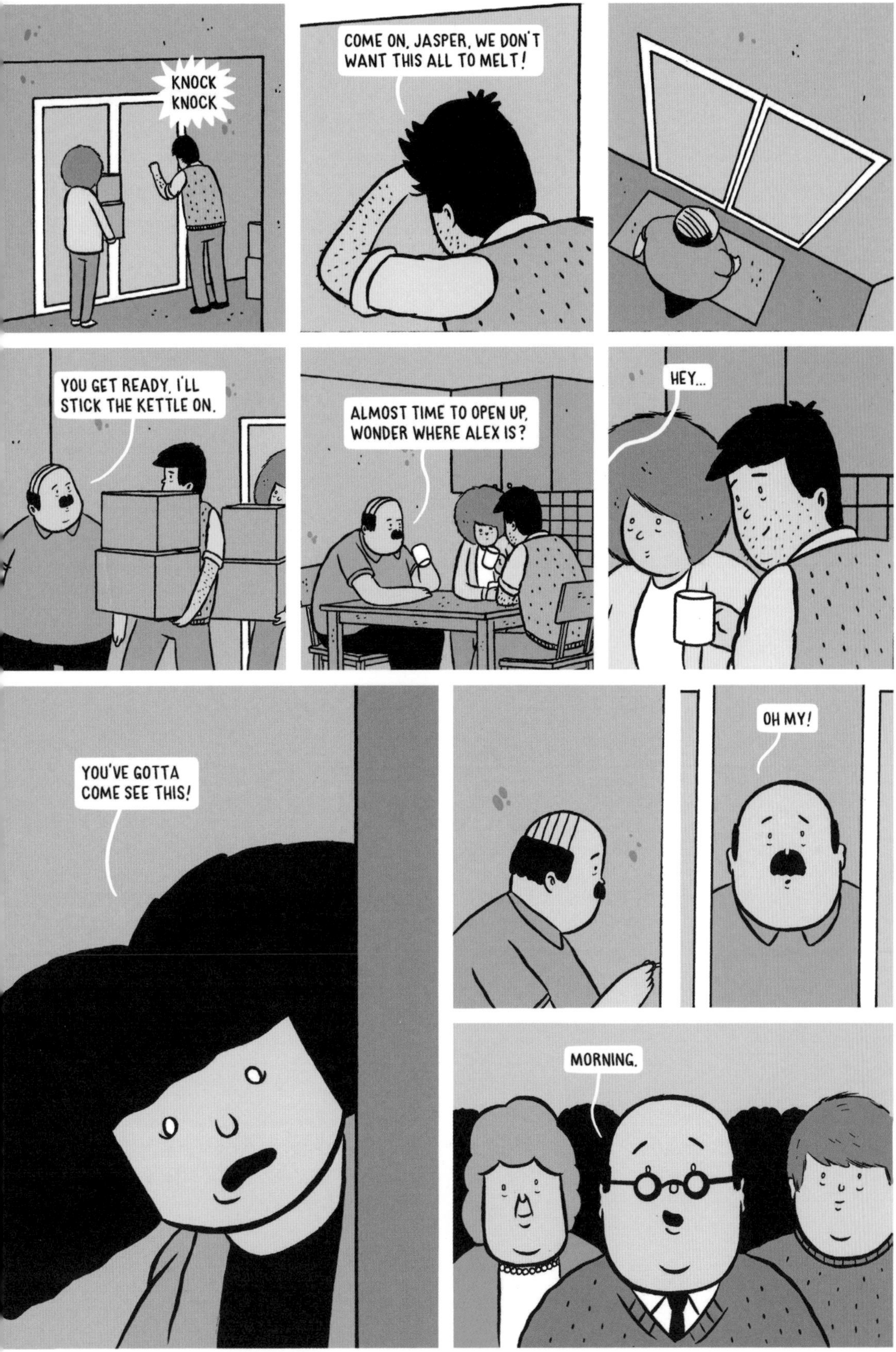
KNOCK KNOCK
COME ON, JASPER, WE DON'T WANT THIS ALL TO MELT!
YOU GET READY, I'LL STICK THE KETTLE ON.
ALMOST TIME TO OPEN UP, WONDER WHERE ALEX IS?
HEY...
YOU'VE GOTTA COME SEE THIS!
OH MY!
MORNING.

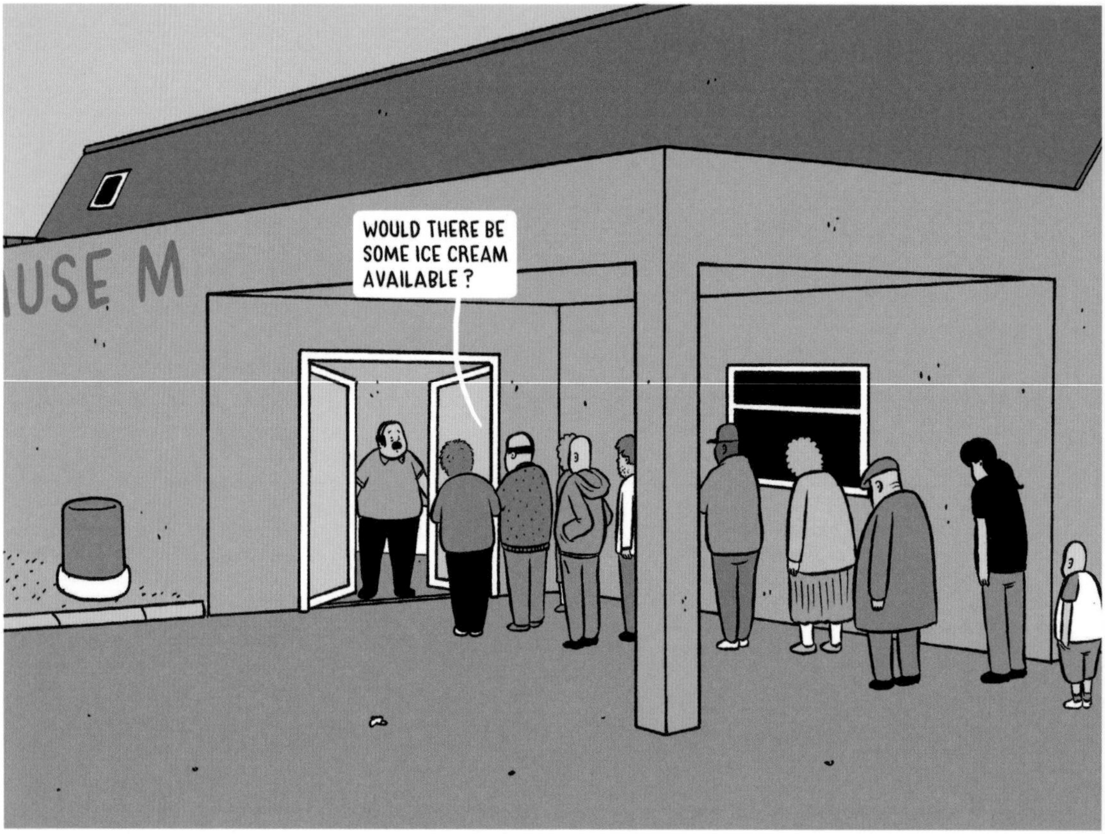
USE M
WOULD THERE BE
SOME ICE CREAM
AVAILABLE ?

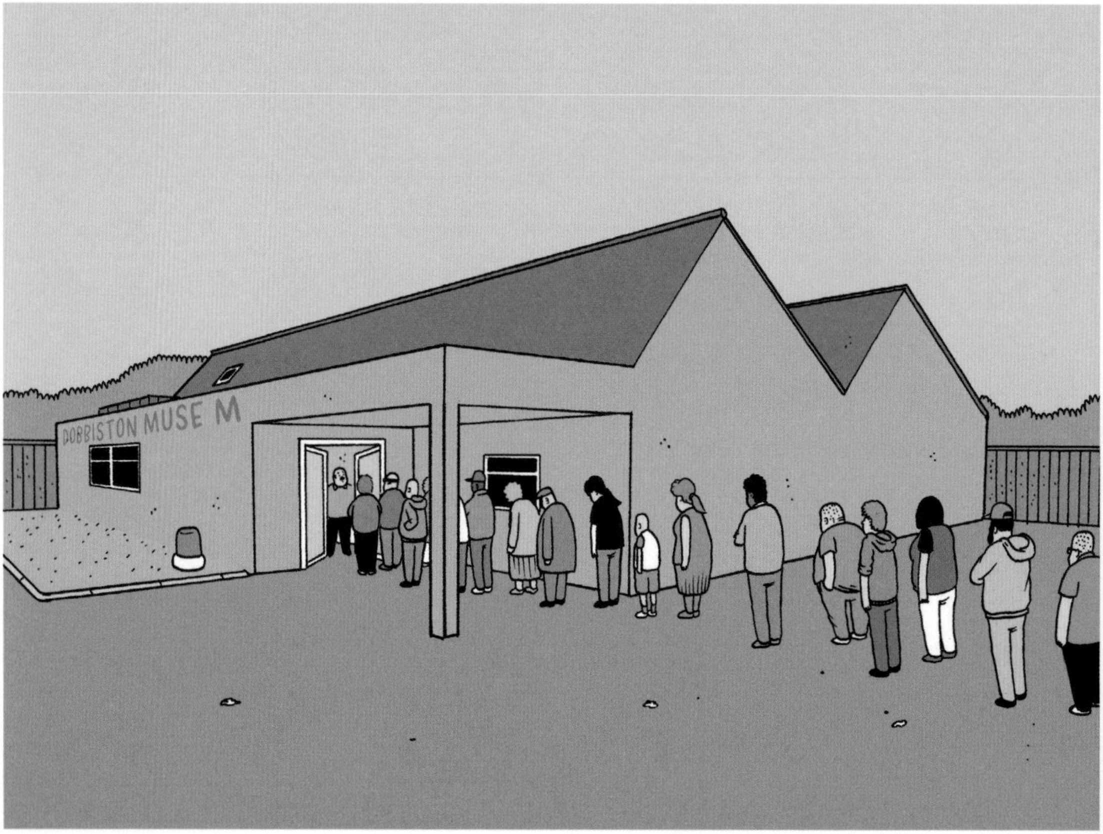
DOBBISTON MUSE M

AND SO...

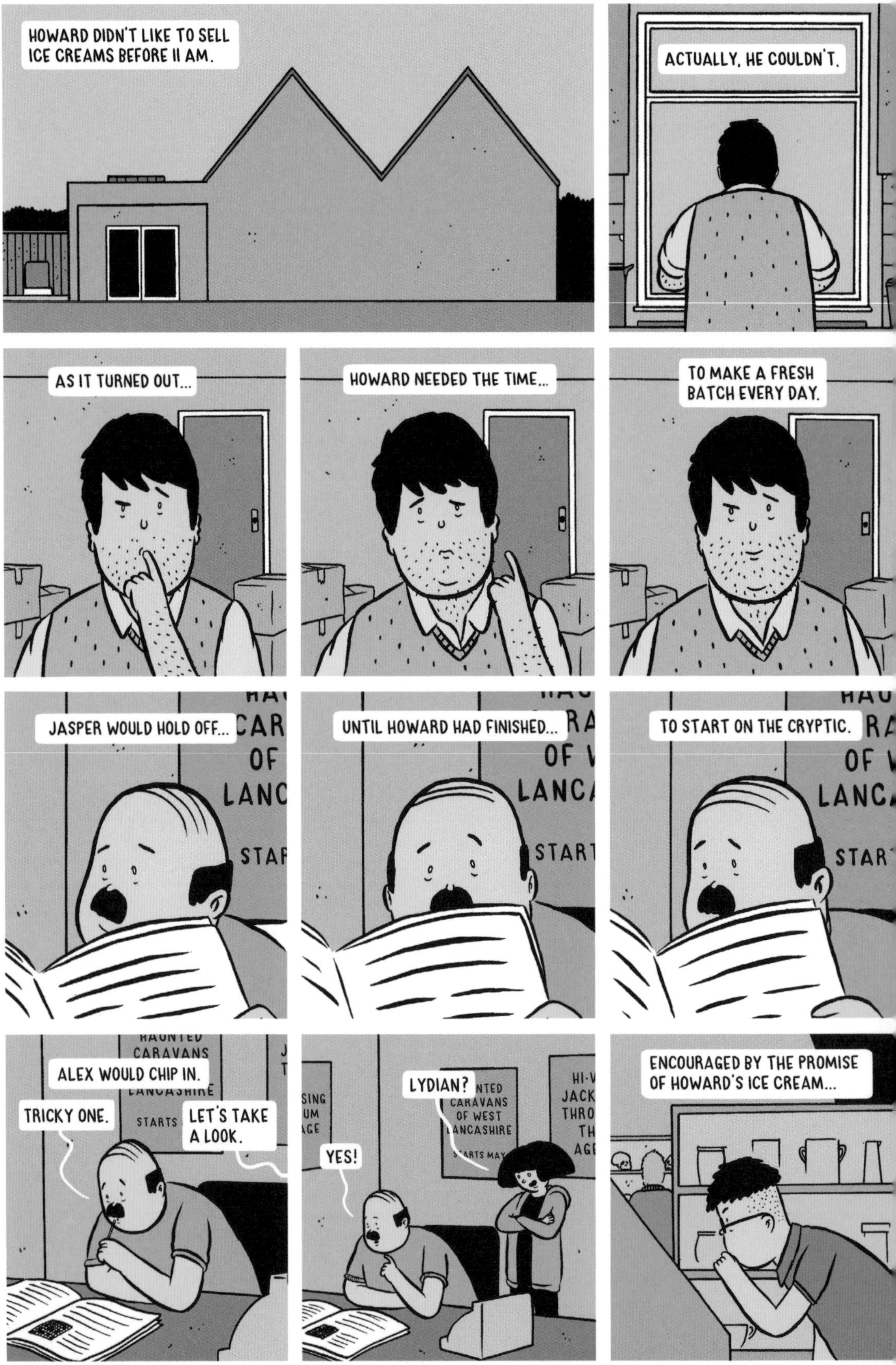
HOWARD DIDN'T LIKE TO SELL ICE CREAMS BEFORE 11 AM.
ACTUALLY, HE COULDN'T.
AS IT TURNED OUT...
HOWARD NEEDED THE TIME...
TO MAKE A FRESH BATCH EVERY DAY.
JASPER WOULD HOLD OFF...
UNTIL HOWARD HAD FINISHED...
TO START ON THE CRYPTIC.
ALEX WOULD CHIP IN.
TRICKY ONE.
LET'S TAKE A LOOK.
CARAVANS
STARTS
LYDIAN?
YES!
CARAVANS
OF WEST
ENCOURAGED BY THE PROMISE OF HOWARD'S ICE CREAM...

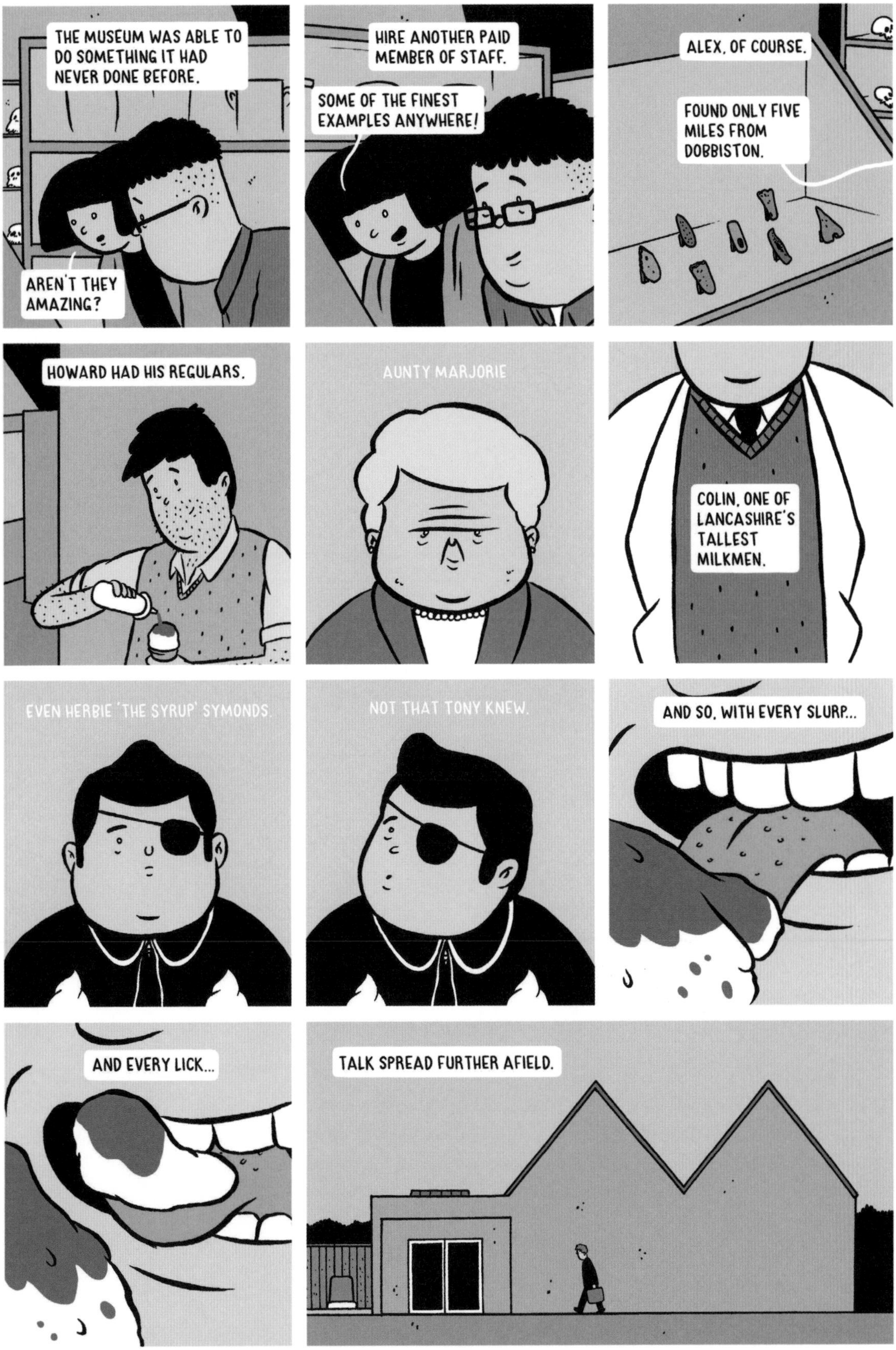
THE MUSEUM WAS ABLE TO DO SOMETHING IT HAD NEVER DONE BEFORE.
AREN'T THEY AMAZING?
HIRE ANOTHER PAID MEMBER OF STAFF.
SOME OF THE FINEST EXAMPLES ANYWHERE!
ALEX, OF COURSE.
FOUND ONLY FIVE MILES FROM DOBBISTON.
HOWARD HAD HIS REGULARS.
AUNTY MARJORIE
COLIN, ONE OF LANCASHIRE'S TALLEST MILKMEN.
EVEN HERBIE 'THE SYRUP' SYMONDS.
NOT THAT TONY KNEW.
AND SO, WITH EVERY SLURP...
AND EVERY LICK...
TALK SPREAD FURTHER AFIELD.

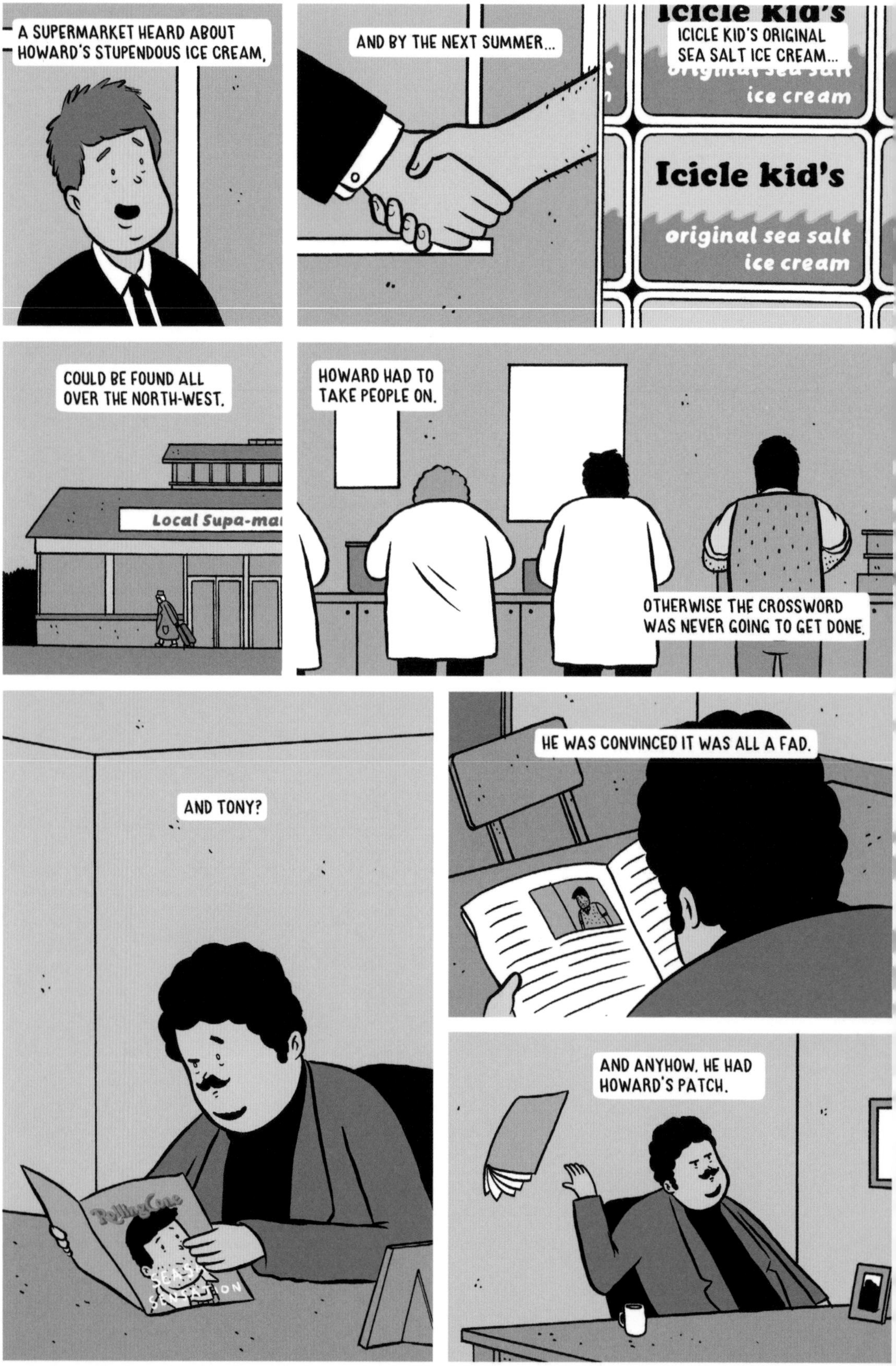
A SUPERMARKET HEARD ABOUT HOWARD'S STUPENDOUS ICE CREAM,
AND BY THE NEXT SUMMER...
Icicle kid's
ICICLE KID'S ORIGINAL SEA SALT ICE CREAM...
ice cream
Icicle kid's
original sea salt
ice cream
COULD BE FOUND ALL OVER THE NORTH-WEST.
Local Supa-ma
HOWARD HAD TO TAKE PEOPLE ON.
OTHERWISE THE CROSSWORD WAS NEVER GOING TO GET DONE.
AND TONY?
HE WAS CONVINCED IT WAS ALL A FAD.
AND ANYHOW, HE HAD HOWARD'S PATCH.

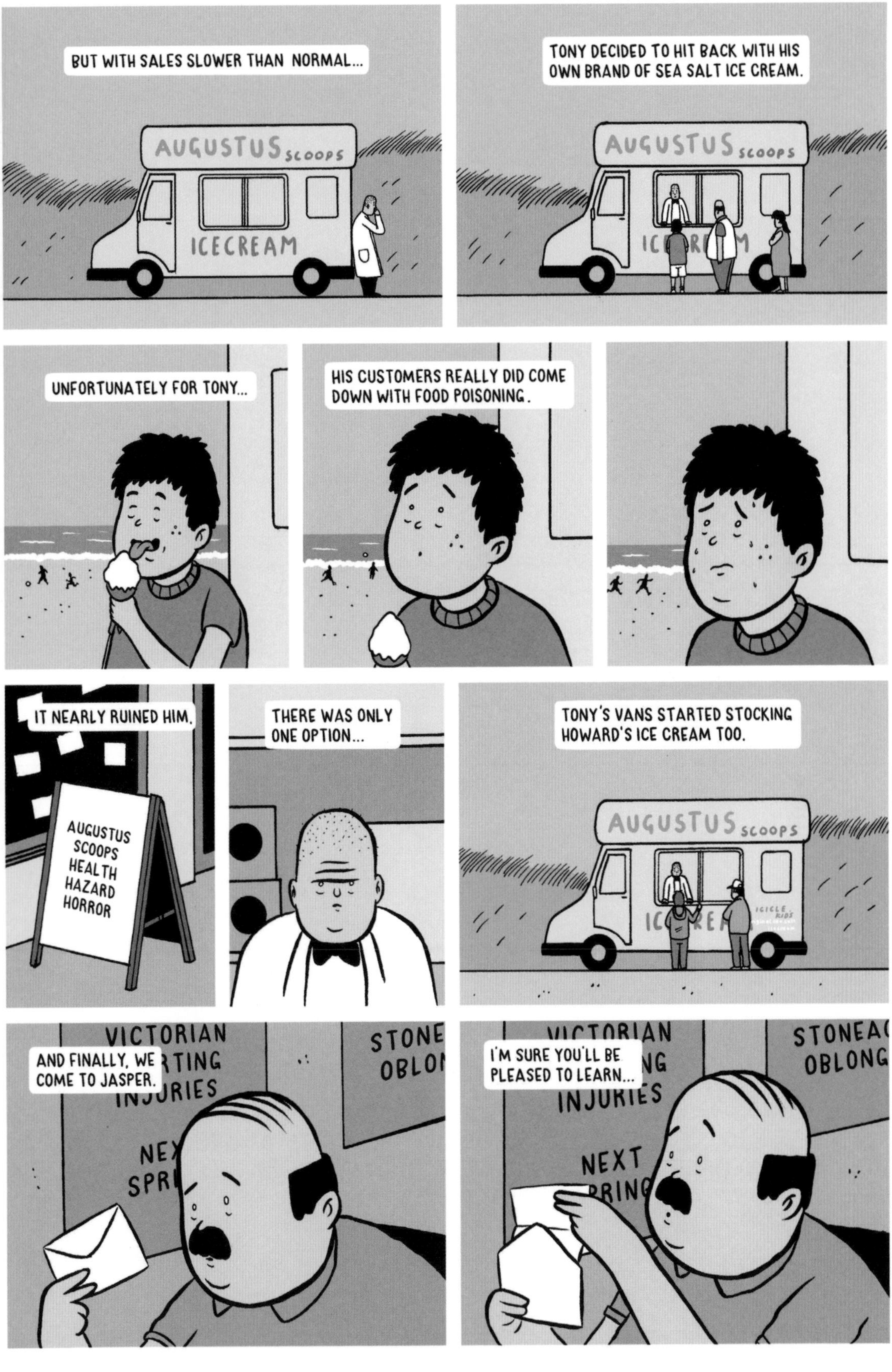
BUT WITH SALES SLOWER THAN NORMAL...
AUGUSTUS scoops
ICECREAM
TONY DECIDED TO HIT BACK WITH HIS OWN BRAND OF SEA SALT ICE CREAM.
AUGUSTUS scoops
UNFORTUNATELY FOR TONY...
HIS CUSTOMERS REALLY DID COME DOWN WITH FOOD POISONING.
IT NEARLY RUINED HIM.
AUGUSTUS SCOOPS HEALTH HAZARD HORROR
THERE WAS ONLY ONE OPTION...
TONY'S VANS STARTED STOCKING HOWARD'S ICE CREAM TOO.
AUGUSTUS scoops
AND FINALLY, WE COME TO JASPER.
VICTORIAN
INJURIES
I'M SURE YOU'LL BE PLEASED TO LEARN...
STONEAGE OBLONG
INJURIES
NEXT

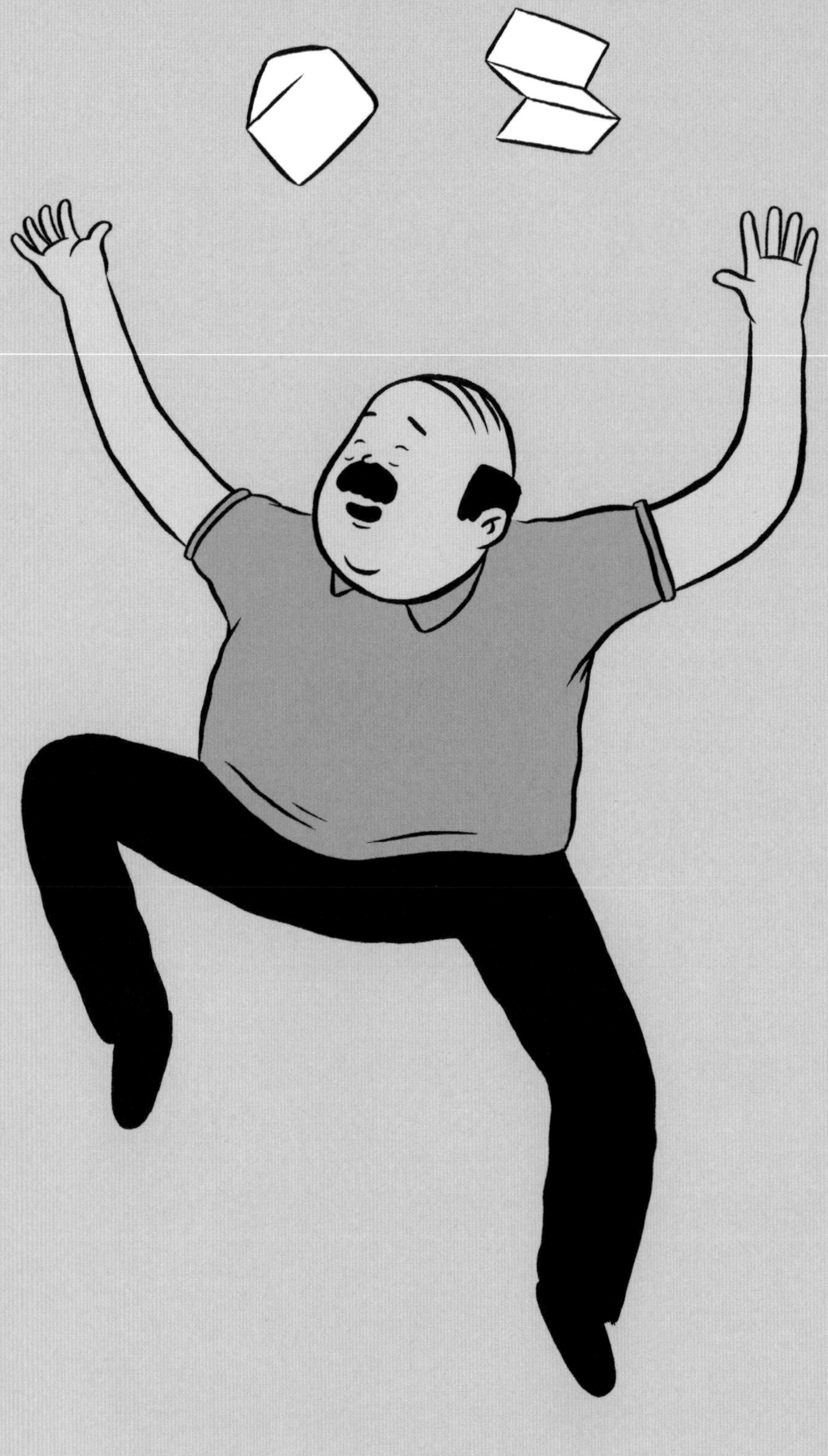

JASPER GOT HIS MOUNTAIN BACK.

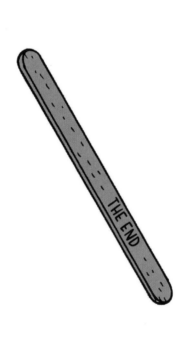

THE END

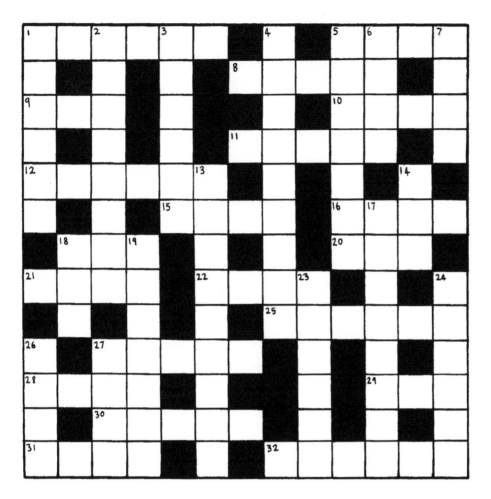

ACROSS

1 FRED IDLED AROUND AS HE PLAYED THE VIOLIN (6)
5 NOT EVEN WORTH A BET (4)
8 SOUNDS LIKE YOU'LL NEED YOUR BROLLY BUT IT'S NOT THE WEATHER (5)
9 GUN BRANDISHED IN A CHARMING WAY (3)
10 ANNUAL EYE ARTIST GET TOGETHER (4)
11 AGRICULTURE APPEARS IN COAT OF ARMS (5)
12 EGG BEATS THE SPOON TO THE TROPHY (6)
15 EARTH FOUND IN SOIL AND DIRT (4)
16 MAN LIES ABOUT BEING SURROUNDED BY WATER (4)
18 LANTERN TRAPS INSECT INSIDE (3)
20 PASS THE TEST WITH A TOP CARD (3)
21 CONTROVERSIALLY, EDWARD STARTS TO PLAY WITH SOME GYROSCOPE (4)
22 FEWER THAN ONE HUNDRED CLICK FOR A NEW TASTE (4)
25 GET DOWN TO IT. WHY? IT'S RUGGED (6)
27 DON'T CIRCLE BROKEN ROUND PAINTING (5)
28 HUNGARIAN WRITES BACK WITH NERO RIB TICKLER (4)
29 IRON OUT THE RIGHT SIDE OF A PARTICLE (3)
30 MY CONTRIBUTION WAS A PUN, IT CAUSED CONFUSION (5)
31 I HEARD THAT HIPS DO LIE, IF YOU KEEP DRINKING (4)
32 CHARLIE BROWN IS ON HIS OWN IN THIS STRIP (6)

DOWN

1 TROUSERS THAT CATCH YOUR ATTENTION (6)
2 BREAKING THE BARRIER WHICH HOLDS BACK THE PROCESS OF GETTING OLDER (8)
3 LAURA WAS TERRIBLE AT PLAYING BY THE RULES (6)
4 FEARFUL OF THE RUMINENT PLAYING THE GAME (9)
5 I PLAY WITH A MOP IN A GREEK CITY (7)
6 DEREK CONFIRMED THE CHANGE OF COLOUR (4)
7 CERTAIN ABOUT RUSE (4)
13 POLICE DEPARTMENT INITALLY ARE IN THEIR ELEMENT (9)
14 JUST SHORT OF A GALE FORCE WIND DROVE ME TO DRINK (3)
17 IAN CUT WITH A SCYTHE TO FIND AN ANCIENT RACE (8)
18 DAD GOT CONFUSED ABOUT THE SUM (3)
19 SOUNDS LIKE THE TYPHOONS ARE MAKING MONEY (7)
23 KICK ASS KATE EATS THE RADIUM (6)
24 YOUNG BIRDS IN A RING (6)
26 SOUNDS LIKE SPIDER'S HOMES ARE GRADUALLY DECREASING (4)
27 HOLIDAY INCLUDES SWIMMING SILENTLY IN THE RIP TIDES (4)

MATTHEW DOOLEY IS A CARTOONIST
FROM THE NORTH WEST OF ENGLAND.
HE WON THE 2016 JONATHAN CAPE/
OBSERVER/COMICA GRAPHIC SHORT
STORY PRIZE. THIS IS HIS FIRST
GRAPHIC NOVEL.

CHOCODIP

CYBER-ICE

STR🍓WBERRY
TORPEDO

RASPBERRY BATON

ST GEORGE

TOMBSTONE

HELTER SKELTER

PINK SHAZAM

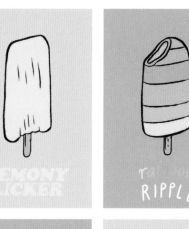

LEMONY LICKER

rainbow
RIPPLE

CASTLE

cherry cheesecake

DINO

PHARAOH

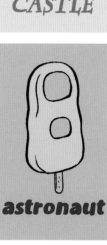

astronaut

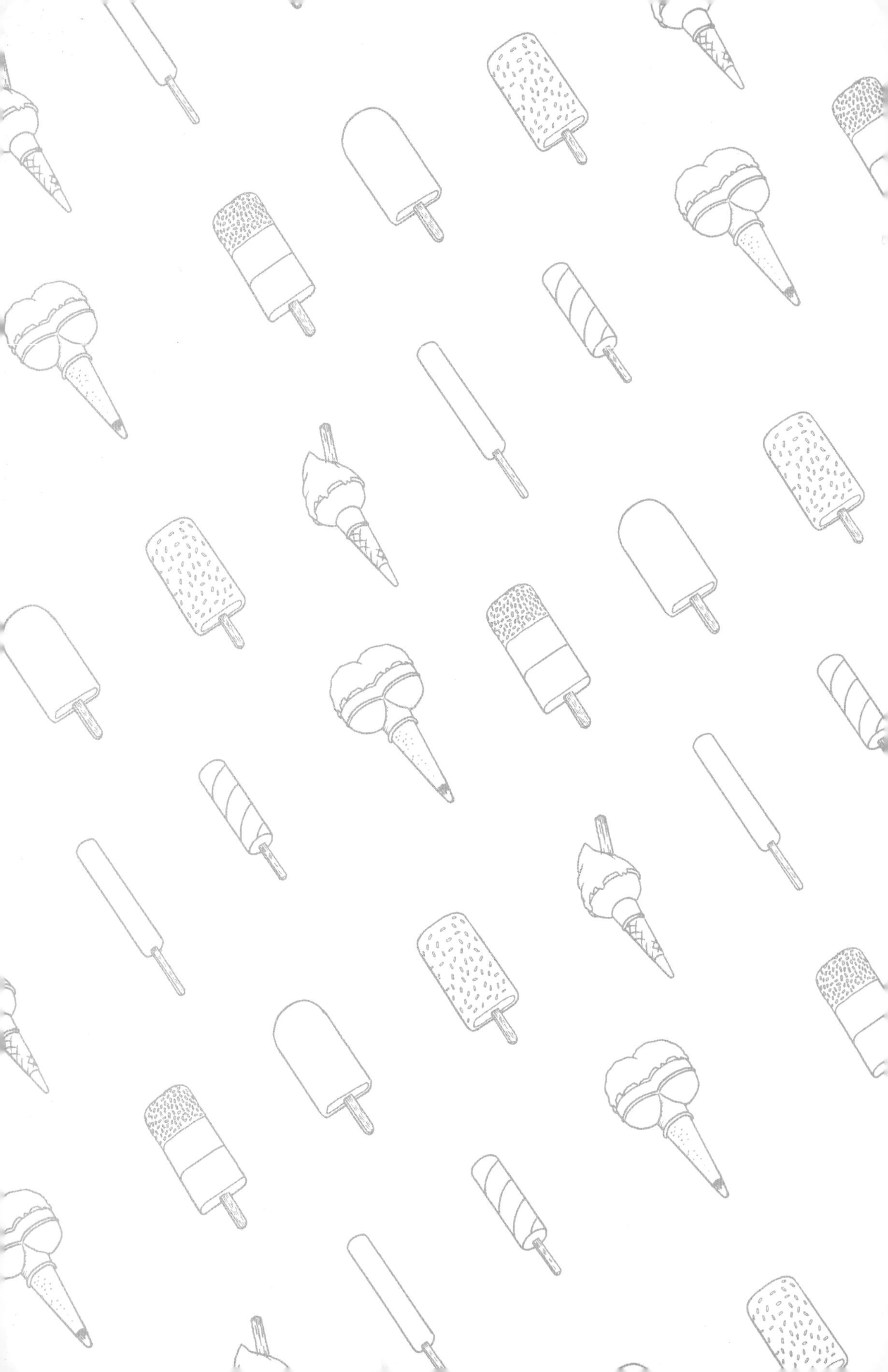